Margaret Wade Campbell Deland

Sidney

Margaret Wade Campbell Deland

Sidney

ISBN/EAN: 9783743304949

Manufactured in Europe, USA, Canada, Australia, Japa

Cover: Foto ©ninafisch / pixelio.de

Manufactured and distributed by brebook publishing software (www.brebook.com)

Margaret Wade Campbell Deland

Sidney

SIDNEY.

I.

"Yes," said Mrs. Paul, "they are really the most extraordinary people. Mortimer Lee began to be queer as soon as he was married, and his wife was always a silly sort of woman; their living in the south on account of her health was one of her absurd ideas,— it was entirely unnecessary. She was born here in Mercer, you know; that house they live in now was left her by her grandfather. When she died, Mortimer Lee came back to it with Sidney. He made the excuse that he wanted the child to be brought up near her mother's people (though they've all died out now), but I think that he wanted to get back to Mercer himself. I knew him before he was married. Ah, he was very different in those days. Marriage ruined him. Marriage has more effect upon a man's character than upon a woman's. Just remember that, sir!"

Alan Crossan laughed. "And always for the worse?" he suggested.

"Some men cannot be worse," said Mrs. Paul significantly; "but for Major Lee, all these theories of his developed after he met his wife."

"They were the effect of her death, though, were n't they?" the doctor asked.

"Of course," answered his hostess sharply; "but if he had n't had such a wife to die, he would not have been so affected. She was a woman of absolutely no sense, I tell you, — some people called her handsome, though I never could see it; but that he grieved so wickedly for her shows the result of having lived with her for ten years. For really, you know, by nature, Mortimer Lee is no fool?"

"Well, no," said the young man, smiling.

"I did n't see him while she was alive," proceeded Mrs. Paul, — "they lived somewhere in Virginia; Sidney must have been about three years old when her mother died, and he came back; let me see, — yes, he has been here twenty-two years, certainly. Dear me! I did not realize that Sidney was so old. He took her education in hand as soon as she could talk; and you see the result. She is her father over again."

"Is she?" the doctor said. "I remember that she was unlike anybody else when we were children, before I went abroad; but that was fifteen years ago."

Alan Crossan sighed. There had been many changes in these fifteen years; scarcely anything remained as he had known it then. Only the two old houses, Mrs. Paul's and Major Lee's, looked as they had looked when he and his mother had come to say good-by, before they sailed for Germany, where he was to be educated. His mother had died there, leaving him at twenty to drift down into Italy, where the years had wrapped him in a lazy dream, and where he had studied a little, painted a little, and fancied that he had thought a great deal. Indeed, this sunny life might have gone on indefinitely, if the sharp distress of another man had not aroused him to the thought of coming back to America. With that thought came a realization of the uselessness of his life, and a desire for the new interest of action. To be sure, he had practised his profession in the little Italian town where he had first met Robert Steele; but it had never absorbed him, any more than his violin had absorbed him, or his woodcarving, or his painting. He was at heart a dilettante, he told himself; but this reflection did not disturb him, for he declared that he was no more responsible for his disposition than for the color of his eyes, and he was almost as powerless to change the one as the other. But when he came to observe, curiously, though with sympathy, Robert Steele's pain, he began to be half ashamed of himself because he had never suffered, and never very greatly cared about anything.

"Odd," he thought, "that it is the sight of trouble which makes me want to live more earnestly; for the deeper you live the more trouble you have. But I suppose trouble is a man's birthright, and instinct makes him seek it. Well, I am going home, and I am going to do some work in the world before I die."

Such an impulse was amusing, he said, but that did not change his purpose. "I will go back to America with you," he announced to Mr. Steele. "I shall make a well man of you yet, Bob. I shall be your physician: all rich men have a physician at their elbow, and, thank Heaven, you're a rich man now. Don't groan,— it's a good thing. But if it distresses you too much, why, my fees will doubtless be a comfort. Yes, we'll go back to Mercer. There are half a dozen families there who will have to employ me, out of sentiment. That's the advantage of being the son of your father,— it creates sentiment. And they all know you, of course. I tell you, old man, you'll be a coward if you don't go back there and live it down. Come, now, when shall we start?"

There was a cheerful certainty about this young man's determinations which made people incapable of resisting them. His friends yielded to his wishes with protestations which were not often serious, because they were known at the outset to be useless. Robert Steele was too sad and too indifferent to protest; and so it came about that they found themselves, that autumn, settled in Mercer, in a house that belonged to Alan, which an obliging tenant had just vacated. The doctor had to admit, however, that sentiment did not move the half-dozen families as it should have done, and patients came very slowly.

But Mr. Steele, at least, had not been forgotten. The young man who had invested trust money in a certain company of which he was himself a director, and then, seeing that values were about to fall, had refused to sell without proclaiming the future depreciation of the stock, was too extraordinary a person to be forgotten. If Robert Steele had embezzled half a million dollars, the community could scarcely have been more startled and horrified than when it learned of his abnormal honesty which had permitted five thousand shares of stock to become worthless in his hands. The money he had invested had been his mother's, and that Mrs. Steele's death was hastened by her bitter and futile anger at her son's wicked quixotism could not be doubted, least of all by her son. The misery of that time left its imprint upon his soul, and it was the sarcasm of fate that at the end of two years the stock which had been thought worthless slowly regained its value. What did he want with money, while his mother's reproaches still rang in his ears?

It was at this crisis that Alan had found him in the little sunshiny Italian town, sick in mind and body, and blurring the misery of memory by a certain daily prick in the arm. He had begun this use of morphine to make bodily pain endurable, for he had been very ill, and after that the tortured mind demanded it. To the doctor, Robert Steele had at first been merely an interesting case. A man strong enough to perform an act of moral heroism, but weak enough to seek relief in morphine, was an anomaly which suggested defective cerebration to the physician. But after a while, the sweetness of Robert's nature, his noble ideality, appealed to Alan with a demand for respect which grew into reverence.

"I cannot understand it," he acknowledged frankly to the sick man. "You were a fool about that stock beyond a doubt, but it was a glorious folly; and you are a coward now, with nothing glorious about it. But here I am, going back to America with you. Well, such capacity for enthusiasm proves that I am still young."

This dull November afternoon the doctor had been telling Mrs. Paul of certain noble traits in Robert Steele, for whom she had nothing but contempt, and he had spoken of Major Lee's kindness to the sick man, to which she replied that that was only because Mortimer Lee was himself unintelligible; and from that their talk had drifted to those theories which had been developed in the life and education of the major's daughter.

A chill mist had brought an early dusk into the garden outside, but there was a fire smouldering on the hearth, which made a little halo of brightness about Mrs. Paul. The room was full of shadows, although the Venetian blinds had been drawn up to the very tops of the long windows, so that the gray afternoon light might delay Davids with the lamps as long as possible. That John Paul, sitting close to one of the windows, his big head showing like a silhouette against the pale background of the sky, could not see to read his paper did not trouble his mother at all. Of course he had not protested; to John Paul's mind there were very few occasions that were worthy of protest. But his mother was aware that he had put his paper down, and was waiting for the lights. Indeed, it would have been hard to name any circumstance in her own house of which Mrs. Paul was not aware. She made no comment upon it, however; instead, she repeated Alan's words.

"Fifteen years ago!" she said, lifting one delicate hand to shield her face from the fire. "Is it possible that you have been away fifteen years?

Shame on you! You deserve to find yourself forgotten. Indeed, I should have forgotten you ten times over, except that I knew your father so well. Yes, you are right in saying that Sidney was different from other children; perhaps it was because she knew so few of them. That was another of Mortimer Lee's beautiful theories, — that she should not know girls of her own age. I suppose he was afraid she might acquire some healthy ideas. But he need n't have been. Good sense is not catching. Look at Sally Lee. I've done my best for her. I suppose I've seen her nearly every day for twenty years, — but she will always be a goose. She can't develop brains in her old age. I call Sally old, in spite of her ringlets. Dear me! why is it that an unmarried woman does not know how to grow old?"

The flicker of the fire showed a glimmering smile in Alan's eyes. He was standing with his elbow on the high mantelpiece, looking down at the keen old face before him.

"I am very fond of Miss Sally," he said. "She belongs to the salt of the earth."

Mrs. Paul lifted her hands impatiently. "Good?" she said, — "of course; but, Lord, how uninteresting goodness can be!" Her careless glance rested on his face, and lengthened into a steady look. "Alan," she declared, "you are really a very handsome man. You remind me of your father."

The doctor smiled, — and amusement will always save a man from embarrassment; "I thought I looked like my mother?"

"Oh, your mother?" she said carelessly. "I'm

sure I don't remember her well enough to say. Yes, you have a beautiful face; but there is nothing behind it. It is the face of a dreamer. It would serve Mortimer Lee right if Sidney fell in love with you; but she sha'n't. I suppose you have about two cents to live on? But, seriously, I hope great things from Robert Steele's being in town."

"Great things?" said Alan lightly. "For whom? Sidney?"

"Of course for Sidney," returned the other. "For whom else?"

"Well, there's Miss Sally; and as Sidney is never to marry" —

"Oh, fudge! Sally! Don't talk to me about Sally," interrupted Mrs. Paul. "If the young man has lost his wits, you had better never take him to the major's again, — that's all I have to say. And as for Sidney, of course she'll marry. We all know what paternal plans amount to when a girl falls in love," — she seemed to brush aside an invisible feather. "Beside, she must marry. What is going to support her when her father's gone? And he can't live forever. He's quite old now; sixty-five, at least. Yes, Robert Steele's money is just the thing that family needs. I hope you will make him call there often."

"If you remember Robert Steele," returned the doctor, "you will know that you can't arrange things for him. And if you decide that he is to fall in love with Sidney, it will be the very thing he'll not do."

"Fudge!" cried Mrs. Paul again. "My dear Alan, you don't know what you are talking about.

He can't help it. Neither could you, if you had anything to support a wife upon."

"But poor Steele," protested the doctor, — "why should you want his heart broken? If the major is in earnest that Sidney shall not marry, and if she agrees with him" —

"Of course he is in earnest, and of course Sidney agrees with him," Mrs. Paul broke in; "but a theory cannot change the order of nature, my young friend. Really, I almost lose my patience when I think of it. Of all ridiculous notions! A girl must not marry, forsooth, because her husband may die, and so she may be unhappy. As though to be a widow with plenty of money were the hardest thing in the world!"

"You have not found it so?" inquired Alan amiably.

"You are impertinent, young man!" declared his companion, and then she laughed. "I suppose that is the reason I like you. But these ideas of Mortimer Lee's, — I am sure that they grew out of some disappointment after his wife's death. I shall never believe that such a man as he could blast his whole life because of a chit of a girl, — though I have no doubt that he was attached to her. He may have loved some one else, for instance, but thought, because he was a widower, — a man is really settled when he is a widower, — or perhaps — But why do I talk to you? You don't know anything about Mortimer Lee; I do. I watched him in those days, I can tell you. Johnny's father had just died, and naturally I — understood him. Lord! how little sense men have!" She drew her eyebrows together, and frowned, absently, at the fire. The room was quite dark now, and under cover of the shadows John Paul yawned. He had risen, and stood like a spot of burly darkness against the fading oblong of the window. He was not interested in the conversation about the Lees: perhaps because the topic was far from new; perhaps because he was wondering how that speech upon the tariff, which he had put down when it grew too dark to read, had ended. With his hands behind him, he stood, while his mother talked, staring out into the forlorn and frosted garden, which lay in shivering nakedness under the cold sky. This garden, inclosed by its brick wall, extended behind the house, as well as in a narrow strip on each side of it. In front, below the drawing-room windows, there were no flower-beds; only a bit of decorous lawn ending in three terraces, and then a hedge along the low stone wall upon the street, which some twenty years ago had been a country road; but the street had been graded, so that now the old house was high above its level. The dreary outskirts of the bustling little manufacturing town had pushed closer and closer upon the house; a mill loomed up in the street below, and now and then a belching flame from a giant chimney sent a flare of light through the fan-shaped window above the white front door, or a fitful gleam across its brass knocker and knob. The hall within was wide and cheerless, although it had plenty of light; the leaded windows on either side of the door threw two lines of fluctuating brightness across the old

Turkey carpet; and opposite the drawing-room door — for the house was not double — there was a wide, low window, full of many small panes of glass. It looked only upon the blank of the garden wall, dark with ivy, and across a small grass plot on which upon a pedestal, was a sadly rusted iron Magdalen with a cross upon her knees. The sunshine poured through this window for a little while in the morning, and the dimity curtains were always pushed back, that all day long the hall might have as much light as possible; yet it was never anything but gloomy; dark family portraits in tarnished frames followed the wide staircase, and a faded engraving of the Trial of Effie Deans, hanging between the entrance to the dining-room and the green baize door of the drawing-room, added to its solemnity. Under the staircase stood a row of tall old fire-buckets, and a rosewood table for the candles and lamps, which, however, were never lighted until a certain hour, no matter how the late afternoon might darken with fog and mist.

Mrs. Paul's rules were not to be broken by such things as wind and weather. And as for cheerlessness, — her house suited her, she said, and other people were not obliged to live in it. It did suit her, although sometimes she resented the loud intrusion of the approaching town, but it was more with the petulance which is an occupation than because of any genuine annoyance. The felting in the windows, and the green baize door closing with noiseless tightness, shut out the clamor of the street below. Furthermore, there was always the consciousness that, if she wished, she could move away, as half a dozen other families had done; their estates being swallowed up by streets, and their dignified old houses turned into mills, or factories, or great tenements. When money is to be considered, human beings often display a curious indifference to the roofs which have sheltered their joys and sorrows and their sacred death-beds. But it was not any sentimental regard for her old house which kept Mrs. Paul here on the hill, nor was it altogether the feeling of superiority in being loyal to traditions to which her neighbors had been faithless.

Her sense of duty, she declared more than once, was really morbidly strong. "Of course," she said candidly to Miss Sally, "you and Sidney are not fit companions for me, and Mortimer Lee never chooses to come to see me; but what would you do without me? Heaven knows what would become of Sidney if I were not here to teach her manners. No, I will not give you up."

Little by little, all her interests had centred upon the major's household. It was ten years since the last of her older neighbors had moved away; and although no one knew that they had ceased to remember, or were themselves forgotten, these friendships belonged only to the past.

"Yes," Mrs. Paul explained to the doctor, "my first thought is for Sidney. With a simpleton for an aunt and a wicked infidel for a father, what would become of her if it were not for me? And I mean that she shall be married, I can tell you that,

—if it were only to teach Mortimer Lee a lesson! Everybody knows Robert Steele's folly, but it's all over and past. I'm not one to remember a man's sins against him. Besides, he has his money back again, and this time he'll keep it. Now, remember, you are to take him with you to the major's every chance you get. I shall invite him to meet Sidney here, too. It won't be the first time I've given Providence a hint. Johnny knows that. I was bound he shouldn't have her, for Sidney must marry a rich man, and Johnny hasn't a cent, except what I choose to give him."

John Paul shrugged his shoulders in the dusk, but did not speak.

"It's a pity he isn't well," she continued. "What did you say was the matter with him?"

"I did not say," Alan answered briefly.

Mrs. Paul laughed, with an impatient gesture. "Oh, you young doctors!" she said, "your importance is most amusing. I suppose you use it instead of sense? There! go home. I'm tired of you. I wish you would see that that medicine is sent in for Scarlett. I hope you appreciate my friendship in letting you experiment upon my maid? Johnny!"

"Yes, mother," said her son, coming to her side, as the door closed behind the doctor.

"I will play a game of draughts with you," she said, pushing her straight-backed armchair a little farther from the fire: "there is time before tea. Just fetch the table, and ring for Davids to bring the lamps."

John Paul rang the bell and silently brought the

small table, with its inlaid checkerboard of ivory and ebony; as he did so, the baize door opened, and Davids stood like a lean shadow against the dusk of the hall behind him.

"You may bring the lamps," said Mrs. Paul, beginning to arrange her men, the old-fashioned rings flashing upon her hands.

"It is not," said Davids, moving his shaven jaws with deliberation, "a quarter to six."

Mrs. Paul looked up. "I think you might as well bring them," she said, half apologetically, "if they are ready."

"They are not yet lighted"—he began to say, with respectful stubbornness, but John Paul interrupted him quietly.

"Bring the lamps," he said; and the man went at once to get them.

"I can give my own orders, thank you!" cried Mrs. Paul angrily. "You take too much upon yourself, sir! Please remember that this is my house."

She was still frowning when Davids returned with two tall lamps whose ground-glass globes faithfully imprisoned the light. He put one on either end of the mantel, and then, with a noiseless step, brought a footstool, and arranged a screen between his mistress and the fire, which had brought a delicate flush to her soft old cheek. After that he lit the candles in the sconces and put another lamp on a table at Mrs. Paul's elbow, so that in a moment the room was flooded with soft light.

This drawing-room of Mrs. Paul's was handsome,

and almost interesting; but the wainscoting above the bookcases built into the wall made the corners dark, and there was no cheerful litter of home life about it. A bust of the late Mr. Paul stood between the further windows, and over the mantel there was a painting of a very young girl in a white gown and pink ribbons. This was Annette, the child who had died, and for whom, it was said, Mrs. Paul had not grieved. Indeed, she had seemed angry at the child rather than at fate. She never spoke of her, but silence is sometimes more bitter than words.

All this was more than twenty-five years ago, when John Paul was less than twelve years old, and had been sent away to boarding-school that he might not be a nuisance to his mother. Mrs. Paul did not often look up at this picture, even when she was alone, and she had been heard to say carelessly that a woman could live her youth over again in her daughter, whereas a son —

But Providence arranged those things, she supposed.

II.

WHEN Mrs. Paul's door closed behind Alan Crossan, he stood a moment upon the steps thinking. A bell had rung in one of the factories, and down in the street a group of tired girls chattered shrilly as they turned toward their homes. Alan, looking through the arbor which covered the flight of stone steps down the terraces to the gate, could see them, and the cobble-stones of the street, and the dingy doorways opposite. It was only through the arbor one caught a glimpse of it all, for on either side of the gate, along the wall, was the high blackthorn hedge.

Just now, heavy drays, loaded with rattling iron rods or bales of dirty cotton, rumbled slowly past. A hand-organ, a block away, broke into a sharp jingling tune; one of the mill-girls began to dance, and there was a shout of noisy laughter from her companions. Alan Crossan frowned. It set his teeth on edge, he said to himself, — the bleak skies, the bald and vulgar streets, and the shrewd wind clattering through the branches of the trees. The doctor was tired. He had been in the almshouse infirmary all the morning, and then had come home to find Robert Steele sunk in the deepest depression.

Of course Alan understood its cause. As his friend made a better and better fight against his controlling weakness; as, steadily, he pushed his morphine further from him, he not only suffered physically, but he grew more aware of his cowardice, and the burden of that thought seemed to fling his soul into the dust of shame. Ordinarily, Alan's glad courage was quick to cheer and comfort the sick man, but this dark afternoon he had felt incapable of the exertion of cheerfulness, and so had wandered out, rather aimlessly, and had found himself, towards dusk, in Mrs. Paul's drawing-room. She amused him, and that, he declared, was good for his moral nature, so it was a duty to call upon her often. As he stood now watching the jostling crowd in the street, the remembrance of Robert's loneliness oppressed him; but he found himself thinking of Major Lee's library and Miss Sally's kindness, rather than of his own power to help his friend. He was in that frame of mind where a man likes to be made much of. "I will go and ask Miss Sally to give me a cup of tea," he said.

He thought again of Robert, as he opened the heavy iron gate and found himself in the street, and he declared that he was a brute to leave his friend alone. But he did not turn back.

Major Lee's house was on the other side of Mrs. Paul's garden wall. Its long-unused driveway (for the major kept no carriage) circled about a little lawn before the porch, and then opened upon a side street, which was really only a lane. Back of the house there was a great tangled garden, inclosed, like Mrs. Paul's, by a brick wall, — it was much larger than hers; beyond it was a pasture, and then a hillside crowned by sparse, open woods; beyond that were the rolling hills of the tranquil country, untouched as yet by the taint of trade.

The confusion of the bustling town did not intrude here, as it did at Mrs. Paul's. Perhaps this was because of that large silence which seemed to hold the life within.

"How little the major talks!" Alan thought, as he came through the lane, and looked up at the great gray house, set back in its walled courtyard, "and Sidney only listens. How gracious that bend of her head is, when she listens! Miss Sally talks, of course, but she does not say anything, and her voice is so pleasant."

The Lees' house was larger than Mrs. Paul's, being double and with low wings on either side. The veranda, with its four white pillars reaching above the second story, gave it a certain stateliness, in spite of a look of dilapidation and neglect.

"The fact is," Mrs. Paul had once explained to Robert Steele and the doctor, "Mortimer Lee has no money for repairs. He saves every cent for Sidney, Sally tells me. But I believe he grows poorer and poorer each year. I don't understand it, unless Sally is wasteful about her housekeeping, which I am sure is very likely, for she has less sense than any one I know. She tries to make both ends meet, but"— Mrs. Paul closed her lips with decision, though with the look of being able to say more, if she chose; which indeed was true, but, frank as she was in expressing her opinion of the major's sister, she would have been incapable of parading her anrangements with Miss Sally, whereby she listened every day to a French novel, or a history, or a newspaper, and Miss Sally, in consequence, accumulated a little fund, which she called — although Mrs. Paul did not know it — her "poor money." Sidney, quite unconscious of payment being made, sometimes took her aunt's place, although only when it was history or the news.

"French novels won't hurt *you*, Sally," Mrs. Paul declared frankly; "you are too old and too silly."

So Miss Sally, with her delicate and gentle face tingling with blushes, read many strange things to the handsome old woman in the carved armchair. That Miss Sally often went home and washed her little hands with vigorous and tearful protest and with a burning sense of degradation Mrs. Paul never knew, but she would have been delighted had she discovered it.

Housekeeping for Mortimer Lee, with his Virginia ideas of living and his narrow income, was not easy; but Miss Sally was always joyfully content, for was not money being put aside, little by little, for Sidney's future support? Beside, the pleasure of having her allowance for household expenses go sometimes a little further than she had dared to hope, in making her brother and her niece comfortable, filled her faithful life with a reason for being. They were so patient with her, she thought, these two shining ones; they let her love them all she could, though she was so different and so dull. How often she thanked God, with tears, for the blessing of being able to give them all her humble life!

The doctor walked across the sharp cobble-stones of the courtyard, up between the two ailantus trees which guarded the wide flight of steps, and rang the bell. He could hear its echoing jangle through the long hall, and then, a moment later, Miss Sally Lee's light, hurrying step. Some wet leaves drifted heavily down from ivy which had matted thickly across the lintel of a window, and on the other side of the house a shutter banged drearily. The premonition of cheerfulness within made him shiver in the raw wind. He was glad to take Miss Sally's cordial hand, and then follow her along the hall and into the library. As they opened the door a gush of firelight danced out, and lit two sudden stars in Sidney's eyes, as she glanced up from her seat in the corner of the old sofa by the hearth.

The room was full of the dusky glow of the fire, for the lamps had not yet been lighted; it glimmered on the bindings of the books which lined the walls and on the heavy furniture, and it lit a mimic flame in the darkness against the window-panes.

"Sit down, dear Alan!" cried Miss Sally, pushing a chair toward the fire before the doctor could prevent her. "How is poor Mr. Steele, and won't you tell Sidney she must not try to read by firelight? I was just going to fetch her a lamp when you rung."

Miss Sally's small, anxious face and timid manner always caused Alan to think of a deprecating bird, and made him want to stroke the somewhat ruffled plumage of her hair and dress, and bid her never fear. Instead, he remonstrated with Sidney. "By this flickering light?" he said. "Why, I am astonished at you!"

She had been bending down, so that the fire could shine on the page of her book, and her smooth cheek was scorched in spite of her protecting hand.

"I just wanted to finish a paragraph," she explained, smiling at his reproaches and closing the book quietly.

"What is it?" said the doctor. "What! Von Hartmann, and in German? To ruin your eyes for that sort of thing, Sidney, reflects upon your judgment."

"I did n't understand it very well," she said, "and I did n't like to give it up."

"Of course you did n't understand it," Alan declared, with the instant irritation of a man who sees a charming young woman do a thing which is not charming. Sidney Lee and German pessimism were not compatible; it was like running a steam engine through a flower garden for a girl to study that sort of thing, he had said to himself more than once. "Nobody understands it who has a healthy mind," he continued. Sidney only smiled. "At least no one should want to understand it," he amended, beginning to be good-natured again.

The lazy sweetness of Alan Crossan's temper forbade annoyance for any length of time, so, as he began to talk to Miss Sally, he dropped his solicitude for Sidney's brown eyes, and banished her unpleasant course of reading from his mind.

The cordial firelight, the faint scent of many leather-covered books, mingling with Miss Sally's mild chatter, rested and comforted him. He began to think — for it was not necessary to follow her words — of how he would brace Robert Steele when he went home, and his intention was so genuine that it made him forgive himself for having left his friend alone all the afternoon. From a word caught now and then, he knew that Miss Sally was saying kindly things about Mr. Steele. That she did not know the secret of his illness did not trouble Alan; he was quite certain that her sympathy for suffering did not depend upon the cause of the suffering; and so, sure of her interest, he burst out into praises of Robert which made him forget that he had been selfish in leaving the sick man.

"I admit," he said, his face full of charming animation, "that his action about that money was absurd; we all acknowledge that. But the motive was noble. And after all, it's the motive that counts. He threw away trust money, and the world calls that sort of thing dishonorable; but he did it from a strained idea of honor. Think how brave a man has to be to turn the world's standards upside down! When you come to think of it, though, that's what all great men have done. Yes, Bob is a man capable of greatness. I am so glad you and the major are good to him, Miss Sally. His own people are very cold; Kate Townsend is civil to him (those Townsends on the other side of the river are relatives of his, you know), but no one else is. The Draytons in Ashurst are his cousins, but the colonel has n't noticed him since he returned, and of course Steele won't go there without an invitation. As for me, I am that anomaly, a man without relatives, — except the Pauls, they are far off cousins, I believe; — so I have no one who will show him kindness and appreciation, and that sort of thing. But the fact is, there are not many people big enough to appreciate Steele, anyhow. Not that I believe much in relations," he went on, amused by Miss Sally's horror of such a sentiment; "the tie of blood is purely conventional. Sometimes people are friendly in spite of it, but not often. I am convinced that if Mrs. Paul should recollect that her husband was my grandfather's cousin she would treat me as badly as she does John, so pray don't mention it, Miss Sally?"

"Oh, I won't, Alan," she responded, in an anxious flutter; "but I 'm sure you are wrong. Dear Mrs. Paul would only love you more. But you must always feel sure that we love you. Your mother was a dear friend of mine, although I was so much younger than she. I shall always remember how kind she was when I came here first, just a girl, and so distressed at my brother's unhappiness."

Alan did not speak. The reference to his mother silenced him. Her memory was the one deep and sacred thing in his life, the one sorrow of his cloudless years, whereby he was a richer and better man. He felt the pity in Sidney's eyes, although he did not look at her, and he almost forgave her Von Hartmann; or rather, he almost forgave the major, who was responsible for Von Hartmann. The reality of Alan's own sorrow revealed his unconscious flippancy when he once told Mrs. Paul that Major

Lee's grief of twenty-two years was like a fly in amber: it might be perfect, but it had no vitality. He could not let Miss Sally speak of his mother again.

"Do you know Katherine Townsend?" he said to Sidney, in a changed voice. She was staring into the fire, her chin resting in her hand and her elbow on her knee.

She shook her head. "No," she said.

"You don't know many girls of your own age, do you?" he asked.

"No; you see all the people we used to know have moved away, except Mrs. Paul. Not that I ever knew any children very well. Somehow, I did not need to know children, when I had father; and now there are nothing but tenements around us."

Miss Sally sighed. "Dear me!" she said, "and what dreadful places they are, the tenement houses! There is so much suffering among the mill people."

"You enjoy it, dear," interposed Sidney, smiling a little, with her serious eyes on Miss Sally's troubled face. "What would you do without your sewing-school and your visits to your sick people? She will make you go to see them, too, Alan."

"Do you go?" he said, watching the firelight shining in her eyes.

"Oh, no!" cried Miss Sally deprecatingly; "no, indeed, Sidney could n't go. You don't know how sad it is, Alan."

Sidney shook her head, with a shiver. "No," she said. "It is dreadful to think that there is suffering, — but to go to see it!"

"But if by going you make it less?" Alan persisted, too interested to be displeased.

"But you know it cannot really be helped," she answered gravely. "The facts of life are not to be changed by a bowl of soup or a bottle of medicine. Of course there is the pleasure of giving, — to the giver; but that is really all there is."

"Altruism is another name for selfishness, then?" Alan said, laughing.

"Perhaps so," she admitted; "or perhaps it's something worse than that; those people had far better die — they are no good to the community or to themselves — but you philanthropists try to put aside the laws of nature, and keep them alive!"

"That," observed Alan, "is as inhuman a sentiment (I beg your pardon, Sidney) as I have often heard."

She looked troubled. "But it is true," she said gently. "Oh, I am glad my garden walls are high, and shut sad things out. I — I saw a baby's funeral to-day, aunty; and oh, the poor father and mother were taking the baby's little rocking-horse out to the grave with them, to leave it there, I suppose."

"What pathos there is in that," said the doctor, — "that putting things on the grave! It is a sort of compromise with death."

Sidney nodded, but Miss Sally was full of interest. "Did you notice where the funeral came from, my dear? Was it from Mary Allen's, do you think? But you don't know where she lives. It came out of Dove's Lane, you say? Oh, yes, — yes, I'm afraid it was her baby. I heard that it was sick. I must go to see her, to-morrow; poor, poor thing!"

Sidney looked up at the doctor and smiled. "That is the way she does," she said.

They did not talk of the pitiful little funeral any longer, for Miss Sally's kind eyes were full of tears, and Sidney shrank from any mention of pain. The sight of her aunt's concern seemed to fill her with silent impatience; she frowned at the fire, and for a while no one spoke.

The logs had smouldered into a dull glow, when Miss Sally rose to bring the lamps. Alan sprang to his feet to help her, but Sidney, lifting her eyes from the red ashes, only glanced back into the shadows, and said she had not realized that it was so dark. Miss Sally, however, refused Alan's aid, and the two young people fell again into silence, until a step in the hall made a sudden gladness flash into Sidney's face, and she rose to welcome her father. Alan could hear the murmur of their voices in the hall, and then they entered together; the major standing for a moment in the doorway, like a wavering shadow, while he put his glasses astride his nose, and peered through them at the guest in the chimney corner. Then he extended his hand to the young man, in silent and friendly greeting.

His eyes were only for Sidney, but he smiled at Alan when he heard Miss Sally, as she came in with the lamps, tell the doctor that he must stay to tea, and he said gently, "Yes, surely, surely." From the hollows under his shaggy brows, eyes as dark and shining as Sidney's own watched her as she and

Alan talked. It seemed as though every motion and glance of hers fell upon the shrine of his heart; he smiled when she did, for very joy of seeing his darling pleased. He did not listen to what the young man said to her, although sometimes he bent his white head in gracious attention; he took no part in the conversation, and did not speak again until they rose to go in to tea.

Then he said, "I called upon Mr. Steele this afternoon, Alan."

"Did you?" cried the doctor, his face brightening with surprise and pleasure. But the major did not pursue the subject just then.

"Will you give my sister your arm, sir?" he said courteously.

As he spoke, he offered his own to his daughter, and gravely followed Alan and Miss Sally to the dining-room. This formality was as much a part of the major's precise and silent life as was his daily walk to the bank or his cigar at seven. Family rudeness, which goes by the name of affection, was impossible in Mortimer Lee's household; that the stately walk through the wide, bare hall was to a most frugal tea-table was of no importance, and could have no effect upon these decencies of life, — at least in the major's mind.

The doctor had taken tea here frequently since his return to Mercer; for when he had called first, the major, holding his hand silently for a moment, had said, "Let us see you often, Alan. I loved your father, sir." There was something in the old man's voice which made Alan's eyes sting for an unaccustomed instant, and he had come, very often. Sometimes, after having taken a great deal of tea from Miss Sally's little thin blue cups, and eaten many slices of bread, he would, as he went home, stop to satisfy his appetite at a convenient shop; for there was a marked absence upon the major's tea-table of those things which appeal best to a hungry man, although, to be sure, there was a great show of silver, and plenty of glass dishes cut into wide, unequal stars. But it was a pleasure to Alan to be there, even if he stopped at an eating-house afterwards.

The dining-room was behind the library; its corners were cut off to make convenient closets for Miss Sally's jellies, thereby turning the room into an octagon. It was large and always seemed dark because of the heavy sideboard, the big armchairs, and the bare and shining mahogany table, although the walls were covered with a light paper in a wide, faint pattern of green palm leaves, and the chintz hangings in the windows were pale and faded.

The major and Miss Sally were at either end of the table, and Sidney sat opposite the doctor; as usual the group was very silent. The major had but few interests; Miss Sally had no opinions; and Sidney's serene indifference to the world needed no words. So, the doctor, eating his bread and drinking his tea, could, without the interruption of conversation, look at Sidney and enjoy himself very much for a whole hour, for Mortimer Lee did not understand haste.

Sidney had a habit, which delighted Alan, of looking up at him from under her level brows, thinking her own thoughts all the while, but smiling with a grave, impersonal kindliness. Alan could even forget German pessimism when she looked at him in this way. That he ventured sometimes to return her calm, wide-eyed gaze never disconcerted her, which made him perhaps less happy. Now, in a gown of some vague color, that shimmered a little when she moved, Sidney sat dreaming over her bread and honey, quite unconscious of the young man's eyes; the quaint little rosy garland about her cup, or the Chinese pagoda on her plate, interested her as much as he did. The soft color on her cheek was like the flush of clover, and the shadows from her shining hair rested on a smooth white forehead; two lamps on the sideboard and the candles at either end of the table did not light the dining-room very well, so there were many shadows on the young face.

Miss Sally's little maid, who always looked as anxious as her mistress, waited on them as noiselessly as though she were only a small gray and white shadow herself; it was in one of the pauses, while she removed the plates, that the major said again, "Yes, I called this afternoon upon Mr. Robert Steele. I am sorry that he does not look better."

"Yet he is improving," Alan answered. "But you know it is hard lines, Major Lee. There are plenty of people to call him a fool; though a man can bear that, for who is going to decide what is wisdom and what is folly, in this world? But when it comes to being called a rogue" —

"True," said the major, — "true."

"Oh, how can any one be so wicked as to think that he meant to do anything wrong?" cried Miss Sally warmly.

"It occurred to me," proceeded the major (his sister's questions did not often require an answer), "it occurred to me that it might perhaps be painful for the young man to be alone so much" — He paused; it struck him that such a remark might indicate that he thought Alan neglectful of his friend, so he hastened to say, "And you are of necessity absent occasionally, needing recreation from your professional duties," — Alan smiled, — "so I ventured to ask Mr. Steele to make us a little visit. My sister will, I am sure, see that he is made comfortable; and with my household and your frequent calls he will be at least less lonely."

"I hope he said he would come," said Alan joyously. "Ah, he is a good fellow! I know you will like him and find him delightful."

"Most certainly," returned the major, lifting his eyebrows a little. He had not asked Robert Steele for his own pleasure.

Miss Sally, however, was saying to herself in dismay, "A visitor, and eggs thirty-five cents a dozen!"

"He did not say definitely that we might expect him," proceeded the host. "Doubtless he wishes to consult his physician. I depend upon you to present my request in more attractive terms than I was able to do."

"Oh, I shall insist upon his coming," answered

the doctor cheerfully; "it will be the best thing in the world for him. Miss Sally, you will rob me of a patient!"

"Pray," Major Lee protested, "pray do not make my invitation insistent. The young man must not be driven into it. I could not refrain, however, from asking him to come, he was apparently in such a sad state."

That suggestion of a "sad state" sobered the doctor. Perhaps before urging him to come to his house, the major ought to know of that weakness which Robert Steele called "sin"? So, a little later, when his host had risen to open the door for his sister and daughter, and then had returned to the table for his single small glass of wine, Alan spoke of the cause of his friend's illness with some lightness, but with much tenderness. Major Lee made no comment; he only said again, as he pushed the decanter towards Alan, "I shall depend upon you, sir, to tell Mr. Steele how much pleasure it will give me to see him in my house."

It was evident that he meant to forget the doctor's explanation.

III.

"So the major has invited your Steele to visit him?" said John Paul. "Do you realize what an effort that is to him? I suppose he did it because everybody is so down on Mr. Steele. I am, myself, — confound him! — though I don't think him anything worse than a crank."

Alan laughed and frowned. "You can't appreciate him, Paul, — that's what's the matter with you. But the invitation is odd. Your mother has an idea — But I fancy the very fact of the major's taking Bob into his house shows his confidence in the result of Sidney's training?"

The doctor wanted to be contradicted, but his companion, after a moment's pause to guess the meaning of the unfinished sentence, nodded, and said, "Yes, exactly. Mortimer Lee would not hesitate to bring the most attractive man in the world into Sidney's presence (and I suppose you hardly call Steele that?). She's safe; — more's the pity for the girl."

Alan looked at him with lazy annoyance. To have Paul assume so positively that Sidney's unnatural training would certainly spoil her life irritated him; and yet it gave him a vague assurance, too. The thought of Robert's probable intimacy with the major's family had not been entirely pleasant to the doctor; indeed, the more he had reflected upon it, the less certain he became that such a visit would benefit the sick man. But all the while he was thoroughly aware of the fear which lay behind this thought, and even amused by its pretense, so it did not prevent him from using his utmost influence to persuade his friend to go to the major's; though when, at last, after much urging, Robert consented, Alan took up his violin, and spent an hour, with knitted brows, picking out a difficult movement.

He reflected now that there was no reason why John Paul's assurance that Sidney was safe should be comforting, but it was,—at least so far as Mr. Steele was concerned.

The two men had met upon the little covered bridge that spanned the hurrying river, upon either side of which lay the manufacturing town of Mercer, and now they were walking on together; Alan to the house of an unexpected patient, and John Paul—

"I am going," he had explained, with unnecessary frankness, and with a dull flush upon his brown cheek,—"I am going out to Red Lane to see a little boy. He has some pups. It's Ted Townsend,—brother of Miss Katherine Townsend, you know: nice boy; nice pups."

"Nice girl?" Alan observed, stopping to light a cigarette, his eyes smiling over the sputtering match in his hollow hand.

"Oh!" returned the older man hastily; "yes, quite so. Don't see much of her, of course. She has pupils, and that sort of thing. She has to earn her own living, you know. Steele is her cousin, is n't he?"

"Yes, but she would n't permit him"— Alan began to resent.

"No," interrupted John impatiently, "she won't permit any one,— that's just it. And she has those sisters to look after, and Ted."

"And the pups?" suggested Alan, but John did not notice him.

"Why, think of it, Crossan," he said, taking his hands out of his pockets to gesticulate: "here she is,— Katherine Townsend, a woman who is worth any ten I ever saw in my life (I'm just an outsider, and unprejudiced; you'd say the same thing if you knew her),— here she is, giving music lessons to this little Eliza Jennings in the toll-house. Eliza Jennings is a nice little thing, no doubt, but"—

John Paul wore a fur cap, and as he spoke his forehead seemed to disappear under it in two big wrinkles.

"Does Mrs. Paul know Miss Townsend?" inquired the doctor, after a moment's pause; and his companion's abrupt "No" made Alan's eyes dance. Robert Steele, and the smallness of his own practice, and all the little worries of life could be forgotten when he found anything droll. It was a happy temperament, this, which could banish an unpleasant thought by a merry one. "With it, a man does n't live on a mountain-top," Alan admitted gayly, "but he finds the foot-hills amazingly pleasant."

John had no more to say of the sister of the boy with the pups; yet, as they went past the toll-house, he looked searchingly into the window from which it was Mrs. Jennings' habit to extend one tight, plump hand for a penny. But in John Paul's eyes, the small room within was empty, although, indeed, Eliza Jennings sat rocking comfortably in a big chair, which had a crocheted antimacassar on its back. There was a row of geraniums on the window-sill beside her, which strained the wintry sunshine through a net of scarlet blossoms and broad, vigorous leaves.

"Was it Mr. Paul, ma?" she said, with a sort of gasp, as the fur cap vanished from the small horizon of the toll-window. Eliza's freckled little face grew quite intent as she spoke. It is curious how lasting is the interest in a question of this nature. Eliza Jennings had kept a half look, which meant hope and expectation, upon that window of the toll-house for many months. Yes, it was quite six months ago that Mr. John Paul began to take these very frequent walks towards Red Lane, and in that time Eliza had had many a pleasant nod, or a word or two about the weather, as he handed her a penny for the toll.

With a view to this interest in her life, Eliza could not have lived in a better place than the toll-house. The pedestrian could not come from Old Mercer to Little Mercer save across this bridge. Then, too, as he returned, he must stop long enough to extract a penny from the pocket of his breeches, and where a man is tall and stout this is not done hastily.

The gray toll-house at the end of the covered

bridge did not seem to belong among the smart new houses of Little Mercer, but rather as if it had been pushed out of the older town when the bridge first crossed the river, and was now looking back with regret. There was a yard around it, inclosed by high palings, which were always dazzling with fresh whitewash. In summer, poppies, and bouncing-bets, and bachelor's-buttons pushed between the bars, and gazed with honest sweetness at the foot-passengers, for the garden was always full of riotous color and perfume.

Now, only a few brown stalks stood straight and thin in the snow. The wooden arbor in the middle was reached by a tiny graveled walk, which curled about among the flower-beds to make a respectable length. On this cold November day its seats were piled high with powdery snow, which rose in a gleaming dust when the wind blew from up the river, and then settled in small icy ripples along the floor. But the arbor (in which, during the summer, it was the custom of Mrs. Jennings to serve tall glasses of ice-cream to hot wayfarers) had, even in November, a certain sacredness for Eliza. Was it not here that she had first talked to Mr. John Paul? It was a June day, — ah, how well she remembered it! He had brought little Ted Townsend into the summer-house, through the hot sweetness of the blazing garden, and had begged Eliza to fetch him two glasses of ice-cream.

"Every fi' cents Kitty gives me," Ted said, breathless with anticipation, "I spend here, don't I, Miss Eliza?"

John, in a look across Ted's curly head, good-naturedly shared his amusement with Eliza, who felt her heart beat with pleasure.

"He's just grand!" she told her mother, and Mrs. Jennings agreed with her; "it was real good in him to treat Master Ted," she said, "though I should have thought a gentleman like him would 'a' brought the boy's sister along too; for it would seem right nice to her, workin' all day like she does, teachin' this one or that one;" and Mrs. Jennings was glad that her Eliza could stay at home, like a lady, with only a bonnet to trim now and then for a neighbor. But the little milliner had resented even this small criticism upon the grand gentleman in the garden.

Mrs. Jennings, except where love made her shrewd, was a woman of slow, dull thought, but she began to connect her daughter's sudden desire for improvement in one way or another with that scene in the garden, and not long afterwards, seeing Eliza so faithful in her blundering practice upon the melodeon, she had suggested that her daughter should take organ lessons from Miss Townsend, "an' be a real musician, 'Liza," she explained. "I guess you'll find *he's* musical, too. Besides, she ain't real well off, you know, and I like to help a body along."

"And pray why not?" Katherine had demanded of Mr. John Paul, as he stood indignant and aghast in her small parlor.

"But, Miss Townsend," he stammered, "you — you are " —

"Delighted to have a new pupil," she finished, and laughed.

Katherine Townsend was always cordial and occasionally sincere. This time she was both. "Don't you see," she said, "it would be absurd in me to say I would not instruct little Eliza how to play upon her organ with twenty-two stops. I want pupils, and she wants lessons. Why should we both be disappointed?"

"I — I could find you some pupils; there are lots of people who would be glad"— he began; but there was nothing more to say. Miss Katherine Townsend was a young woman who managed her own affairs. Her little house was quite out of sight of any wistful eyes at the toll-house window which might follow Mr. John Paul's figure to the turn by the big barberry bush, which hid the footpath along Red Lane. To be sure, it was plain enough that Mr. Paul often happened to be going in or coming out from Old Mercer just when Miss Townsend did, but it did not follow from that, that he went to see her. He never paid the toll for her, Eliza had noticed; she always put down her own money in the most matter-of-fact way, and what could be more natural than for the milliner to say, "Well, ma, they ain't hardly friendly. A young gentleman who was waiting on a young lady would n't let her pay her own toll." And Mrs. Jennings assured her that she was right. Indeed, Mrs. Jennings would have assured Eliza of almost anything, so truly did the heart in her large bosom feel all her daughter's joys and griefs. It was not necessary

that Eliza should confide in her; although she had
never seen the diary in which was recorded, in
violet ink, the emotions of an empty and harmless
little life, Mrs. Jennings knew all, with that maternal
instinct which is not dependent upon knowledge.
Perhaps the only thing she had not guessed was her
daughter's desire for a confidante. Eliza had often
thought how happy she would be if she could only
"tell" some one, — granted, of course, that the day
might come when there would be anything more to
"tell" than that there had been a cheery good-morning or a laugh about Ted's passion for ice-cream, and
granted also that the confidante should not be her
mother. With such indifference is maternal devotion too often received! Sometimes, in a pleasant
dream, while she trimmed a bonnet behind the geraniums in the window, or watched the light from
the river ripple upon the low ceiling, she thought
how much she should like to tell Miss Katherine
Townsend that she had "given her heart away."
She often pictured the scene to herself, as she sat
rocking and sewing, in that delightful misery which
only the sentimental young woman knows; and she
would sometimes drop a tear upon her ribbon, which
always brought her back to practical life with anxious haste. But although Miss Townsend was most
kind during the weekly music lesson, this confidential talk never seemed possible. There was a look
behind those gray eyes which forbade intimacy, and
sometimes made Eliza's thick little fingers tumble
over each other on the keys, and her heart beat with
a sort of fright.

"It's perfectly ridiculous in you, 'Liza," said Mrs. Jennings impatiently; " she ain't got any more money than we have, so I tell you! Yes, and them three children to bring up, too. It was different enough when her pa was alive. There! I'm sorry for her. But you do make me real provoked at you, when you act as if you were more 'n half afraid of her. She ain't situated so as to be proud."

And indeed Miss Katherine Townsend would have been apt to agree with the mistress of the toll-house. There was much anxiety and hard work in her plain and quiet life, much keen disgust, and weariness with many things. But below all this, which may be forgotten, there was a dull regret which she never put into words. It was in her mind this cold, bright afternoon, when the doctor and John Paul had gone over the bridge, and then out along the turnpike into the country.

Katherine had come home from a lesson, tired, she said to herself, of everything; which was but another way of saying that she was feeling the lack of some absorbing occupation of mind. These music lessons were necessary, but never pleasant; Katherine had too much self-consciousness ever to find teaching a delight for its own sake. Ted had run down the lane to welcome her. He had forgotten his coat, in excess of affection, and Ted's colds were a constant anxiety to his sister. Carrie and Louise were squabbling in the upper hall; and the one maid-of-all-work came with heavy, slipshod tread to the foot of the stairs, to say that the flour was out and the coal low.

Why did the girls squabble? Why did Ted cough? Why were Maria's aprons always dingy? "Father's house ought not to be like this; father's children ought not to have such voices." Something seemed to come up into Katherine's throat, but she only stopped to kiss Ted, and break up the small quarrel by asking her sisters to see that his shoes were not wet. Then she dropped down upon her bed until tea-time. She hid her tired eyes in the cool pillow, although with no thought of tears. Miss Katherine Townsend was not one of those women to whom can come the easy relief of tears. Beside, she had nothing to cry about. This thought of John Paul, she said to herself, was too familiar for emotion, and too impersonal. She was only sorry that he was not a braver and a stronger man.

"And yet he is so good," she said, with that same feeling in her throat, — so good, and honest, and kind. Oh, what shall I do if I cannot make Ted a brave man!"

Of course this young woman understood John's attentions to Ted; she knew what those accidental meetings on the bridge meant to the big, slow, simple man; but what was she to infer if he never put his meaning into words? What she did infer, and what made her manner such that these unspoken words seemed more and more impossible to John, was, that he was unwilling to marry upon the small income which Mrs. Paul gave him; and that he was too indolent or too cowardly to take his life out of his mother's hands, and live it as he chose, with poverty if necessary, but with love. For, knowing the sort of life which John Paul led, and knowing too that it was not the natural bent of the man, her conclusion was that he led it because it was easiest. She knew just how his day was passed. There was the warehouse in the morning, where he sat in a little glass office, but where the old head clerk never dreamed of going for assistance or advice. She "preferred to give her own advice," Mrs. Paul had declared contemptuously. John read the letters, but Murray answered them as he saw fit; his ostensible employer, meanwhile, studying his English newspaper, or writing scholarly and stupid articles upon free trade ("which might be the ruin of the house, if anybody ever read them," grumbled Murray). Besides this, the mornings were good times to look up the pedigrees of favorite dogs. One of these researches among kennel-books resulted in a present to Ted of the mastiff puppies, which greatly inconvenienced Ted's sister. In the afternoon, John could walk, or ride, or read more newspapers, and dream much of Katherine Townsend.

But she, here alone in the cold November dusk, thinking of this lazy, comfortable life, said to herself that it served him right that, after such a day, he had to spend his dull evening until nine listening to his mother's tongue, while they played at draughts by the drawing-room fire, "and just because he has not the courage to break away from it all!" Although in her heart she added "and love me," yet her indignation was that which every earnest mind feels at the sight of neglected possibilities, and not at all the smaller pain of wounded self-esteem.

Perhaps her inner consciousness, however, that he did love her made this finer attitude of mind possible.

But Katherine, in her bitter thoughts, was not just. She did not understand that this sort of life may begin in a sense of duty, and end in the habit of content. John Paul had gone into the warehouse for his mother's sake. How glad he would have been to do the work there heartily and earnestly, and how completely his mother had pushed his desires aside, Katherine did not know, and would hardly have respected him more had she known. She could not guess the gentleness of this silent man, nor imagine that he shrank from disappointing his mother, even though he hurt his self-respect by the sacrifice.

But little by little, habit had blurred that pain. John was thirty-six, and for years he had been living on the very small allowance which his mother chose to make him. He had never felt that he earned it, unless indeed he earned it by sitting in silence beneath her gibes, to which he had become so accustomed that he could think his own thoughts all the while. One of the best things he had ever written upon the tariff had been thought out during a game of draughts, while Mrs. Paul had railed about Miss Sally Lee until she was white with anger.

One other thing Miss Townsend overlooked: John had no motive for action greater than this self-sacrifice upon which he was throwing away his soul.

"If Katherine cared anything about me," he said

to himself, "if she would even look at me, I'd fling the whole thing over in a minute."

So this makeshift of life went on, and John Paul made no effort to do anything but endure. He wished he had known Miss Townsend before; perhaps she would have cared for him when he was younger. John felt very old and very dull now, and the only thing he could do was to comfort himself by seeing Ted often, and hearing him talk about Kitty, which was certainly not very satisfactory for a lover.

IV.

Mrs. Paul had a moment of great astonishment when she learned of Major Lee's invitation to Alan's friend. Miss Sally had been her informant; but instead of being thankful for a bit of gossip and a new interest, she was angry that no one had told her sooner.

"He invited him day before yesterday?" she said. "Why are you so secretive, Sally? Why did n't you tell me before?"

"I have not had a chance to come in," Miss Sally explained, gently. "I have had so much on my mind about the kitchen, you know, and" —

"Much difference it will make in what the poor young man gets to eat," interrupted Mrs. Paul, "whether the kitchen is on your mind or not, Sally! And as for not having had a chance to come in, why did n't you make a chance?"

But Mrs. Paul was really too much delighted with the arrangements of Providence — "for such things are providential," she declared — to find much fault with Miss Sally. She was full of interest and pleased expectancy.

"Young Steele can't live in the house with Sidney," she reflected, "and not fall in love with her; the mere fact that Mortimer Lee does n't want him to will insure that. Well, I shall do my part. No one can say that I ever shirk a duty!" She lost no opportunity to inquire about Mr. Steele; his health, his frame of mind, his manner. "All those things mean so much to a girl," she thought, impatiently.

When John Paul came in to tea, one evening, a day or two after Robert had gone to the major's, she was instant with a question.

"Did you go to call upon Mr. Steele this afternoon? I wonder if you would know enough to make a call upon any one unless I sent you! Well, why don't you answer me?"

"Yes," said John.

"Yes?" cried his mother. "Are you as sparing of ideas as you are of words, Johnny?"

"I saw him."

"Well? What? what? what? Can't you tell me about it? Here I sit alone all day, and you make no effort to entertain me. Your weight is not confined to your body, my friend. The only really interesting and curious thing about you, Johnny, is how you can be so dull, and yet be my son. Was anything said?"

"Nothing much," John answered, slowly. He was thinking at that moment of Katherine Townsend.

"I'll warrant,—if you were there. Johnny, you've less sense each year. I suppose I must put it into plain words. Did Robert Steele seem impressed by Sidney? There, you can answer that!"

"No," said John.

Mrs. Paul struck her hands sharply together. "Either you are blind or he is," she declared.

Indeed, there seemed to be no one from whom she

could gain satisfactory information; least of all could she learn anything from Sidney herself, although the girl came more than once, in her aunt's place, to read aloud, which gave Mrs. Paul an opportunity to ask questions.

But Sidney's absolute unconsciousness baffled her. Coming in out of the icy wind, which blew the snow in drifts along the path, and ruffled her hair about her forehead, she looked at the older woman with serene eyes, and a face on which the delicate flush, as fresh as the curve of a sea-shell, never deepened nor changed. Sometimes her level brows gathered in a fleeting frown. It was not pleasant to talk so much of Mr. Steele, she thought; it was enough to have him in the house; and the best thing to do was to forget his presence, so far as she could.

"I don't like to think about sick people," she said once, in her placid way; "it is so disagreeable."

Miss Sally, to whom the remark had been made, was distressed that her darling should be annoyed, although, to be sure, she said bravely, "Is it quite kind to feel so, love?" But that little protest made, she did all in her power to keep Mr. Steele out of her niece's way. Robert was perfectly aware that she did so. He felt Sidney's aversion, without realizing that it was not for him, but for his suffering, and the consciousness of it threw him back with infinite relief upon Miss Sally's gentleness and pity. She, at least, did not despise him; and he even began to tell himself that her friendship was an incentive to fight for his honor and his manhood.

Perhaps his first week at the major's was the

crisis of Robert Steele's struggle for liberty and self-respect; but the last clutch of the old habit struck sharp into his heart. He was, however, far nearer freedom than he knew, for he was so absorbed in wrestling with this horror of weakness that he did not stop to remember how rapidly Alan was reducing his morphine. He was blind to everything which might have encouraged him, and quite unable to perceive his own progress. He felt as though he were remaining stationary, or even drifting, little by little, further away from hope. He spoke afterwards to Alan of his mental condition at that time. "It was a horror of great darkness," he said. "I felt — you know the old illustration — as though a maelstrom were roaring for me, to suck me down into furious blackness of night, and then as if I were beating my way out along a side current, only to find that it too was whirling round the same terrible centre."

Here, in this despair, Miss Sally's little friendly, timid hand was reached out to him. Her kindness seemed greater, perhaps, for Sidney's coldness; but its cheer and strength no one knew save Robert himself. So it came about, when he had been at the major's two or three days, that he and Miss Sally began to sit together in the parlor across the hall, and leave Sidney and her father alone in the library.

Robert did not talk much; it was pleasure enough just to listen to Miss Sally's mild voice, so full of confidence and respect. She, it must be admitted, talked a great deal. Once she told him, and it soothed him inexpressibly, that she thought he had been so noble and so brave about — that money. He must forgive her for speaking of it, but she did think so.

That Miss Sally was as ignorant of finance as little Susan, singing in the big, sunny kitchen, made no difference to Robert Steele; although perhaps he did not probe her knowledge by a question because he feared to discover its shallowness. He was quite content to sit here, in the long-unused parlor, making no effort to talk, only listening dreamily to her pleasant chatter. It was not a cheerful room, save for her voice, even when the afternoon sunshine streamed through the leafless branches of the ailantus trees, and touched the faded yellow damask of the old furniture and the gray paper with its scattered spots of gilt. Sometimes the sunshine rested in a glimmering dust upon the half-length portrait of a very beautiful young woman, who lifted a stately head and throat from a crimson velvet wrap, and looked with calm, level eyes over the heads of the people in the room, and out into the golden light behind the trees. Robert looked persistently at this picture while his hostess talked, although the same indifference which he had seen in Sidney chilled him in the face of this woman, long since dead, and made his heart shiver for the warmth and comfort of Miss Sally's kindness.

They had been sitting here together the first Sunday of Mr. Steele's visit, when it occurred to Miss Sally that it might be a pleasure to him to see Mrs. Paul, and so she proposed that he should go to call upon her.

"I'm afraid it is dull for you," she said, apologetically, — "just to talk to me. Mortimer never comes in here, because of Gertrude's picture, you know, — he does not like to see it; and he and Sidney always spend their Sunday afternoons reading and studying, or they would beg you to come into the library with them. But I am sure you will enjoy seeing Mrs. Paul. Won't you go?"

To Robert, pale, sad-eyed, and ashamed, there seemed but one thing to do, and that was to be guided by any one who would take the trouble to lead him.

"If you wish it," he answered; "and if you will go, too."

So they started out together; Robert walking ahead to make a path through the snow for Miss Sally, and feeling a trembling dignity in this slight assertion of care for some one else. Feathery thimbles fell from the rusted hinges as he pulled open the door in the wall, and a wreath of snow shaken from the twisted branches of the wistaria powdered his shoulders with misty white. He laughed, and made light of Miss Sally's fear that he might take cold. This, too, was good for him.

"Now what in the world," Mrs. Paul was saying, observing them from her bedroom window, "does that Sally come with him for?" However, she made haste to take Scarlett's arm, and welcomed them, a moment later, at the fireside in the drawing-room. "So good of you to come to see an old woman," she said, smiling at Robert under dark brows which had not yet lost their delicate arch.

"And it was good in dear Sally to show you the short way between our houses; but you must not let Mr. Steele trespass upon your kindness, Sally, by keeping you here now, if you are needed at home?"

"Oh, no," said Miss Sally, cheerfully, delighted at Mrs. Paul's consideration. "I can stay just as well as not, thank you."

"How fortunate!" returned her hostess, with the suggestion of a shrug; then she turned her shoulder towards Miss Sally and began to talk altogether to Robert.

Here, too, was solace. With Mrs. Paul his past was all a matter of course. It was a little amusing, perhaps, — an excess of virtue is apt to be amusing, — but it could not change her friendliness, nor that charming cordiality which could forget his amiable folly. Robert Steele felt braced into a glow of confidence and hope; not even the pang of disgust with himself, which came when his hostess cleverly turned the conversation upon Sidney, could rob him of that thrill of courage. In his heart he was thanking Miss Sally for it; but how could Mrs. Paul fancy that?

Alan Crossan, of course, had a clearer understanding of Robert's frame of mind; he knew that it was time to look for strength and courage, whether Miss Sally had been kind or not; but he was none the less pleased, when he called at the major's, to know that his friend had gone out with her. The doctor had dropped in to see Mr. Steele, he said, and was delighted to learn that "Bob was beginning now to gad about." He found the major and his daughter alone in the small room beyond the library, where the old man kept his dearest books and did some little writing, and where Sidney had learned all the bitter lessons which his life could teach. Sunday was the best time in the week to these two friends; the beautiful, silent hours marked Sidney's spiritual growth, because in them she looked deeper and deeper into her father's love. Miss Sally never thought of sitting with them, even when she did not go to church; and they had no callers, except once in a while when John Paul came in, and ate a piece of Miss Sally's plain cake and took a glass of wine from the decanter, which, more out of regard for ancient habits of hospitality than because of expected guests, stood on Sunday afternoons on a side-table in the library.

This December day was cold and bright; the wintry sunshine crept about the long room, gleaming on the silver collar of the decanter, and fading the glow of the smouldering logs in the fireplace. The major was tired, but he let Sidney lead him over to the old sofa and arrange the cushions for his head, more for the happiness of her tender touch than for rest. Then she had brought a hassock to his side, and a book, and without words they were very happy.

Major Lee would have been dismayed if he had seen his daughter ungracious, yet, as he rose to welcome Alan, he felt vaguely that Sidney regretted "this pleasing interruption" (it was thus he answered the doctor's apology) less than he did. It was she who said, in her glad young voice, "You must wait until Mr. Steele comes back, Alan;" and the major could do no less than beg him to be seated, adding, "And you will take tea with us, sir?" Of course the young man accepted the invitation; indeed, he had counted upon receiving it.

"It's very good of Miss Sally," he said, "to devote herself to Steele in this way, instead of going to church. But what will Mr. Brown say? His name is Brown, is n't it?"

"Perhaps next Sunday she will induce Mr. Steele to accompany her to church," the major answered.

"She will not have to urge him," Alan declared. "He is one of those naturally religious people, you know. He goes to church as a matter of course."

"Ah?" returned Major Lee. Mr. Robert Steele's eccentricities did not interest him.

But this mention of church-going introduced a subject upon which Alan wanted to speak to the older man. To be able to express his own opinion on one or two points would be an escape for the irritation which the major's attitude had aroused in him.

"To bring up a girl in this way is outrageous!" he had said to himself a dozen times since he had come back to Mercer; for Alan knew all about the major's theories upon education. Miss Sally's quick and tender and somewhat shallow nature made reserve about herself impossible, and her abundant kindliness claimed her friends' affairs as her own. So, very long ago, Mrs. Paul had been told that Sidney was never to marry, and why; and, naturally,

Alan Crossan's mother had known; and Mr. and Mrs. Brown, down in the little rectory of St. James the Less, — although, indeed, that the clergyman was aware of Mortimer Lee's unholy project was not entirely due to Miss Sally. The major himself had had one keen, clear word with the young man concerning his daughter's training, and Mr. Brown, sorry and disapproving, had yet, in his calls upon Miss Sally in her brother's house, respected the father in the infidel, and made no effort to save Sidney's soul.

Little by little, Major Lee's purpose had become a subject of half-amused, half-indignant gossip. Probably he was not aware of it, but it would not have troubled him at all had he learned it. There was nothing in this world now which could trouble Mortimer Lee, if Sidney were well and happy. Very literally, he lived for her. To show her how to live, he was content to bear life. If the sight of his enduring pain could save her from pain, it was enough.

Sidney, he had said, was to be taught to seek for truth; to do without illusions; to look the facts of life full in the face. She was to judge, emotionally, first, whether it was probable that there was a beneficent and all-powerful Being in a world which held at the same time Love and Death; and next, with inexorable logic, she was to find a universe of law, empty of God. Reason, with relentless and majestic steps, trampled upon many things before this conviction was reached. It pointed out the myths and absurdities of the Bible; it left no hope of personal immortality; it destroyed the Christ of Christianity. It demonstrated that morality and expediency were synonymous. It counseled negation instead of happiness. More than all, it pointed out the mad folly of love in a world where death follows love like its own shadow.

As a result, Sidney was sincere, but not earnest; which is perhaps inevitable, when one believes, but does not feel. She simply took her father's word, and so her unbelief was not her own, but his.

Major Lee had not dogmatized his infidelity; it was his opinion that dogma in negation was as unphilosophical as the dogmatic assertions of theology. He had only shown his daughter certain terrible facts, in a terrible world, and then subtly guided her inference. He had been careful to point out to her the falsehoods, and wilful blindnesses, and astonishing egotism of Christianity, and with this to present the calm reasonableness of law.

That Christians called Law "God," Sidney knew; but what they felt when they said "God" was unknown to her. With all his fairness, Major Lee had never been able to tell his daughter that. He had spread his life, like a strange and dreadful picture, before her eyes, and she had seen, with terror, that it had been blasted by love and death. Love, he had declared, was the certain road to despair; and she was instant to put his deduction into words,— *therefore, never love.*

This conclusion of hers was as unaffected as the most spontaneous impulses in the lives of other women, and it became perfectly natural. Rappaccini's daughter, it will be remembered, found, in course of time, poison her daily and necessary food.

Alan Crossan, seeing the result of Major Lee's teachings in Sidney's serene indifference and in her understood determination never to marry, had burned to attack the sad old man. Yet, oddly enough, though his indignation was no less, he had felt of late a growing disinclination to antagonize Sidney's father. So, instead of rushing into argument upon the wisdom of love, he found himself considering that skepticism from which, he was assured, the major's morbid theories sprang.

"You never go to church, do you, Sidney?" he began.

"Yes," she answered, "occasionally. I like the music."

"Oh," said Alan, rather blankly, "I thought, from something you said once about belief, that you would hardly go."

"It has nothing to do with belief," Sidney explained. "I never think of that, except sometimes."

The major looked up at his daughter in silence.

"I think of it," she said, quite simply and gravely, answering the question in his eyes, "when I see the power which it has. Oh, the lifted-up look one often sees! Poor little Mrs. Brown, the light in her face on Easter, — you know their eldest son died just before Easter? — it meant absolute confidence. And then to think it is only belief, and not knowledge, which causes such confidence! It is wonderful, even if it is not real."

"Yes," observed the major, "it is certainly most interesting that a self-created illusion will sustain the soul in such a crisis, even temporarily. Yet it always fails. It cannot outlast the capacity of the brain for nervous exaltation. Mrs. Brown's resignation did not last, you remember, — poor soul — poor soul!" The major, with his long white fingers pressed together, looked absently at the spark of sunshine in the little worn ring upon his left hand.

"I don't think you ought to call belief unreal," the doctor protested. "True or false, it is real to the believer."

"You mean the hope of immortality and reunion, and all that?" Sidney asked, a little disdainfully. "Do you think that is often real to people?"

"Yes," he said; "but all the belief in the world cannot overcome the weakness of human nature."

The major smiled. "You are right. It cannot change facts; assertions will not conquer the inevitable."

"And, Alan," cried the girl earnestly, "surely, if its belief were genuine, human nature is great enough, love is great enough, not to be so horribly selfish as to mourn; — if it could *really* believe that death did not end all, and there was a heaven and happiness. They have to say so, the Christians, — and I suppose they think they believe it, or else they could not love any one, you know; but you can see that it is not lasting, as a reality would be, for they mourn just as much as the people who have no illusions. The talk of the church about immortality, and meeting again, and Easter, why, it seems to me like taking hasheesh : but the burning pyre, and the smoke, and the flames are there, all the same."

Alan did not answer her. His mother was in his heart. Had he not loved her enough to rejoice in her happiness, if, in his soul, he had believed that she was happier, — that she *was* at all? Instead — and the memory of those empty days came back like a sickness of the soul. Perhaps Sidney was right, and his belief was not genuine.

"You are not a Christian, are you, Alan?" Sidney asked, suddenly.

"I don't know," he said, smiling. "I suppose I am. But I prefer to keep my illusions, if you please ; so I don't examine myself very critically."

"How can you say that!" cried Sidney. "How can you even think that perhaps your beliefs are illusions! Either, it seems to me, a man would have to believe with all his heart, and not know that he was blind to facts, or else see the truth of life and make the best of it."

"Or the worst," Alan answered, lightly. "There was Steele's father; every one says he was a most unhappy man. He was a freethinker, was n't he, Major Lee, — what would be called an agnostic, to-day?"

"Yes," said the major.

"And you, — you are also an agnostic, are you not?"

The major looked at him, with mild patience in his eyes. "I do not call myself so. I do not know enough; I have not yet compassed the sum of my own ignorance."

Alan felt instinctively that Sidney's father regarded him with disapproval, and as one who spoke of great things flippantly. A little color came into his dark cheek, and he made haste to comment upon the fact that Robert Steele, with such a father, had a deeply religious nature. "I don't mean that he is one of your stiff sectarian fellows," he explained, " only that he is so devout that he can worship anywhere — from a Quaker meeting-house to St. Peters. Very likely he gets it from his mother; she became a Roman Catholic, you remember. It was always a surprise to me that so intelligent a woman could be a Catholic."

The major smiled. "But religion and intelligence have nothing to do with each other, my young friend."

Alan laughed. "Very little, I acknowledge."

"Oh, how can you say that, and still call yourself a Christian!" said Sidney.

"I suppose," observed the major, courteously, "that the doctor would spare himself the pain of knowledge."

"No," answered the girl, looking with tender gratitude at her father, "it is only knowledge which spares pain."

"And so," Alan declared, amused and half annoyed, "you are to have no pain in life, Sidney, because your knowledge has taught you to cast out the things that comfort other people, and save them from the fear of death, — I mean the belief in God and immortality?"

He had risen, and was standing in his favorite

attitude by the fire, his elbow on the mantel and his hand grasping his coat collar. His dark, sensitive face was flushed a little by the glow of the logs. The sunshine had quite gone, and the dusk was beginning to creep in from the garden. "How can any knowledge spare such suffering?" he went on. "It is bound to come to us all; we cannot cheat life, or lose the anticipation and the fear of death. Where was there ever a happy soul, except a child?"

"Here," said Major Lee; he touched Sidney's shoulder as he spoke. There was something in his voice which made the young man start. The passion of tenderness in the worn old face sobered him into earnestness.

"But some time,"—he stammered, "some time — even if she loves no one else"—

"She will lose me? Yes. But that is regret, not grief. Affection for a parent is natural; it is the instinct of the animal; it is not — *love*."

His voice shook with sudden excitement, and he said that word with the awe of one who takes the unspeakable name upon his lips.

"But," Alan protested, "you make it appear that love is the curse of life!"

The major was silent.

"You forget," insisted the young man, "that love is its own exceeding great reward, — it is worth the pain."

"You have, of course, experienced both love and grief, that you speak so positively," said Mortimer Lee, his face darkening in the shadows.

A sharp reality came into the moment. Alan knew that in the sense in which the older man spoke he had never felt either. "No," he answered, "but I know that life is beautiful and good where there is love, — I mean the love of a man and woman : it is not always fierce and terrible ; it does not of necessity involve the unreason of passion ; and it does glorify existence. But life is still good, even when death takes love out of it."

"I do not call that love," said the major, "which can be taken away and leave — anything ! Passion, truly, is but the incident of love, but love and the worth of life end together." The momentary agitation had left his face ; he even smiled a little at Alan's excitement.

"But," persisted the young man, confused, by Major Lee's contempt and his own lack of words, into contradicting himself, "we *must* love. It means ambition and hope, and all that makes life worth having. Why, life without it, or without any comfort in religion to help a man meet death, — life is tragedy !"

"Has that just struck you ?" said the major.

V.

"Now, Sally," said Mrs. Paul, "I want to talk to you about Sidney; just put that book down, will you? Are you in such a hurry to get back to Mr. Steele that you want to plunge into it at once? Or is it that you are so charmed with 'Entre Nous Trois?'"

Miss Sally's quick disclaimer only made Mrs. Paul shrug her shoulders.

"You have not enough sense, my dear, to appreciate it; it can't be called innocence, at your age."

They were sitting in the little room which opened out of Mrs. Paul's bed-room: in it she wrote her notes, or received her head clerk from the warehouse, or looked through her housekeeping accounts. Davids knew that room well. He knew that when Mrs. Paul sent Scarlett to summon him there, it was with the intention of finding fault. "Law, now," he had often remarked to Scarlett, "if Mr. John only knew how to handle her as I do! Give in just a bit here, and stick it out there, and let on you're more 'n half offended, and law! she comes round in a minute. But Mr. John would rather bear her tongue than argufy. People that keep such close mouths," said Davids, with a reproachful look at the little silent serving-woman, "are exasperating. I ain't one to deny it, for all I think of Mr. John."

Miss Sally often read aloud in this small, severe room, — so small that Mrs. Paul, sitting by the window which overlooked Major Lee's library, with her back to the reader, shut out a great deal of light, and made it necessary that Miss Sally should hold the book close to her eyes. Just now, however, Mrs. Paul had turned a little so that she might look at her. "For I want you to pay attention, if you know how, to what I am going to say," she had explained; and Miss Sally had put down the novel with a sigh which was at once relief and apprehension.

Mrs. Paul permitted herself, in this room, something which was an approach to *négligé:* the bit of lace which did duty for a cap upon the soft puffs of her white hair was missing, and she wore a wrapper of changeable silk, lavender and black, with an edge of black fur down the front and around the throat and wrists; her white, delicate hands were without rings. "The morning," announced Mrs. Paul, leaning back among her cushions, listening to the French novel, "is for work, and jewels are for the leisure of a drawing-room. Thank God, I understand the proprieties of life, or how would Sidney ever be taught? No one, Sally, not even Mortimer Lee, insists more upon the observance of propriety than I do; but you can make a goose of yourself about it, and that is just what you do, in looking after Sidney and young Steele."

"I?" said Miss Sally, startled into self-defense. "Why, I don't know what you mean, dear Mrs. Paul!"

"What should I mean," cried the other, "except

that you are with him all the time, — not Sidney! You seem to think a girl must not sit with a young man, or walk with him, or let him so much as look at her. All very well, to a certain extent, but are you never going to give him an opportunity? I declare, one would think you were in love with him yourself."

"Opportunity?" faltered Miss Sally.

"Yes," answered Mrs. Paul, emphatically. "He has been at the major's nearly three weeks; he must have been impressed by Sidney, if you had ever permitted them to be alone for a moment, so that she could talk. She can't, with your chatter going on, Sally; you know that as well as I do. With this absurd idea of propriety, you never leave them for an instant."

Miss Sally's face flushed a dull and painful red, and then faded into breathless pallor; in her astonishment, she even gasped a little, with a sob in her throat. She was used to being found fault with, but she never could get used to the pain of it.

"Mrs. Paul," she said, "I don't know what you mean; I — I never thought of propriety. Mr. Steele is not very strong, and I have tried to take care of him. Sidney does not want to talk much to him, and Mortimer is so much occupied that he cannot entertain him; it would not be polite to leave him alone, so I try to be with him. And as for Sidney, it never could make any difference how much she talked to Mr. Steele or to any young man; you know she will never care for anybody."

"I know you are a fool, Sally," said Mrs. Paul,

calmly. "If this has been stupidity on your part, instead of anything better, — I gave you credit for something better, you see, — all I can say is, you can't plead ignorance any longer. Arrange things a little. Lord! have you no imagination? Send Sidney over with a message to me, this afternoon, and ask him to see her through the garden."

"But I have n't any message, and Sidney would not" —

Mrs. Paul sat up quite straight, and tapped her foot for a moment.

Miss Sally was too fluttered to continue.

"Well, you will send her over here this afternoon; remember! Now read; that's what you are here for. I gave up any hope of conversation long ago." And Miss Sally, in a trembling voice, began.

She would have been glad if she had been allowed to explain a little further. She would have repeated once more that unforgotten talk with her brother, to show how impossible it was that Sidney should ever fall in love with any one, no matter what "opportunity" — Miss Sally flushed as that word came into her mind — was offered.

She went on reading quite steadily, but that scene of twenty-two years ago rose before her eyes. How much younger Mortimer was then, but how old he looked that night! She had gone upstairs to put Sidney to bed, and her brother had entered just as the child lisped after her aunt, her sleepy head on Miss Sally's shoulder, "God bless dear father and aunt Sally, and make Sidney a good girl, for Jesus' sake. Amen." In the dusk of the fire-lit room, his sister saw a strange expression on Mortimer Lee's face, but he only said, quietly, "When the child is asleep, Sarah, will you be so good as to let me see you in the library?" With what a light heart she had gone down-stairs to hear what he had to say, — she was young then, only seventeen, — with what high hopes of usefulness and comfort and love for the little motherless baby and the bereaved and lonely man! He was walking restlessly about his library; his face was haggard, and bitter lines were deepening about his lips. He stood still when his sister entered. "Sit down," he said curtly. "I have something to say to you. I heard the child praying when I came into her room. It must not happen again, Sarah."

"But — but, Mortimer" — Miss Sally answered, trembling, for his face frightened her. "I thought I ought to teach her to say her prayers. Do you mean that you are going to, brother?"

"I!" he said, and laughed. "Yes; yes; that's it. I am going to teach her, my dear."

"Then you will hear her say her prayers?" she asked. It seemed perfectly natural to her that the child's father should claim the sweet task. Major Lee looked at her with pitying impatience.

"You do not understand me, Sarah. Sidney is to have no religious instruction."

His sister opened her lips to speak, but dismay robbed her of words.

"I will not have this folly of prayer in my house," he continued, — "at least for the child. You may pray, and believe, and suffer, if you want to; your life is your own. But Sidney is mine. She shall know that this God you talk of and this pretty hope of immortality have no more foundation in reason than her fairy stories. No miserable egotism shall induce Sidney to address her puny wishes to the First Cause, nor make her fancy that she is immortal, so that she may dare to fasten her soul on some other soul, which at any instant death may snatch away from her. Without your God and this idea of immortality she will not love, and so she shall escape suffering."

Miss Sally could not argue; she could only protest. She clung, sobbing, to his arm, which never relaxed to take her to his heart.

"Oh, Mortimer, don't — don't say those things! Oh, spare the child! Don't take God away from her. She can't live without God. And oh, let her love somebody, Mortimer, if it's only me!"

"Love you?" he said sharply. "Of course, that sort of affection, — certainly. I was not speaking of that. She will be fond of me, undoubtedly. I meant — *love!*"

He groaned as he spoke, and Miss Sally dared not look at him. "Oh, brother," she entreated, "don't say she must never marry! People are happy who care for each other. You and Gertrude were happy."

"You think people are happy, do you?" he answered. "It is only observation, not experience, which draws such a conclusion. There is not, — listen, Sarah, — there is not an hour of a day, no matter how heavenly happy it may be, when the fear of death, the terror of the certain parting, does not strike upon a man's heart. It stains every hope, it darkens every thought; and that you call happiness!" He pushed her away from him, and began again that terrible walk up and down the room.

"But, Mortimer, dear brother, listen!" she cried, the tears rolling down her cheeks. "God makes up for it afterwards, when we meet those we love."

"We do not meet them," he said, turning and looking at her with stern eyes. "What! could life be endured one instant if I thought *she* was — anywhere? Could I wait long enough to think before I followed her — to search for her — oh, to search for her!"

He dropped his face in his hands. It seemed to Sally Lee as though she dared not breathe until he spoke again.

"So you think your God would add that misery too? Well, if it makes you happier, child, — but keep it to yourself. If your imagination can create a Being who permits love and death in the same world, and yet is not a — I suppose you can find some comfort. But not one word to Sidney, remember. I am going to save her from love, and then perhaps she will forgive me that she has this cruel and damnable thing called life."

He left her without another word, and Miss Sally heard the key turn in the door of his little room beyond the library. As for her she sat down on the edge of the sofa and cried as though her young heart would break, for her brother and for the baby who was to be the subject of his unnatural and unchristian grief. "If only I can be good, the dear child cannot help coming to the Saviour," she said, between her sobs, "because she will see how He helps and comforts me. Oh, I will try to be good. And if I'm happy when I am married, she will know that Mortimer is all wrong."

But Christianity taught Miss Sally no subtlety, only simple-mindedness; so how could she contend with the clear and clever reasoning which, little by little, drew hopes and illusions from before the eyes of the growing girl, and displayed the baseness and bitterness of life, while at the same time Sidney's instinct showed her in her father's character, that this cruel knowledge was compatible with spotless honor and gracious sweetness! As for the other way in which Miss Sally was to teach her niece, the gradual years had blurred her anticipation of marriage; for, like all those mild souls who are born old maids, she had cherished the conviction that marriage was a woman's duty, and looked forward to it as a matter of course. Now, at nearly forty, although, from force of habit, vague thoughts of it flitted through her mind at times, she had ceased to think of it as a probability; the cares of housekeeping and the interests of other people made her assume and feel a sedateness far beyond her years; and so, instead of precept or conscious example, she simply loved.

It all came back to her as she sat reading the unsavory novel; and if Mrs. Paul had not been so interested in the plans she was making for Sidney, she might have noticed the vagueness of the reader's voice.

"I should just like to tell her there is no use in thinking of Sidney's falling in love," Miss Sally was saying to herself. "Mortimer would never permit it, and how could I seem to bring it about against his wishes — and Sidney!" It seemed to Miss Sally, in spite of her theories about the sphere of woman, improper to think of Sidney in such a way.

"Do go," Mrs. Paul said, suddenly, in the middle of a sentence, "and send Scarlett to me as you go down-stairs. Lord, what a book! There is sorrow enough in real life without having tragedies in novels. I want to be amused, if you please. I hope you will make a better selection next time."

Miss Sally's horrified protest that the choice had not been hers delighted Mrs. Paul.

"No, I suppose not," she said. "You haven't sense enough. Every woman of the world should read such books, so as to make allowance for life and learn to be charitable; it is a religious duty. But you will never be a woman of the world, my dear!"

"I think," returned Miss Sally, timidly, "a bad book can't teach us charity if it amuses us too."

Occasionally this gentle and not very sensible little creature made a remark implying a moral bravery of which she could not have been supposed capable.

"I could n't let her speak of wicked books in that way," she thought, as she went down-stairs, her heart pounding with fright.

She gave Mrs. Paul's message to Sidney, and dared not omit adding, "Perhaps Mr. Steele will walk across the garden with you, my love?"

"No," said the young woman, looking at him with wide, calm eyes, "I will not trouble Mr. Steele."

He had risen with quick pleasure, but at Sidney's words he shrank back. "She does not want me," he thought, and with bitter gratitude his mind returned to Miss Sally. The thought of her kindness was like wine to a resolution which sometimes flagged; it never failed him when the struggle was hard. How much this courage which came with the thought of her, was due to increasing bodily health Robert Steele never asked himself.

When, late that afternoon, Sidney opened the green baize door of Mrs. Paul's drawing-room, she found her sitting by the fire. She seemed to be expecting some one, the girl thought; at least, as Sidney entered, she looked beyond her into the hall. "Well?" she said; and then, "Did you come alone?"

"Yes," Sidney answered, brightly. "Aunt Sally told me that you wanted to see me."

"That Sally!" said Mrs. Paul, under her breath. "But why did you not ask that poor, forlorn Mr. Steele to come with you? I'm sure he can't find your aunt's conversation very interesting; my drawing-room might be a little more entertaining."

"I did not think of amusing him," said the girl. "Aunt Sally proposed that he should walk across the garden with me, as though I were afraid to come alone!" She smiled, but Mrs. Paul made an impatient gesture.

"Well, never mind now. (I'll see Sally to-morrow!) Sit down, my dear."

"Can't I read to you?" Sidney asked. "You are alone, and"—

"I'm always alone," said Mrs. Paul, sharply; "don't say foolish things. No. I want to talk to you."

She waited while Scarlett placed before the fire a screen, made of a fan, which had nymphs and shepherds painted upon it. Then she leaned her head against the carved and uncomfortable back of her chair, and looked up at Sidney. Her keen dark eyes had an unwonted gentleness in them.

"My dear," she began, "you must be a little more thoughtful for your poor sick man. Talk to him sometimes; it must be very dull when your father is not at home, if you never speak to him."

Sidney raised her eyebrows. "I don't like to talk to him," she announced, calmly; "he isn't exactly ill, but to see any one who is not quite well is not pleasant. It isn't as if I were aunt Sally, and could make him more comfortable, you know."

The frank selfishness of this did not disturb Mrs. Paul. "I do not want you to make him more comfortable," she said, with a short laugh, "but don't ignore him while he is your father's guest. Why, I am driven to entertaining him myself. I am going to ask you all to take tea here,—Alan and all. I suppose Mr. and Mrs. Brown must come; that is the nuisance of the clergy,—you have to invite them; and of course you and Mr. Steele. He seems a most amiable young man?"

"Yes," Sidney answered, with something as near carelessness as can come into the voice of a young woman when speaking to her elders and betters.

"And — Mortimer Lee. Perhaps he will be willing to do me a favor, for once? I don't ask him very often. It was three years on the 18th of last July since he entered this house."

"But father never goes anywhere," Sidney explained.

When that strange resentment came into Mrs. Paul's voice, Sidney's happy readiness to reply forsook her; instead, there was something like anger in her serene eyes; what right had Mrs. Paul to seem to disapprove of him?

"Don't I know that?" cried the older woman. "I knew him long before you were born, young lady! And he would have been a great deal happier man to-day, if he had had more sense. There! don't talk about it; it irritates me to talk about such folly, — a man like Mortimer Lee to make a hermit of himself! Stop, I say, — don't talk about it! But I suppose he can do this, at least; it is n't asking very much."

"I hope he will come," Sidney said. "It will be so pleasant if he will come."

"It will be pleasant, if you behave as a well-bred young woman should, and endeavor to be agreeable to my guest; and also if you wear a decent dress, as befits your father's daughter. What have you to wear?"

"I have that muslin, with the blue ribbons," the girl answered, doubtfully; "or I suppose aunt Sally might get some new ones, — another color."

"Nonsense," said Mrs. Paul; "you are not a miss in your teens; pray have some sense." She stopped, and frowned. "If you had not so much wicked, wilful pride, I would buy you a proper gown. Sally does n't know how to dress you. But I tell you what I will do. Hush! don't begin to protest; it is most unladylike to protest. I have some dresses in the garret, — old ones, child, old ones, — and Scarlett shall shape one over for you. I have my reasons for wanting to see you properly dressed, for once in your life."

"Oh, but, Mrs. Paul," said Sidney, "I would rather wear my muslin."

"Well, I would rather you did n't wear your muslin," interposed the other, grimly. "Now, say no more about it. We will go and look at them, at least. Just ring for Davids; we must have candles; the garret is dark by this time."

"Had n't we better wait for daylight?" Sidney said, anxious to put off the evil hour; but Davids was already listening to his mistress's orders.

"Tell Scarlett to take up two lamps; and do you light all the bedroom candles, and put them on the red chest of drawers, over against the chimney-breast, so that the light will fall on the big mirror; and make haste, — make haste!"

Davids was as incapable of haste as Major Lee himself, but Scarlett came hurrying in, a moment later, to say that the lamps were lighted, and to precede her mistress to the garret, a flaring candle in a tall silver candlestick in each hand. Davids gave Mrs. Paul his arm, and Sidney, annoyed but helpless, followed them through the hall and up the wide, winding stairs. The silence was broken only by the soft thud of Mrs. Paul's stick, or a sharp word to Scarlett lest a drop of wax should fall on the faded Turkey carpet.

In the garret, Davids had drawn an armchair to one side of the old cheval-glass, which, as the candles gleamed and flickered across it, seemed a pool of misty light among the shadows under the rafters. On the chest of drawers, which stood against the great unplastered chimney-breast in the middle of the room, were two lamps with frosted globes, which looked like moons glimmering in a mist; Scarlett had put some candles there, also, and on a shelf above the mirror a candelabrum dropped a wavering plummet of light into its mysterious depths. But the garret was quite dark, except for this spot of brightness about the three women. The stains and streaks on the yellowing plaster of the walls had faded into the dusk, and one could scarcely see the spider-webs between the rafters, or the strange array of "things" on shelves and pegs; there were three warming-pans in a row upon the wall, — no one knew how long ago their brass had been polished last; at one end of the room old-fashioned bonnets hung, cavernous with shadows, and seeming, when the candles flickered, to nod, as though ghostly heads whispered and chattered together; and hanging above the presses were portraits of the forgotten dead, which no one had the courage to destroy.

Mrs. Paul sank, a little breathlessly, into the chair by the glass, as Davids left her and noiselessly closed the door behind him. "Now!" she said, with great satisfaction. "Open the blue chest first,

Scarlett. I think — I think it is in that." Scarlett, on her knees by the blue chest, lifted out the piles of clothing within it. " No, no, not that," Mrs. Paul commented, impatiently, " not that; have you no eyes, Scarlett? That quilted satin petticoat was my mother's, Sidney; look, child! She wore that when she rode into Washington, on a pillion, behind my grandfather, to see Congress assemble. Nor that! Lord, Scarlett, have you no sense?"

" The chest is empty, madam," answered Scarlett. It was curious to see the eager look on Mrs. Paul's face, when there was but a dream in Sidney's eyes, and quiet indifference in Scarlett's voice and manner.

" Then look in the big press," Mrs. Paul directed. " It is the lavender brocade, with bunches of flowers; don't you know?"

When it was found, and shaken from its folds of years, and she had helped Sidney put it on, the servant began to be interested. Mrs. Paul leaned back in her chair and watched them. The yellowing lace ruffles in the sleeves scarcely touched the girl's white elbows, and the flowered bodice would not meet across her young bosom. But the high-heeled satin slippers which Scarlett produced fitted her quite perfectly, and the full skirt was long enough, the train twisting itself about her ankles as she turned and looked into the clear darkness of the mirror.

" There is a taffeta scarf there," said Mrs. Paul, plucking at Sidney's sleeve, and then pushing aside the lace in the square neck, her wrinkled hand seeming to lose its whiteness where it touched the girl's soft skin; "just put that over her shoulders, and then lace the bodice across it— Lower, lower! Don't cover her throat. Don't you know better than to cover her throat? Now, hold the candles so that I can see her!"

Scarlett moved the candles upon this side and upon that, the lights and shadows falling on the distressed young face and the gleaming folds of the old brocade.

"It seems to me," Sidney said anxiously, and trying to draw a long breath, "that the muslin would be better; this is quite stiff, Mrs. Paul, and tight, — truly it is."

"Nonsense," said Mrs. Paul, impatiently. "I went to parties before you were born; I know what is proper for a young woman to wear. Of course Scarlett shall alter it. You don't think, Scarlett, that a band of black velvet about her throat?— Jewels can't be thought of."

"No, madam," Scarlett answered, the candles shining on her little worn face as she walked around the girl. "She's beautiful! It does remind me of other days, madam!"

The two old women had apparently forgotten the young creature, with her protesting eyes. "Make a courtesy, Sidney!" cried Mrs. Paul, shrilly; "but you don't know how! There, take my stick, Scarlett;" and rising stiffly, her head held high, her lips breaking into a smile, she lifted her plum-colored silk skirt daintily and sunk back, with the sweeping bend with which long ago she had greeted one lover or another.

"Do you remember, Scarlett?" she said, falling into her chair with a sigh which was almost a groan. "I was as young as you, Sidney, when I saw your father first, — it was before he was married. It was nothing to me, of course, there were so many young men; I don't know why I should happen to remember it. I wore a yellow satin that night. You could n't do that with your color; there are few women who could stand it. Do you remember, Scarlett? There! the gown is beautiful; but you must n't let it make you vain. Fine feathers, you know. Yes, it must be altered a little; women dress so foolishly nowadays. Now, come downstairs. I want to see you walk across the drawing-room. A woman manages a train by inheritance; if your mother was used — Well, come downstairs, — come downstairs. Scarlett shall do your hair the night you come to tea. Don't interrupt me; in my young days, chits of girls did n't interrupt their elders." There was a strange excitement in Mrs. Paul's face. "It will be beautiful, Scarlett. What?" In some dim way it was not Sidney who stood, young and flushed, with eyes like jewels under her shining hair, but she herself. "And this is the way I held my fan," she said, opening the ivory sticks upon Sidney's round arm. "There, swing it — so! Can't you look across it and then down again, at your hands. Oh, not like a Sunday-school child repeating its verse. Lord, Sidney!"

Sidney laughed. "But it is easier to look straight at you, Mrs. Paul," she said. Then the little procession moved across the sagging floor, and down the stairs to the drawing-room. Sidney, still reluctant, but young; for the soft colors, the shimmering folds, the cobwebs of lace, were a glimpse into a new world.

"You seem too pleased with life, Sidney," declared the old woman, watching her with puzzled irritation. "I did not look like that when I walked down a drawing-room, I can tell you. Oh, Alan Crossan? Here, what is the matter with Sidney? What will keep her from looking so — good?" She laughed as she spoke, with a droll glance.

The doctor had entered, with an unheard announcement from Davids. "A little further instruction from Mrs. Paul," he observed, critically, while beneath his eyes Sidney stood with a new, unpleasant consciousness of being embarrassed. "A little more attention to your example cannot fail to remove obtrusive goodness. And yet, do you know, I doubt if it would be altogether an improvement?"

Mrs. Paul laughed, her keen, dark eyes sweeping him from head to foot with charming insolence. "You are impossible!" she said. "Sidney, you can go upstairs, now. She does n't get her timidity from Mortimer Lee, I can tell you," she went on. "I suppose it is Gertrude Randolph over again. And yet, there is a certain way in which she can carry her head that promises hard things for young Steele."

"Steele?" questioned the doctor, frowning.

"Yes, my friend," cried Mrs. Paul, "and I am doing my part, I can tell you. I have opened that Sally's eyes, and — well, we shall see. That is, if the young man is not a fool, — though they generally are. How is he, your Steele?"

"Better," returned Alan, cheerfully. "I left him just a moment ago talking to dear Miss Sally, by the library fire. They said Sidney was here, and I came to bring her home to tea."

VI.

Mrs. Paul's unusual softness as she talked to Sidney that afternoon, had its natural reaction when she played at draughts with John Paul in the evening.

"He's that badged," said Davids, when he left the mother and son at the tea-table, and came out into the serenity of Scarlett's shining kitchen, "that it does seem like as if he must jaw back. But he ain't said a word, except to tell me to fetch him some more curried roe. Well, thank the Lord, he can eat." Scarlett's invariable response of silence filled the man with such wrath that he almost forgot his sympathy with his master. "A woman'd better have a tongue," he said, "even if she can't use it no better than *she* does!"

But John Paul found so much comfort in his curry, and in studying out a phase of the fishery question which it perhaps suggested, that Davids' sympathy was really unnecessary; John did not even remember his mother's anger over night. There was nothing to remind him of it, for he never saw Mrs. Paul in the morning; only Scarlett, and sometimes Miss Sally, were admitted to her bedroom while she breakfasted.

He took less time than usual that day over his coffee and paper, although breakfast was a most important affair to John Paul; for he was in haste to jot down those ideas about the fishery trouble, so that later in the day he might go and talk them over with Katherine Townsend. Indeed, such was his interest in his bit of work, and his impatience to have, he said to himself, the benefit of Miss Townsend's clear criticism, that he started out over the old bridge quite early in the afternoon.

Little Eliza, staring from the toll-house window, answered his cheery nod with a flickering color in her round cheeks. "Had your music lesson, Miss Eliza?" he called out, and waited good-naturedly in the wind while she ran to open the door that she might answer him.

"Pretty cold, isn't it?" he asked, beating his hands together, and looking back across the bridge. "Seen Miss Townsend come out from town yet?"

"No, sir, not yet," responded Eliza; "she comes late to-day, Miss Townsend does. Thursdays she doesn't pass the toll-house before half past four, sir."

"Pshaw! what did I start so early for?" he thought. He was uncertain what to do. He might go on, and wait for her in the parlor of the house in Red Lane; but though Ted was a first-rate little boy, and the brother of his sister, talk of pups did sometimes pall. "What time is it now?" he asked, bending his head so that he could look through the low doorway and see the fat Dutch clock ticking above the dresser. "Twenty minutes to four! I wonder if you 'd let me wait in your pleasant sitting-room, Miss Eliza? I — I 'm a little early for a call I wanted to make, and, — "

"Oh!" cried Eliza, after a speechless moment of delight.

So Mr. John Paul entered, and from the kitchen pantry what did Mrs. Jennings hear, "just as sociable and friendly like, but, ' *Won't you take off your coat, Mr. Paul?* '"

"It gave me such a turn," Mrs. Jennings confessed afterwards, as she and Eliza talked it all over, "that I was like to sit right down on the floor. And wasn't I thankful that I'd put them cakes in the oven!" For they had cakes and tea, in the little sitting-room with the antimacassars on the chairs and the geraniums in the windows; and it was all, Mrs. Jennings declared, just as genteel and cozy as could be. Of course, after she brought in the little hot brown cakes, the mistress of the toll-house, in a discreet and proper way, retired to the pantry, where, with overflowing eyes and palpitating bosom, she could hear the whole conversation.

What that half hour was to Eliza and her mother John Paul never knew. "Thank God, you was at home, 'Liza," Mrs. Jennings remarked more than once; and then she excused the warmth of her words by saying that most people would say Providence, she supposed, but, for her part, she only said Providence when things didn't go right and she wanted to find fault. "And you can't find fault — the other way!" said Mrs. Jennings, piously.

When it was time to go, John Paul, in the goodness of his heart, said many pleasant things of the gay little room, and complimented the cakes and the geraniums, and even the hens in the yard. Mrs.

Jennings was so thrilled by his condescension, and so tearful with admiration of her daughter's " pretty manners," that she began to make plans for his next visit. " For he 'll come," she said, nodding and winking, as she and her daughter sat that night by the little air-tight stove, which smiled redly through its square mica eyes, and filled the room with a cheery glow.

" Law, ma ! "

" Yes," continued Mrs. Jennings, — it was her habit, before going to bed, to sit thus by the stove, in a wadded short gown, with carpet slippers on her ponderous feet and a cup of tea in one hand, — " yes, he enjoyed it, — he said he did. So he 'll come again ; you mark my words."

" Did he say he enjoyed it ? " Eliza murmured, meditatively, although she had herself repeated to her mother those very words when the door had closed behind John Paul ; but it was a pleasure to hear them again.

" Yes, he did," declared Mrs. Jennings. " ' Thank you for letting me come in,' he says. ' It 's been very pleasant to wait here,' he says. ' I 've enjoyed it very much.' What do you call that, 'Liza ? "

" And then he said that about the cakes," added Eliza, dreamily.

" Yes, then he said that about the cakes," her mother assented, with great satisfaction. " You 'd ought to have asked him to come again and have some more ; still, it 's best to be sought, I will say ! "

" Oh, ma ! "

" And then you talked all that about your music

lessons. Well, now, it does seem to me I would n't 'a' kept on like you did about Miss Townsend?"

"But he was asking about my lessons," Eliza explained.

"Yes, but you need n't 'a' gone on praisin' her," said Mrs. Jennings, in a discontented voice. "There! I do get out of all patience with her; and yet when she's here, I don't know why it is, but I never seem to know just what to say. Well, never mind her. Only, next time he comes, do let on that you've something else to talk about than her." She twirled her teacup round, and then looked searchingly at the grounds. "There's a man there," she said, pointing with her stubby forefinger at the bottom of the cup; "he's a visitor! See those grounds!"

Eliza shook her head. "I don't believe he'll ever come again," she said, with mournful common sense.

But Mrs. Jennings pressed her lips together in a mysterious way. "I understand such things, 'Liza. I know a man don't say to a young lady, 'Thank you for letting me stay,'—*letting* me, says he,— without some meaning in it. Would Job Todd say it, d' ye think? I guess not!"

In spite of her good sense, Eliza's spirits rose, or at least she allowed herself to enter into the enjoyment of her delusion. She blushed and smiled in the firelight, until Mrs. Jennings shed tears of happiness at her darling's happiness.

"Oh, ma," the little milliner said, rising with a happy sigh, and standing a moment before the glass, —"oh, ma, if I just was n't freckled!"

But Mrs. Jennings pushed back the soft hair from her daughter's forehead with a loving hand. "There, now, deary, don't think of that. My! if your skin was n't just so soft and fair, you would n't freckle. Freckles is a sign of beautiful complexion under 'em."

This was so comforting, Eliza smiled again. John Paul little knew what a commotion and joy his visit had caused; had he known, possibly he might not have trespassed upon Mrs. Jennings' hospitality again, even to the extent of coming in to buy a bunch of geraniums for Miss Townsend, later in the winter.

On this especial afternoon, however, he only knew that it had been a pleasure to listen to Eliza's raptures about her teacher. ("She's just splendid!" Eliza had said, and sighed for want of better words.) Indeed, the expression was so much in his mind that he found himself smiling as he joined Miss Katherine Townsend and asked her to let him go as far as Red Lane with her. He had the most casual way in the world of asking such favors; it was almost irritating, unless one happened to know that it was his method of disguising his shyness.

"You have a most ardent admirer in your toll-house pupil," he declared. "I — ah — stopped there a moment."

Katherine's smile was like sudden sunshine; she knew quite well why Mr. John Paul had stopped at the toll-house. "She is a good little thing," she said, "and her mother is delightful. Mrs. Jennings told me, when she engaged me," — John winced, —

"that she was always glad 'to give the benefit to people that was real poor and had to work hard.'"

"Confound her!" grumbled John Paul, "do you call that delightful?"

"Charming!" returned Katherine, gayly. "I told her that I was very much obliged to her, and she said in the most comfortable way, 'Well, never you mind; may be you 'll get settled down one of these days!' She had the respectable mechanic in her mind's eye, I 'm sure."

She laughed as she spoke. One could easily believe, however, that Mrs. Jennings would have hesitated at that final suggestion. There was a look in this young woman's face which puzzled and irritated the mistress of the toll-house, in spite of her knowledge that the Townsends had as little money as she had. That slight immobility of the upper lip, which gives piquancy as well as a hint of hardness to the whole face, or, it were more exact to say, a promise of justice without sentiment, gave also a look of pride which the carriage of her head accentuated. As Mrs. Jennings had confessed to her daughter, she never knew just what to say to Miss Townsend; so naturally enough she disliked her.

They had almost reached Red Lane when John stopped. "Are you very tired?" he asked. "Could you walk a little further out into the country? That grove of birches on the Perryville Plank Road must be marvelous."

There had been a storm of sleet in the morning, which, as the cold deepened, had frozen on the trees, and now in the late afternoon, when the gray clouds lifted in the west, and a flood of ruddy gold poured over the white landscape, the icy branches blazed with all the jewels of Aladdin. The pools of ice by the roadside caught a sudden red, and the fringe of windy clouds in the east quivered with rosy light. The birch grove would be beautiful, John thought; its trees were so slight that they would bend like wonderful feathers under the weight of ice, and in this glow of gold gleam and glitter as though powdered with the dust of a thousand diamonds.

It would be interesting to know how many men, in offering themselves to the women they love, use the subtile, or passionate, or tender sentences with which they have beguiled their imagination for many a day. Instead, the flutter of an eyelid, a broken word, or a beautiful silence may tell all!

John Paul had composed the story of his love in his own mind a dozen times in the last month, only to sigh as he ended it and say that he was a fool; she would never look at him, except with that contempt in her kind gray eyes which he could not understand. Nevertheless, he knew precisely at what point he meant to take her hand and tell her that he had loved her ever since he had known her — and — and would she let him take care of her now, and of Ted and the girls; and that no man had ever loved a woman as he loved her; and all the other statements usually made upon such occasions.

Who then could have been more astonished than John Paul to hear himself say, as they walked along the road, which was bordered with wild blackberry bushes, bending into a glistening network of ice,

"The respectable mechanic — must he be a mechanic?"

Katherine Townsend flashed a quick look into his face, but how could he see that, with the sun shining straight into his near-sighted eyes?

"Yes," she said, lightly, "I am inclined to think he must be. To tell you the truth, Mr. Paul, I have come of late to feel an immense amount of respect for him, — I speak generically, my acquaintaince with him being, unfortunately, limited to the piano tuner at the other end of Red Lane, and Mr. Job Todd, who built the kennel for the puppies."

"But, Katherine, I — I meant" — John began to say, his voice quite hoarse, and in his agitation striking at a frozen mullein stalk with his cane; but she interrupted him, with a ring in her voice which made him stumble with astonishment.

"You see, they amount to something in the world, these simple, hard-working men. Oh, since I have had to teach, since I have really seen what living is to most men and women, since I have understood the meanness of luxury, I have burned with contempt for my old, lazy, easy life, — the time when I did nothing for myself, and just let people wait upon me and take care of me."

John Paul's face stung; there was something in her voice which said that these words about herself were for him. A woman, plodding through the snow, looked towards them with that dull curiosity with which wayfarers regard one another, and John wondered if his face betrayed the ache in his heart.

"You are severe," he said.

"I can't help it," she answered; and then a moment later, "The iron has entered into my soul, Mr. Paul. The unevenness of life has seemed too horrible to bear. I think — I hope that if I were suddenly to have plenty of money again I should keep on doing something to earn it, and not be lazy, and indifferent, and satisfied with a small, ignoble, comfortable life. Oh, I feel this so about Ted. If I can but teach him to be a *man;* to feel the shame, the disgrace, of dependence, either upon one person — me, for instance — or upon one class in the community. He must earn his own bread, and not take one crumb or one cent more than he gives, somehow; — I don't care how; by his brains or his hands; only he must be independent. I try to make him feel it now, although he is just a little boy." She stopped, and put her hand up to her eyes a moment. "There is such a glare on the snow," she explained, in an unsteady voice.

"Miss Townsend," John said, "it seems to me that you are hardly fair to the man whom the accident of birth places in a position where work is not necessary" — But she interrupted him.

"Birth never places us where we should not work; our own weakness or cowardice may let us take advantage of circumstances that we have nothing to do with. Oh, I despise such men, men who are satisfied with small, useless lives, and take what they do not earn."

"I am afraid you are a socialist," John answered, but his face was white.

Katherine shook her head. "I am a Christian, — that is all."

"You are not fair!" he burst out. "For instance, I — my mother " —

"Yes? Well?" she said, for he had paused; to defend himself made all her scorn personal, and killed his hope.

"You know my position," with an impulsive gesture. "It was my duty to go into the warehouse, no matter how much I hated it. I don't work, I know, though I should have liked to; but why should I have consulted my own wishes (I had n't the motive then that I have now), why should I have made her miserable?"

"Why disturb your own comfort? Is n't that what you really mean?" Katherine said, with bitter lightness. "But perhaps I don't call things by the names that you do."

"What do you call it, Miss Townsend?" John asked, quietly.

"I don't think my opinion is of any consequence," she said, but she bit her lip to keep it firm.

"It is everything in the world to me, Katherine."

Her contempt scorched his face, but somehow there was a strange comfort in it, which he did not stop to analyze.

"Please do not call me Katherine, Mr. Paul," she commanded, with an attempt at gayety, "even to show that you are friendly in spite of my candor. I — to tell you the truth, I should call such an attitude as yours toward your mother, selfish and — cowardly."

John started as though he had been struck in the face; to be sure, that talk about Ted and herself had meant it, but to put it into words! They had reached the grove of birches, and stood looking miserably at the sparkling trees. The wet folds of the clouds had quenched the sunset light, and a low wind, blowing up from the river and wandering across the hills, made the mail-clad branches creak and rattle.

"It is beautiful;" Katherine said, vaguely, looking into the glittering mist of the woods with unseeing eyes.

"Very," John answered, with his back to the trees; "I am astounded by your use of words, Miss Townsend."

"Why should you be?" she cried. "Look, *cowardly:* how many times have you told me that you have kept silent rather than have a discussion!"

"Never when there was a principle involved," he interposed, doggedly.

"There is always a principle in everything," she declared. "More than that, deeper than that, you have preferred the ignoble comfort of your life to working hard and honestly at anything." John saw the sheen of tears in her eyes. "And selfish? Can you for one instant claim that this effacement of yourself has been for any one's peace and comfort but your own? Have you ever, by one single protest, *helped* your mother? Forgive me for speaking of her, but you asked me, and I have to be honest. You know as well as I do that there is a point in the relation of parent and child where the parent grows no older, apparently, but the child ceases to be young, and at that point there has to be an adjustment of ideas which is not agreeable. But what are you to call the child who will not assert his individuality because it would be unpleasant to do so? Indeed, I don't know any other word than selfish. Oh, it seems to me that so many, many wrong things are done under the name of self-sacrifice!"

John did not speak. The branches of a tree creaked shrilly; some oak leaves, stiff with a glaze of sleet, rustled, and bits of ice fell sharp upon the frozen snow.

"If I can only keep Ted from such twisted morality!" she ended.

John said something between his teeth. "I wish you would be so good as to drop Ted; you mean all this for me, of course. But you are cold. I ought not to have kept you standing here. Let us go back."

They turned, and began to walk silently towards Red Lane. Katherine could not talk; she had spoken out of a full, hot heart, but she knew very well what the reaction would be. She saw herself beaten with self-reproach and helpless regret. They had almost reached Red Lane, when John said gently:—

"I want you to believe that I value your sincerity. It has hurt you to say all this."

"Not at all," Katherine answered, holding her head high; "the truth is never hard. I have felt that we were friends, and "—

"And it is only right that I should know what you think of me?"

"Yes," said Katherine.

VII.

ALAN CROSSAN, as Miss Sally said, was really devoted to his friend. There had been scarcely a day since Robert had come to the major's that the doctor had not called to see him. "And it's so nice for Sidney and me," Miss Sally asserted, in one of her long, pleasant talks with Mr. Steele. "To think, now, that he should have taught her to carve so beautifully! But then Sidney could be taught anything. I've always said that."

They were in the long parlor, which was only a little more dreary than usual, with the gray rain sweeping in against the front windows under the dark roof of the porch, and spattering down the chimney once in a while upon the fire. Except Miss Sally Lee's kind face, the soft-coal fire was the only cheerful thing in the room; it burned with a dancing whirl of flames in an old-fashioned grate, which had two brass balls on its hobs, and an iron back wrought into the flaring rays of a broad-faced sun. On the high black mantelpiece stood an ormolu clock, with a dome-like glass shade to protect the figures of Iphigenia and Diana; it had not moved a gilt hand across its fretted face for years. Robert Steele watched it now vaguely, listening to the rain and to Miss Sally's chatter. He was thinking of her rather than of what she said. She was so upon the outside of what was greatest to her, so ignored and unnoticed, and yet so true and good, that she stirred his pity and then his tenderness. When to tenderness he added gratitude, it is no wonder that the quiet little spinster was transformed in his eyes. "Yes, 'a noble woman, nobly planned,'" he thought. Yet he did not finish the quotation; he could not, despite his convictions, looking at the simple, gentle face, matter of fact and incapable of subtlety, with mild eyes under sleek brown hair, which she wore in old-fashioned bands over her ears. But though she might not warn or command, at least she comforted him, because, he said to himself, she believed in him; he did not reflect that she believed in every one, even in Miss Sidney Lee, whose neglect of her aunt filled him with indignation. Nor did he realize that to be one's self neglected will sometimes bias the judgment. With this thought of Sidney, he glanced, reluctantly, towards the portrait at the other end of the room: here was the same insolent sweetness, the same serene selfishness, the same charm which stung him into anger and, he said, dislike. Yet he still looked at the painting, with something beneath his anger, which he called content. It was so much better to be with Miss Sally, he thought, than to see that look in the face of Miss Sidney Lee.

"You are so much better," he heard Miss Sally saying; "and when you are well, just think what good things you will do with that money." Robert had made some dreary comment upon his money, and it was thus Miss Sally received it, following out a suggestion she had made some time before, but which she had taught Robert to feel was his own.

"If the thirty pieces had come back to Judas," he answered, "do you think that the establishment of a lazaretto would have washed them clean?"

"But it is not the same kind of thing," said Miss Sally, with a little awe at the allusion, but much good sense; "and it's time for you to have your beef-tea, anyhow."

"I think," returned Robert, smiling at her with wistful eyes, "that your good opinion is better for me than beef tea."

"I'm afraid," she said, with a gleam of fun (it was wonderful how, under kindly influences, she was developing a harmless gayety which had never been called out when it might have better matched her years), — "I'm afraid that you couldn't live up to the good opinion without the beef tea." She nodded and smiled with a small assumption of authority, and then went to fetch it, coming back presently with a tray on which was a frail blue bowl of soup and a glass of sherry.

"How are you so wise in caring for people, Miss Sally?" Robert asked, watching her spread a little table at his side. "You know just what to do for everybody."

"Well, I am an old woman, you know," she answered brightly. But it was strange how young she looked with the glow of the fire on her face, although there were some threads of gray in the knot of ringlets at the back of her head.

"You are not old," Robert protested loyally; but

nevertheless he was astonished when she said she was but thirty-nine. "You are so wise," he explained, with the simple candor which Miss Sally had been quick to appreciate, "so wise and kind, that I had thought you were more than thirty-nine. I am thirty-five, you know, and you are so much wiser than I am."

Miss Sally blushed. "Oh, but indeed I am not at all clever. When I think how much Mortimer knows, and Sidney, I feel as if I really belonged in the kitchen with Susan. But you?" she added, with sudden constraint, — "why, I thought you were only Alan's age."

It was curious what an instant change of atmosphere this mutual knowledge caused. Miss Sally began to wonder if she had been quite polite in telling a man as old as Mr. Steele what he ought or ought not to do. She began to feel a little awe of him. Perhaps he had thought her forward? Robert, too, was aware of a subtle difference. He became more assertive; sympathy and confidence meant more from a woman so nearly his own age than from one as much his senior as he had supposed Miss Sally to be. A friendship which holds within it the possibility of something warmer than friendship is always attractive, whether the possibility is recognized or not. Robert, hearing at that moment Sidney's voice in the hall, said to himself that while he was honored with Miss Sally's regard it made no difference whether Miss Sidney Lee ignored him or not. But he felt suddenly old and tired, as the room darkened with a dash of rain against the windows, and Sidney and Alan entered.

As he looked up at them a surprising thought first presented itself to him. Perhaps it sprung from Sidney's careless glance; but he did not stop to analyze it. His mind went back to the dull rooms in town, the empty days, the weight of undesired wealth, and — being so far recovered — the remembrance with a thrill of fear of the old bondage; but with that remembrance came the thought of Miss Sally's belief in him; and then — the possibility!

"Steele," Alan's voice broke in, — Miss Sally had slipped away, "to look after somebody's comfort," Robert was sure, — "Steele, I have been telling Sidney about your charming cousin, Miss Townsend. I can't persuade her to go and see her. She would teach you lots of things, Sidney; even to read novels, perhaps. Bob, did you know Miss Sidney Lee scorned novels?"

"No, I don't," said the girl; "only I do not read them, Alan. Isn't it a little waste of time to read novels? And Miss Townsend — as she is a teacher, I suppose she is positive, and " —

"And what, pray, are you?" cried Alan. "No, really, she is delightful. I called on her last night, which is more than you've done for a month, Bob. School-ma'am? Not a bit of it! Simply a charming woman, though worldly and decidedly practical."

Sidney smiled with serious eyes. To hear him talk in this way gave her a curious feeling of being left out; she did not understand it. She did not answer him, but waited for him to go on, with that peculiar and silent graciousness which stirred Alan's heart as an unseen and noiseless wind blows red coals into a flame.

"She brought up a question which interested me," Alan proceeded. "I don't know whether to call it ethics or taste. Bob, listen. You look half asleep. She had come across a sketch, or story, or something,— she said it was true,— about a man and his wife who came over in a steamer; I think it was that one which went down on the Newfoundland coast. Well, the man, it seems, was the sole support not only of his wife, but of his mother and his sisters. When the steamer began to sink, it was found that only a few could be saved; so of course the women were to go first. But this fellow's wife would n't move. 'No,' she said. 'You 've got to be saved because of your mother and sisters.' And the man — if you 'd call him a man — actually did go off in the life-boat, and leave his wife to drown! What do you think of that, Steele? Your cousin told me of half a dozen people who upheld him. He saved his miserable life at the cost of his wife's."

"I don't see that he had any choice," Robert answered.

"Bob," the doctor admonished him, "I shall have to order you to bed, if you utter such sentiments; it shows that you are not strong. Sidney, you are not going to agree with him?"

She shook her head. "I think they should have died together. They had a right to themselves. Why should the woman have insisted that her husband should live heart-broken all his days? Oh, she was cruel! She did n't really love him."

"Do you think so?" Robert asked, with that hesitation which always came into his voice when he spoke to Sidney. "I think she loved him divinely, because she wanted the highest thing for him; and what must have been his passion for duty that he could leave her!"

"My dear fellow," said Alan, "the value of an effort is determined by its result, not by the nobility of motive which prompts it. You are both wrong; he should have saved her and died himself. Here's Miss Sally. What do you say, Miss Sally?" And then he told her the story.

"I think they should both have put on life-preservers," answered Miss Sally earnestly; at which they laughed at her, even Robert; yet there was a new consciousness in his heart as he did so, a sort of pity that she had not seen the deeper thing; and with it that tenderness without reason, which excuses and commends at the same time. The laughter, Sidney's at least, made him resentful as well as tender.

Robert Steele, not yet strong, very pitiful, very grateful, was drifting gradually to a position where he should say, "She is so kind to me. I am so sorry for her. I will try to be worthy of her friendship. I — love her!" He sighted this point that rainy morning in January, though it was nearly two weeks later that he fairly rounded it, being then within three days of his departure from Major Lee's house. His visit had prolonged itself far beyond Alan's expectation; indeed, it had been evident to the doctor ten days before that Robert had stayed as long as the most ardent hospitality might desire; but such a thought had not occurred to the sick man. Miss

Sally had assured him, when he protested at the trouble he gave, and said he must go away, that it was a pleasure to have him stay; and Major Lee, courteous, indifferent, almost unconscious of the young man's presence, but never forgetful of that forlorn, half invalid life of which he had had a glimpse, said, too, "Pray do not think of leaving us, sir." So Robert had remained. He had, of course, no inkling of Mrs. Paul's joy in this, as he had not seen her. She had fallen ill, "and when I have a cold in my head," she announced to Miss Sally, "I don't go about making an object of myself." It was for this reason, too, that the tea-party had been postponed, and that she did not know that John had gone away from home for a week; for it was not Mrs. Paul's habit to receive her son in her bedroom, and no one cared to impart the information. Only Scarlett and Miss Sally were privileged to see the undress of their tyrant, and they found her more awful with her white hair drawn straight and tight away from her fierce eyes, and without the softness of lace about her neck and wrists, than when in the dignity of her satin gowns.

She had taken cold the day of the sleet storm, — she remembered the date with angry exactness, — and the Lord only knew when she could be downstairs again, and able to ask the people to tea. Yet Mr. Steele's lengthened stay was somewhat pacifying, and the first time that she was in the drawing-room again, and had had a talk with Sidney about him, she was really pleasant for the rest of the evening, even to Mr. Brown, when he called, as was his duty, to congratulate the richest member of his parish upon her recovery. But all the while that she was listening to him or giving advice ("I never shrink from giving advice," she had declared more than once, which, indeed, was strictly true), she was making many plans for Sidney and Robert Steele.

It was almost a pity, for it would have saved her much disappointment in the future, that she could not at that moment have seen Miss Sally and Mr. Steele sitting by the fire in the yellow parlor. The major was in his library, where, as a matter of course, Sidney had joined him; so these two persons, no longer young, and therefore to be trusted, were alone.

It was a relief to Robert when Sidney left them. That wide questioning look in her frank eyes always kindled in him a hot disgust with himself, and a desire to be soothed by Miss Sally's gentle if ignorant approval. How well she understood his moods, he said to himself, as she fell into a pleasant silence. So long as he did not know that her thoughts were upon the failure of her beef stock to clear, his content could not be lessened. He sat in his usual attitude, his head resting on his hand, and his sad eyes watching the dancing shine of the flames. Miss Sally had drawn a bit of cambric from her green workbag, and was softly stroking the gathers with her needle.

"That is something for somebody, I am sure?" Robert commented.

She nodded pleasantly. "Sidney does n't like to sew," she explained.

Robert Steele sighed. "I suppose you have never known the feeling of self-reproach for neglect of any one you love?"

"Why, I almost think," said Miss Sally, "that love means self-reproach. I don't see how a person can ever be satisfied with what he does for any one he cares for."

"Still, love always forgives love," Robert answered, "even for apparent neglect." He was thinking of that last look in his mother's face, when weakness and fear had silenced her reproaches, and she had — how Robert blessed her for it! — "forgiven" him. Then his thoughts followed the story of his own miserable cowardice. "It is your own forgiveness that it is hardest to get," he said.

Miss Sally looked puzzled; then, with a gleam of that good sense which seems an actual part of a somewhat foolish character, she said, "But I think you forgive yourself when you make yourself worthy to be forgiven by somebody else; not when they do forgive you, but when they ought to. Sometimes, it seems to me," continued Miss Sally, who could not remember an injury over night, "that we pardon things too easily."

Robert sighed. "You are so kind in spite of your justice. You have forgiven me."

"Oh, dear me, Mr. Steele," protested Miss Sally, "I did n't mean — why, of course I was not talking about you; you have done nothing which needs forgiveness; you know what I think about that money."

As for his remorse for his cowardice, it never entered Miss Sally's mind. To tell the truth, she had been reproaching herself for not scolding Susan about the ruined beef stock, and wishing that she had been more strong-minded than to forgive her so quickly.

"If I am ever anything in this world," cried Robert, his face lighting with earnestness, "it will be because you believe in me, Miss Sally!"

"Oh, Mr. Steele," she said humbly, "don't say that. God gives you the strength. I only see it. I sometimes think that I can see such things, because I am a little on the outside of life, you know; and so perhaps I have more time to see what is good in other people."

"If you think that a man is good, it will make him so. He has got to live up to it," Robert answered.

Miss Sally laughed. It was so strange and pleasant, this talking out her little thoughts.

"If you believe in me," he went on, "I will grow into something for your sake. I will build a better future on this miserable past, if you will show me how." Miss Sally put her work down, startled by the earnestness in his voice. His eyes had a strained and hunted look in them, and his lips, under his soft brown beard, were pressed hard together. "And you shall not be on the outside of anybody's life; you shall be in mine, you shall make it!"

"I — I'll help you all I can," she said simply, but her voice trembled; she did not know why, but she was vaguely frightened; she began to sew very fast, and looked toward the door, as though meditating flight.

"I will be something in the world. Oh, care for me just a little, Miss Sally!"

"I — I don't understand," she faltered, and then regained her presence of mind. "I'm sure we all like you, Mr. Steele." But her hands shook, and the needle flashed in and out unsteadily.

"Why, I" — he paused, and put his hands over his face for an instant; he was saying to himself that it was for her sake that he was conquering his sin — "I love you. You have been good to me, you have made me feel that there is hope for me yet, you have given me life — and I love you!"

Nothing could have been more honest than this declaration. No young man who has played the sighing lover for a year could, at that one instant of unrecognized pity and profound gratitude, have felt himself more truly in love than did Robert Steele now. How could he tell that his growing hold upon life was due not only to Miss Sally's belief in him, but also to a firmer pulse and a healthier circulation? And how could the timid, trustful little spinster discriminate? She had had no past experience with a man in love, with which to compare this scene; she merely began to cry with all her might, stealthily wiping her eyes on the bit of cambric, and saying, "Oh, why, my! You must n't talk that way, Mr. Steele!"

Robert had risen, and stood beside her; one nervous hand upon the back of her chair, and the other covering the bit of cambric and her trembling fingers. It would have been hard to say which trembled most. He had always seen her strong for him, and this weakness stirred him profoundly. "Don't you see? I love you. I want you to love me, Miss Sally," — he spoke as gently as to a sobbing child, — "care for me, and for your sake I will try to be all you can desire."

"You've got to have your wine," replied Miss Sally, with sudden determination and calmness. "I don't know what I've been thinking of to let you talk — so much."

She thrust her sewing into the green bag in a resolute way, but her lips were unsteady, and the tears glittered upon her lashes.

"Just say one word," he pleaded. His own earnestness was like wine to him. "Love me, and I'll be worthy of you. Say that you will marry me."

"I — I must think," she said. So many things came rushing into her mind: assured comfort for Sidney and the major; some one who would care for her; a happiness of her own which might show Sidney many things. All this without the slightest thought of love itself. "I *must* think!" she repeated, and, without waiting to hear his entreaty, she slipped out into the hall and up to the darkness of her bedroom. Her face burned and throbbed, and she put her hands up to her throat, as though she could not breathe; a little quivering sob parted her lips. She made haste to light her lamp, for Miss Sally was not one to whom the reserve of darkness was a comfort. Then she sat down on the edge of her high bed, and tried to compose herself; but her breath was hurried, and her eyes blurred once or twice with half-frightened tears.

"I must really," she said to herself,—"I must really take some pellets. I am—I am agitated." A small chest, holding many little vials, stood on the straight-legged dressing-table. Miss Sally lifted the lid and regarded the contents critically. "What would be best?" she pondered, and was not satisfied until she had opened her "Domestic Physician," and, glancing down the list of emotions of the mind, learned that fear, excessive joy, violent anger, and unhappy love might be benefited by—and then a list of names. Miss Sally did not pause to classify her emotion. Ignatia was advised for three of the four conditions, so it was the safest thing to try. Five little white pills were counted carefully into one shaking palm, and then placed upon her tongue, while she stood, the bottle in her hand, awaiting their effect. A moment later she went over to her bedside, and kneeling, buried her face in her hands. She was ashamed that she had not thought of this before. The small pills had no doubt calmed her mind enough for faith. She prayed with all her simple heart for wisdom, then looked up to see that the lamp was not smoking, and prayed again.

It must have been nearly three hours later, when the house had fallen into the sleepy silence of night, that Sidney, sitting by the old hour-glass table in her bedroom, her smooth forehead frowning over some accounts the major had begged her to settle for him, heard a hesitating knock at her door, and Miss Sally entered.

The bare and lofty room was full of shadows, except for the spot of light in which the young woman sat, so, glancing up in a preoccupied way, she did not see that Miss Sally's eyes were red and her mouth tremulous. Miss Sally's gray flannel dressing-gown was short and scanty, and when she knelt by the hearth and stirred the fire she shivered a little.

"It is cold in here, Sidney," she said.

"Is it?" the girl answered tranquilly. With the soft color in her cheek and the swift, warm youth in every vein, how could Sidney know that the little drowsy fire in the wide black fireplace quite failed to heat the big room? There were many draughts in Sidney's bedroom, which had windows on two sides, sagging doorsills, and a great chimney, and the room was cold, — so cold that on the small fan-lights which capped the windows there was a faint cross-hatching of frost, and when the moon looked in upon Sidney, adding the columns of figures, these wonderful lines and feathers sparkled as though a diamond had been shivered against the glass. A path of moonlight lay across the floor, and touched the pillows and the white canopy of the bed. It glimmered on the brass knobs of the dressing-table, and spread a film of silver upon the oval mirror balanced on the chest of drawers. It showed, too, Miss Sally crouched upon the hearth, and holding up one hand to shield her face from the fire.

Is a woman ever too worldly or too simple, too young or too old, to desire sympathy in a love affair? A man rarely burns to pour even a successful love into any other man's bosom; but a woman must say, or look, "My life is not uncrowned." The acceptance or nonacceptance of the crown is the usual excuse for such confidences. Miss Sally felt vaguely that her niece was altogether remote from love and loving, and yet, she must talk to some one!

"Sidney," she began.

The girl glanced at the forlorn gray heap beside the fire, and noted, with the cruel exactness of youth, that Miss Sally's hair showed some white threads about the temples. "Well, dear?" she said.

"How do you think"—Miss Sally seemed absorbed in following the pattern of the brass fender with her eyes—"that a woman knows she is in love?"

Sidney put down her pen, and stared at her aunt with undisguised astonishment. "I am sure I don't know! How do you suppose?" There was the impersonal interest in her voice with which an inhabitant of another world might question a state of mind he could never know. "Who has been asking your advice?"

Miss Sally shook her head miserably. "I've always thought, at least it has seemed to me, that one would feel, if she fell in love,"—Miss Sally blushed—"that she could n't have any life in the future without—the other person; and as if she had not been alive in the past, not having had—the other person. And yet, you see, Sidney, there are so many other things?"

"What other things?" Sidney asked, curiously. This odd conversation did not suggest anything serious; it only amused her. Miss Sally never needed a premise, and was incapable of reaching a conclusion, so her niece was not apt to look for meaning in her chatter.

"Well, if you like a person very much, and he likes you very much, and he will make you happy, and he needs you, and you think it would be pleasant,— only of course life would be pleasant, anyhow, but not *as* pleasant,— in fact — well, if you want to — Sidney, I suppose that's a kind of love?"

Sidney flung her head back with a laugh, closing her account-book with a soft bang. "I don't pretend to know what love is. but I know what it is not! Has your Mr. Steele been asking your advice? Has he fallen in love with anybody? He had better ask father's advice." A quick gravity came into her face as she spoke of the major.

Miss Sally shook her head. "You know I don't think as brother does?"

Perhaps if she had not just risen from her knees, she would not have invited argument by even so mild an assertion of her opinion. Very long ago, she had given up discussion upon such subjects, and put her theories into an unselfish life. In earlier days she had tried argument once or twice, but had been quickly worsted by her brother's logic, given in Sidney's silver voice.

"It's better," Miss Sally had assured herself with wistful humility, "for little minds to leave great things alone; somehow, if I meddle with them, it is n't only I that am ridiculous, but the great things are, too." That she referred to her belief now showed how deeply she was moved.

"I think people are happier when they love each other," she said.

"If they believe themselves immortal," Sidney

answered, with that pitying contempt which affection keeps good-natured, "or if they can forget death."

"I think," answered Miss Sally, rising and looking at her niece with another kind of pity, "that if they remember the dear Lord, they can trust the rest." She was so earnest, she almost forgot that she had been asking advice for herself. "If they just take God into their lives, darling, they need n't fear death."

Sidney smiled. "Dear!" she said, putting her strong young arms about the little figure; and the amusement in those starlike eyes silenced Miss Sally.

VIII.

It was sadly a matter of course that Sidney should forget that half hour by her bedroom fire, and Miss Sally's troubled look. Like every one else she was used to her aunt's inconsequence; that Miss Sally should have discussed the symptoms of falling in love meant nothing more practical than did her views on political economy, when she suggested that all the money in the world might be divided, so that there should not be any more poverty. "Well, at least," she had explained, blushing but persistent, "it would be more like the golden rule." Only Robert Steele had had the insight to know how brave she was to stand by her little foolish opinion, and it was he, now, who knew the meaning of the blush that flickered in her face when any one spoke to her.

There was a look of half-frightened importance, and a fluttering delight, in Miss Sally's eyes the day after Robert had told her that he loved her, which, however, had no relation to love. She was undeniably pleased, but as for accepting Mr. Steele, — that was another matter. Yet there were so many reasons for it, she said to herself, absently dusting the library for the second time. "It would be a good thing for Sidney, oh, in so many ways! And if I

still lived here" (it did not occur to her to say
"we"), — "if I still lived here, I could take better
care than ever of Mortimer. And oh, what pretty
dresses Sidney should have!" And there was something as near malice as could come into her gentle
soul, when she reflected, " How surprised Mrs. Paul
would be!" To Robert himself she had only said,
looking hard out of the window, as she handed him
his beef-tea, in a sidewise, crab-like manner, "Please
to wait a little, Mr. Steele; please to let me think."
She looked so small and frightened that, with a
warmer wave of that impulse he had called love, he
answered very tenderly, "Yes, Miss Sally, — only
do not give me up."

The pleading in his voice seemed to his listener
irresistible; she had the same desire to make him
happy which she felt whenever she stopped to comfort a crying child in the street, and give it a penny
and a kiss. But she could not frame the words
for which he asked. Instead, he heard her in the
hall, and caught the major's patient impatience as
she fussed about his coat. "Fussed" was the uncompromising word which flashed into Mr. Steele's
mind; yet he knew very well, as he resented his
own thought, that had that care been expressed in
his behalf he would not have called it "fuss." He
was to leave Major Lee's the next day, and as the
two households were almost one, it was only proper
that he should go that afternoon to say good-by to
Mrs. Paul; the strain of expectation made it hard
to sit alone in the parlor, and Miss Sally seemed
suddenly occupied upstairs, so it was a relief to go
out.

He found Mrs. Paul just getting into her carriage, a bad moment for pleasant commonplaces, or indeed for anything, — a moment at which Davids, diplomat as he was, always quailed. She was angry that Robert Steele should see her thus, muffled in hideous wraps and supported by her man-servant; looking — no one knew it better than she — old, and awkward, and pitifully feeble. Yet the quiet way in which Mr. Steele took Davids' place, and with wonderful gentleness lifted her into the carriage, disarmed her pride by its appeal to the suffering body. She glared at him through her veils, and said grudgingly, "Come, get in. You might as well call upon me in the carriage as anywhere else." Yet when he had seated himself opposite her, and Davids had slammed the door, pride asserted itself. With weak, uncertain hands, and bitter impatience at the weakness, she pulled the lace back from her face. She was perfectly aware that the soft black folds made a fitting frame for her dark eyes and her shadowy puffs of white hair. Then she smiled.

"Really, this is very nice of you," she said, "though I wonder Sally Lee permitted you to come out alone. She has been a most devoted nurse." She lifted her eyebrows, with that air which says, "I can sympathize with you!"

"She has indeed," Robert answered. He was aware that he spoke warmly, and vaguely dismayed at his own consciousness. "There is no one so kind as Miss Lee," he added.

"True," returned Mrs. Paul, with the slightest shrug under her laces. "Kindness is Sally's *métier*

A woman has to have some peculiarity; goodness is Sally's. It is very monotonous."

"If it were more general, it would not be a peculiarity," Robert answered curtly.

"I suppose you have found it amusing sometimes," said Mrs. Paul, again with that look of *camaraderie* and understanding. "A little of it is amusing; it is only when one goes through years of it, as I have done, — really from a sense of duty, you know, to keep my hold upon Sidney, — that one finds it a bore. Poor little Sally! How well I remember when I saw her first! Mortimer Lee brought her with him to take care of Sidney, when he came North after his wife's death. But it was a pity he couldn't have had a person of more sense. She has encouraged all his wicked ideas, even that folly of never going into the parlor where his wife's picture hangs, you know. She means well, no doubt, but she is so silly; sometimes I almost fear she makes Sidney dull."

She looked at him keenly as she said that. Mrs. Paul knew very well that a little slur is like oil upon the fire, and there certainly was a quick annoyance in his face, which gave her much satisfaction.

"Yes," she went on, "Sally was quite plump when she first came to Mercer, — twenty years ago and more; let me see, she must have been twenty-five, — and she looked for all the world like a pincushion in a tight black cover; she wore a jacket, — shouldn't you know that Sally would wear a jacket?"

Robert Steele tingled under the contempt in her

voice. "Whatever Miss Lee wore must have been suitable."

Mrs. Paul laughed. "I am glad you admire Sidney's aunt, — that is quite proper. But, really, between ourselves, she is amusing? Oh, how I used to admire her moral courage in those days! It was before there was a Mrs. Brown at the Rectory, and Lord! how regularly Sally went to church! Really, you know, Mr. Steele, where an unmarried woman goes with increasing devotion to a church where the clergyman is attractive and also unmarried, it shows a willingness to be misunderstood which is noble. It is a common virtue among old maids; if the clergy could only know how the female mind confounds religion and love, they might not be so hopeful of their converts."

"There was never such a thought as that in Miss Lee's mind!" cried Robert, his face dark with anger. (If only she had given him the right to defend her!)

"Ah, well," said Mrs. Paul carelessly, "it does n't signify. Mr. Brown was too intelligent a man; although once I really did fear — but I had a word with him! I've no doubt he's been grateful ever since; for a clergyman is so unsuspecting that a designing — Who was that young woman you bowed to?"

"My cousin, Katherine Townsend," Robert answered; "and if you will allow me, I shall say good afternoon. I must see her for a moment."

This terrible drive must end. He could not protect Miss Sally, but he need not listen to her maligner.

"She walks superbly," observed Mrs. Paul, watching the tall, straight figure hurrying along the road. "Is she handsome? Who is she?"

Robert, with one hand on the door-knob, gave her antecedents, and said she was not at all handsome; but Mrs. Paul nodded approvingly at the name of Drayton, and forgave the lack of beauty.

"A woman," she declared, "who holds her head like that can afford to be positively ugly. And poor, you say? That is nothing. She's her mother's daughter, and she can't escape the habit of good manners any more than any other habit. And it is manner that counts."

She was reluctant to have him leave her, and as he stood bareheaded by the carriage door she dealt one more blow for her cause.

"Sidney will miss you when you go," she said; "she hears so little sensible talk: for Mortimer Lee with his egotism, — his grief is nothing in the world but inordinate self-love, — is as absurd in his way as Sally is in hers. Good-by, good-by, — let me see you often."

Robert joined his cousin, and walked on with her to make the long-delayed call; but when he went away Katherine Townsend drew a breath of relief. He was so preoccupied, so silently depressed, that it was an effort to talk to him. He had had an instant of dismay in realizing that he perceived a perverted truth in some of the things Mrs. Paul had said of the woman he loved, — " the woman I love with all my heart;" and his dismay was, he declared, because of the weakness of his character, not the weakness of his love. "That is the strongest thing about me, at least," he thought drearily. He brightened up a little when, near the bridge, Alan overtook him. Alan made too many demands upon his friends to admit of anything so selfish as depression. Just now, too, the doctor was full of an impetuous determination to be happy. He had come out to walk with this purpose distinctly in his mind.

It was one of those still, raw days, with a feeling of snow in the air, and a mist settling like smoke along the thawing ground. On hills that faced the south, patches of sodden grass showed here and there through the melting snow. The river had not been frozen over for nearly a fortnight, but its black, hurrying current bore occasional blocks of broken, snowy ice. Alan was blind to the cheerlessness of the day. He was thinking, with an intentness which was a new sensation, of Sidney and her view of life. Not because he feared it, but because it was a part of her charm, this strange and exquisite aloofness from the things which other women took into their lives. He would not have had it otherwise, he told himself, and yet — he was not altogether happy. "We are queer beings, — men," he declared, smiling and frowning together.

He had taken this walk out into the country for the pleasure of thinking about Sidney, but sometimes this pleasant thinking was interrupted by an annoyed remembrance of a certain erratic action of his heart, which he had watched with a good deal of interest for nearly two years now. "That's the worst of being a doctor," he grumbled; "knowledge divides your chances by two. But hang it! I won't think about it." And he dismissed it, as he had often done before, but this time with a new unwillingness to see a thing which might affect Sidney Lee! This determination and the joyous flight of his fancy had brought exhilaration and satisfaction into his face.

"Hello, Bob!" he called out gayly, as he saw Robert walking slowly through the mist; and, as he reached him, he struck him lightly on the shoulder. "Where do you hail from? Been to see the charming Katherine?"

"Yes," Robert answered, "and Mrs. Paul. Alan, what a woman she is!"

"Superb!" cried the other, with a grimace. "Has she been giving you good advice? I observe that whenever she does not set a bad example, she gives good advice."

Robert was in no mood for flippancy. He did not reply, but looked drearily before him and sighed. He was trying to understand his depression. "With such hope of happiness as I have," he was saying to himself, "why can I not conquer what is, of course, bodily weakness?" But he sighed again; it was at such a moment as this that his face was an especial index of his character. Deep, wistful gray eyes, under a sweep of brown hair that fell across his forehead, and required at times a half-backward toss of his head to keep it in its place; a delicate and sensitive mouth hidden in a pointed beard, which concealed a chin whose resolution belied the tenderness of his eyes and the weakness of his lips. It

was an interesting face; not from what it hinted of
reserve, but because of its confiding sweetness. He
was only silent now, he thought, because he had no
right to tell Alan of his new hope.

On the bridge the two men stopped and, leaning
on the hand-rail, looked down into the water. The
river was so high that there was a jar and thrill all
through the tumbling old structure.

"Look here," Alan said, when they had watched
the sweep of the water a moment in silence, "what
a mighty fine girl Miss Townsend is!"

"Why, of course," Robert answered, smiling;
"is n't she my cousin, man?"

"No nonsense about her," Alan proceeded; "no
money; reasonably good-looking; no morbid father
with preposterous theories." (Alan had not yet
reached the point where he could take the major
seriously, although, to be sure, he was apprehensive
that the major might take him seriously.) "I
should think you would be the fellow to say you saw
the hand of Providence in it."

"I don't know what kind of a hand John Paul
would see in it then," returned Robert.

"Oh!" said Alan. "What? Well, I always
knew Paul was a man of intelligence, though he
has no tongue. I'm sorry for you, Bob."

"You need n't be," Robert assured him.

"Now, look here," Alan insisted. "(Come on,
don't stand here in the cold.) There must be some
reason that you did n't fall in love with her, because
it was so plainly the thing for you to do. A girl
who is poor, charming — well, I said all that — and
yet you did n't?"

"I don't see why this does n't apply equally to you," answered the other; "and, furthermore," — he looked at his friend with affection shining in his eyes, — "furthermore, I don't see how she or any other woman could have helped" —

"Bah!" cried Alan. "No, there's a reason for your not doing it. I swear, Steele, I believe there is 'Another'! What?"

Robert's face flushed. Alan was delighted.

"Come, now," he demanded, "out with it!" Then his amusement suddenly faded in the thought of Sidney; he even looked anxious.

"Don't be an ass," Robert began, laughing to protect himself. But Alan was in earnest under his lightness.

"You'd better tell me," he said. "If you don't, I'll think that it is — Miss Sally! There! I've no business to jest about her. But, seriously, you may as well make up your mind to ask my advice, because, you know, you've got to have my consent, and " —

Robert had been breathless for a moment; then he broke in sternly, "You are right; you have no business to use Miss Lee's name."

The doctor looked at him in astonishment. "Bob," — he said, and paused. A woman had brushed past them, coming with hesitating and uncertain steps out of the mist. Alan, seeing her face, forgot his raillery, and forgot too the thought which had flashed into his mind at Robert's words. "Poor soul!" he said; "did you see that, Bob? What a face! — sick with misery. A look like that strikes on your heart like a hammer." He stopped and glanced back, but seemed to check the impulse to follow her. "Poor, forlorn creature! At least we never saw that kind of wretchedness in Italy. The earth was kind, and the air. People were not physically wretched, and to me physical suffering is no end worse than moral misery."

"That is unworthy of you, Alan," Robert began, still confounded by that reference to Miss Sally and hearing only the end of the sentence; then he too looked back at the hurrying shape in the fog. "Hold on a minute, will you?" he said. "She is in some sort of trouble; perhaps a little help" — and he turned to follow the gaunt young figure which had so old and awful a face. Alan tried to detain him.

"No good, Bob; money given that way does no good except to the giver. Sidney says that's the use of all philanthropy."

But Robert had gone, and Alan sauntered on slowly, alone. He smiled as he spoke Sidney's name, and now, as he walked, he whistled softly to himself. Just then, back from the middle of the bridge, and wavering down to the water, came a shrill scream, followed by a splash which sent a shudder through the darkening mist. Alan turned, while the sound still rang in his ears, and ran back. How very long the bridge seemed before he reached Robert! He had one glimpse of him, starting forward as though to jump into the river, and then staggering back, faint with horror, against the side of the bridge. "She climbed upon the rail," he gasped, "and then" —

Alan pulled off his coat, and with one bound swung himself over the hand rail and would have dropped into the water, but Robert clung to his arm.

"No," he cried, "you shall not, you've no right"—

"Let go!" the doctor said between his teeth; he twisted himself from his friend's grasp, and in another moment was in the river. He must have known, even as he jumped, that it was too late, and that Death had already pulled the woman under the water. But he called out to her not to fear,— that he was coming, that he would save her. The echo of that brave young voice surely followed her into eternity.

As for Robert, he stood an instant in horror and dismay, staring at the hurrying river with its flecks of white ice, where Alan, buffeting the water and the mist, was whirling out of his sight. Then he made as though he would follow his friend; then cried out, "My God, what have I done!" then ran towards the toll-house, shouting madly for a boat. But a skiff had been put out. Mrs. Jennings had seen the girl jump, and had screamed to a man upon the shore, with all the might of her little voice hid in folds of flesh. The whole thing was over in ten minutes, and Alan safe on land. But it seemed to Robert Steele as if he lived a year as he stood waiting for the boat to come back. He saw them rowing about,— looking for the woman, he supposed; the suspense was unbearable.

"You're hardly able to stand," Job Todd was

saying to Alan, for it was he who had pulled the doctor into the skiff; "and what made you try to do it, anyhow? A woman's bound to have her own way about dyin', like everythin' else. And in that current you had about as much heft as a shavin'."

Alan was shivering so that he could scarcely speak; but he laughed. "I believe you'd have been the very man to do it, if I hadn't had the first chance."

"Well, very likely I should have been just such a fool," Job admitted modestly, and then leaped ashore to help Alan out of the boat and hurry him up to the toll-house.

"I'm all right," the doctor said to Robert, "but, poor soul — we were too late!" As he spoke, it occurred to him that Robert had been almost at the woman's side when she threw herself into the river. He was too confused by the realization that he had just seen death, and by the shock, just making itself felt, of his plunge into the icy water, to have any thing but puzzled wonder in his mind; but when he was in the toll-house, and Mrs. Jennings, with tears and brandy and hot blankets, was hovering about him, ponderous, but ecstatic, his wonder took definite shape. Why had not Robert tried to save her? Why had he waited? Fear? He refused to harbor the thought. But *why?*

Mrs. Jennings was pouring out her unheeded praises, and regretting that her 'Liza had not been at home to see such bravery, though it "would 'a' been a shock, too, — that poor, dear, beautiful young woman. Job, take a sup o' somethin' hot; it's agitatin' to see such sights, — I feel it myself." So she took the sup of something hot, which Job, having signed the pledge for Eliza's sake, declined. Then she looked at Robert, standing silent, with despair agonizing in his eyes which he never lifted from Alan's face. "I suppose," she said, "you ain't in no great need of anythin'? I saw you on the bridge watchin' her, till this dear gentleman came up. Well, the Lord knows it's pleasanter not to be so feelin' as some of us is. 'Tis n't everybody as could 'a' stood there, and not 'a' tried to save the poor creature. Now, this blessed gentleman here, I see he's one to give way to his feelin's, like me," declared the mistress of the toll-house, weeping comfortably. Then she asked him, being anxious to learn his name, to write in her 'Liza's autograph album. Alan laughed, protested that he did not deserve the honor of Miss Eliza's autograph book, admired the geraniums, and told Mrs. Jennings he believed she'd make a first-rate nurse, especially for any one needing stimulants; but he never looked at Robert Steele.

When the carriage which Job had made haste to order, arrived, it seemed as though Mrs. Jennings' enthusiasm would lead her to bundle herself into it; it made her praises of Alan almost insulting to the silent "coward" — she only hinted at that word — who took his place beside the doctor. But when the two men were alone in the carriage, with Mrs. Jennings' admiration shut out, it was Alan who was silent.

"Oh, Alan," Robert said, in a smothered voice,

"what is right?" The doctor frowned. "I thought — and yet to see you do it — risk your life because of me! And if you had died, what then?" He covered his face with his hands, in overwhelming and passionate pain.

"Please do not give it another thought," Alan answered, with a carelessness which seemed too perfect for disdain; "you see I am none the worse."

"I saw her first," Robert went on, almost as though speaking to himself, and with that singularly distinct enunciation with which a man baffled by conflicting emotions seeks to keep one idea clear in his mind. "I — I watched her there in the water, in an eddy, — I could have saved her then. But I felt so sure — then you came. Oh, what is right? That man in the toll-house would have done it; even that woman said " —

"Pray drop the subject," Alan interrupted, impatient and shivering. The suggestion of Mrs. Jennings was more than he could bear. He was saying to himself, "He was afraid."

"Oh, Alan," cried the other, in an agony, "help me! Was I right? You saw it one way, I another. What is right?"

"I was very glad to do it," Alan answered curtly; "probably you were not strong enough to attempt such a thing. Of course you were wise to hesitate, and — oh, damn it, Steele! Why didn't you do it?" His face was quivering.

Robert looked at him, dimly seeing what his friend's thought had been. He was not hurt. The moment was too great for personal pain.

"I did not try to save her," he said simply, "because I believe that no one ought to interfere with a moral act. The woman had a right to take her own life; it lay between herself and her God."

Alan stared at him incredulously, but his face flushed with shame.

"I dared not interfere," Robert ended, with sad sincerity.

Alan drew a quick breath; then he caught his friend's hands in his own, his voice breaking as he spoke. "Forgive me, Steele," he said.

IX.

Of course, when they reached home, they talked it all over. "Suicide is another name for insanity, Bob," the doctor declared. "To my mind, we have as much right to try to save such a person as to treat a man with a fever." But Robert insisted that no one had a right to say that weariness of life was insanity.

"What about the right and wrong of it?" Alan questioned.

"It is a sin," the other admitted.

"Then," said Alan, "according to your theory, one may only use example and precept, but not interfere with force to prevent crime?"

"If it injures no one but the sinner, I should not interfere; but there are few crimes which do not injure others than the criminal. For instance, if the community did not see it, and no one could be contaminated by his example, I should not feel justified in preventing a man by force from shameless drunkenness. Otherwise, I should prevent him. With suicide, only the principal and his God are concerned."

"Stuff!" cried Alan, with wholesome commonsense. "It depresses the community; and, by Jove! it's given my heart a knock that takes a year off my life. I don't believe any act can be confined in its consequences to the principal. There is always the example."

But Robert would not grant that.

"Bob," said the doctor, his hands clasped behind his head and a cigar between his lips, "I give you up, — I can't follow you; and in the matter of this poor soul, you may be right, — you may be right. But I never should have had the courage to let her drown!"

Robert shook his head. "I cannot seem to see the point," he said after a while, sadly, "at which what is theoretically right begins to be practically wrong. I tell you, Alan, I understand the comfort of making somebody else your conscience. That is the peace of the Catholic Church."

"Stuff!" cried Alan again, good-naturedly.

When Robert went back to the major's, that evening, he was very silent. "Very sad," Miss Sally thought, touched, and filled with self-reproaches for her uncertainty.

She had been trying all day to make up her mind, but to see him now, unhappy — and about her! She *must* decide. She grew more shy; and scarcely spoke, so that Robert almost forgot her presence. It was recalled to him, however, when, with a curious mixture of humiliation and justice, he mentioned at the tea-table what Alan had done that afternoon. Even before her pity for the "poor thing" and pride in Alan could be put into words, Miss Sally's thought of Robert sprang to her lips. "Oh, I am so glad you didn't do it," she said; "you might have taken cold!" There was a half sob in her voice, and an instant resolution to "ask Mortimer" at once. For the first time since he had been her patient, Robert did not find Miss Sally's solicitude sweet.

Mr. Steele was to go away the next day, and although Miss Sally was inclined to be sentimental in the silence of her heart, she knew, vaguely, that she should feel a curious kind of relief when the excitement of his presence was withdrawn, — an excitement felt only since he had declared himself her lover.

"May I come to-morrow, Miss Sally?" he said meaningly, when in the morning he bade her goodby; and she, remembering his low-spiritedness of the night before, could only reply, trembling, "Yes, please."

It was not, however, until the evening of that day that she summoned courage to ask her brother's consent to Mr. Steele's proposal. The necessity of having some sort of an answer ready for her lover, drove her to the library door.

She had waited in her bedroom, growing momentarily more chilly and more timid, until she had heard Sidney's door close, and knew that her brother was alone. Then she went out into the upper hall and looked over the stair-rail, to see that no one was wandering about below. She felt her heart pounding in her throat, and her small hands clasped themselves nervously together. All was quiet; there was only the faint crackle of the fire in the parlor, which still sent a dull glow out into the darkness of the hall. It took her many minutes to go down the wide staircase, but the very effort made something which had a likeness to love stir in her heart.

Major Lee, writing at the square table in the room beyond the library, looked up with surprise as his sister entered. He even put on his glasses for a moment, with a keen glance at the agitation in her face.

"Mortimer," began Miss Sally, "may I have a few words — a short conversation with you?" Only Robert Steele had seen the pathos of Miss Sally's unfailing effort to "express herself well" when talking to her brother.

"Pray sit down, Sarah," said the major, with grave politeness. "I trust nothing has troubled you?"

"I am sure you are very good," Miss Sally answered. She was so silent after that one speech, and her agitation was so apparent, that the major looked at her with sudden alarm.

"Is there anything wrong with Sidney?" he asked sharply, half rising from his chair.

"Oh, dear me, no!" said Miss Sally, relieved to have something to say; then she coughed a little, and gazed intently at the small, scuffed toe of her slipper. "I merely wished to say — to observe, at least — don't you think, Mortimer, that there has been a good deal of snow this winter?"

The major did not smile. This was probably his sister's way of leading up to the needs of the coal bin; poor Sarah had a somewhat tiresome habit of coming to the point sidewise. She seemed to the major like a little hurrying sail-boat, which yet tacked and tacked, in an endless zigzag, before reaching its destination; especially when she wished to make a request was there this rather foolish hesitation.

But Major Lee's unfailing courtesy forbade that he should hurry his sister, so he only replied, "Yes, a great deal; and the skies are overcast, so that it is probable there will be more before daybreak."

"Yes," said Miss Sally, "very true," and then lapsed into silence.

Major Lee's habit of refusing to be interested spared him much. He did not urge her to proceed. He sat brooding and dreaming before the fire; whatever she had to say, good or bad, would come soon enough without a question from him. It did not concern Sidney; that was all he cared to know.

"Mortimer," she began, and stopped to cough behind her hand, "I — I think it is wonderful how well Mrs. Paul keeps; it is really remarkable for a woman of her age."

This needed no reply. The major, gazing at the fire, his chin resting on his breast, was twisting, absently, the thin gold ring upon his left hand.

"What a pity Annette did not live to cheer her!" Miss Sally commented. "Only, perhaps she would have married, and left her mother. Most young women do."

"Yes," said the major, noticing only the pause for his reply.

"Don't — don't you think they do, Mortimer? Don't you think most women marry — more than men do?"

He smiled. "I should think it was about equal."

"But women," Miss Sally explained, "generally, expect to be married. Don't you think so?"

"I suppose," the major admitted, with a politeness that might have softened his words even to a more sensitive hearer, "that they are generally less intelligent than men."

Miss Sally did not see the connection, but she was too intent upon her subject to seek an explanation. "I know, Mortimer," she said, "that you think marriage is a mistake, but — but I can't help thinking Annette might have been happier married."

Her brother made no comment.

"And oh, dear me, if somebody had been living in the same house with her, and — and cared for her, you couldn't really blame her?"

"Pity, Sarah, — pity. One does not blame a child."

"And if he cared, oh, very much," — Miss Sally was too earnest to pause — "and would be unhappy if she — didn't — why, then — and oh, Mortimer, I do respect him!" The major put on his glasses and looked at her in sudden astonishment. This emotion was not because of Mrs. Paul's dead daughter. He was interested, but vaguely alarmed. "You see," she proceeded tremulously, "he has been with us for nearly two months now; long enough for anybody to learn to like him. And when he told me — oh, Mortimer, I was so surprised I didn't know what to say! Nobody knows it, of course; not even Sidney."

Miss Sally's fright had made her eyes overflow, so that she did not see the flush on Major Lee's face.

"What!" he said, in a low voice. "But you say Sidney does not know it?"

She shook her head, in a bewildered way. "No, no; it did n't seem proper to tell her."

Major Lee had risen, in his alarm and indignation. "Certainly not; but are you sure that he has not told her?"

"Oh, no, indeed," answered Miss Sally. "He would n't say a word until — until I said he might. And if you are not willing that I should accept him, Sidney need never know it."

"Sarah," he said, after an empty moment of astonishment, "I thought he spoke of — her?"

"Sidney?" she repeated vaguely. "Oh, no; it's only me."

Major Lee turned sharply away, and walked the length of the room and back before he could trust himself to speak. Miss Sally had risen, and stood watching him. Her brother's relief did not hurt her; it was only natural. "Sarah," he said, coming back to her, "I fear I was abrupt. Pray sit down. I am distressed that you should have been annoyed by this young man. I have been neglectful, or such a thing could not have come about. I will see him to-morrow."

"You — you are so kind, dear brother," Miss Sally answered, trembling very much, and with a look of the keenest perplexity on her face.

"I am much disappointed," the major began sternly. "The young man was my guest. It had not struck me that it was necessary to protect my household from possible annoyance. I must beg your pardon, Sarah."

Miss Sally twisted her fingers together and breathed quickly. "But, Mortimer, I thought — I thought perhaps you would be willing for me to live here, so that I could still take care of you and Sidney?"

It was a long time since Mortimer Lee had experienced such successive shocks of emotion. He looked at her a moment in silence; then he said, "Do I understand, Sarah, that it is your wish to accept Mr. Steele?"

"Yes, if you please, dear Mortimer," she answered faintly.

Again the major walked away from her and back before he spoke. "Sally, of course you shall do as you wish, but — I am sorry."

She looked at him furtively. His voice was so gentle that she realized vaguely the thought behind his words, and yet it eluded her as she tried to speak. "I — I'm sure he is a good man, Mortimer. You don't disapprove of him, brother, do you? I'm sure he will do anything you wish, — only he seemed to want me, Mortimer?" The major smiled. "I know," proceeded Miss Sally, the words fluttering upon her lips, "that you think it's a mistake to — to care; but I've never been afraid of sorrow."

"Have you ever known any joy?" he said. "But I wonder if you can know joy, — I wonder if you can love." He looked at her with sad intensity. "Do you love him, Sally?"

His sister's face flushed from her little chin to the smooth line of her hair. "I — I have a regard for Mr. Steele," she said.

The major threw himself down into his chair. "You are safe. You might as well marry him. And I suppose he has a regard for you? Well, that is as it should be. Never cease to have a regard for him, my dear, and you need not fear the future."

Miss Sally saw that he was amused by something, and she smiled, but with a wistful tremor of her lips. "You are willing, Mortimer?"

He did not reply for a moment; then he said, "I see no reason to object. I hope you will not be too happy, but I think there is no danger, at least for you." Mortimer Lee would not permit himself to think that Miss Sally could not inspire profound love. He took her hand and led her to the door. "Good-night, Sally," he said; and then, taking her face between his hands, he gently kissed her forehead.

The fire burned low before he left it that night, and the wind, rumbling in the upper chimney, scattered the white ashes out upon the hearth.

X.

WHEN Robert saw Miss Sally next, the mists of wonder about his motives had been cleared away by a sharp reality. He found, when he reached home, that Alan had been very ill the night before.

That plunge into the river was a great strain upon a heart already weak, and during the long midnight, alone, the doctor wondered, solemnly, whether he might not die before morning. The next day he was weak and still suffering a little, but, as he expressed it, "all right;" yet there was a dusky pallor in his face which terrified Robert, and made him forget his own perplexities. True, this illness had been because Alan had done what he had refused to do, but his passionate tenderness for his friend forbade even so much self-consciousness as that. He watched the doctor, with a comprehension of his smallest wish which was like a woman's; it was so intent, so absorbing, that he almost forgot Miss Sally and his anticipated happiness. He was, however, reminded of both. They had been talking again of that conflict on the bridge. "Steele," Alan said, "I thought it all out last night. You were right, from your point of view; and it has taught me a lesson, it has revealed the smallness of my imagination to me.

After this, I shall approve of everything you do, on principle. If you murder your grandmother,"— Robert winced, and Alan swore at himself under his breath, — "I shall know it was from a lofty motive." The doctor felt so keenly that his simile had been unfortunate that he made haste to talk of something else. "See here, what made you so fierce to me yesterday, when I spoke of Miss Sally? I don't think I deserved it."

Robert had been sitting at the foot of Alan's sofa, but at that he rose and began to walk about the room, steering his way among chairs, and tables littered with books and papers. "What a room!" he said. There were two stands which held chemicals and retorts; and there was a music rack, and an easel with mahl-sticks crossed in front of an unfinished canvas. "You are a disorderly beggar, Alan!" he declared.

The doctor looked at him keenly. "She's good, but not what you'd call brilliant, and you know perfectly well that I did not mean any disrespect. She's been a first-rate nurse for you, Bob, but scarcely a companion, I fancy?" Alan was very serious. "Is it possible?" he was asking himself.

Robert stood still. "I have never known," he said slowly, "a wiser or a kinder companion. I am a better man, Alan, for this visit to Major Lee's." Had he had the right, with the rush of memory which came at Alan's mention of her name, how much more he might have said, how he would have gloried in saying it! With a backward shake of his head he tossed the soft hair away from his forehead, and his eyes brightened; the happiness in them was unmistakable.

"Great heavens!" Alan said to himself, when, a little later, he was alone. In his amazement he sat up, letting his bearskin cover fall on the floor; he leaned his elbows on his knees, and whistled; then, involuntarily, laughed. "Jove! what will Mrs. Paul say?"

The next day, Robert went hopefully for his answer. Miss Sally, trembling and blushing, was awaiting him in the library. In one word she told him she would marry him, and then left him to the grave and puzzled greetings of her brother.

The major's view of the sadness of love might have found words had Robert aspired to any one save Mortimer Lee's own sister; but instinct was stronger than reason, and he only said, "You are probably not aware that the marriage of a friend is always a matter of regret to me. I cannot therefore contemplate my sister's marriage with satisfaction. Nevertheless, you and she must make your own judgments. I hope you will not be unhappy."

What congratulations! Robert stumbled over his awkward thanks, and was grateful that the major, with a courteous excuse, withdrew to the study, and left him to find his way back to the parlor and Miss Sally; but there he forgot all but his thankfulness.

They had a long and happy talk together. How Miss Sally beamed and brightened! The flattery of her joy intoxicated him with confidence in himself. He was full of plans; she should tell him how she wished the money — "her money," he called it — to be spent, and what would make her happiest to do. Should they travel? Would she like to build? Such deference took Miss Sally's breath away, and frightened her a little, too.

"I thought we could live here?" she faltered; "the house is so big, and, you see, I must always take care of Mortimer and Sidney."

Robert was too happy to be startled by this suggestion. He laughed and shook his head, and said she would have enough to do to take care of him, and talked with eager haste of his gratitude and joy. Miss Sally did not know how to speak; she looked at him with overflowing eyes, but he made her silences eloquent by saying to himself that her sympathy and understanding were perfect. The possibilities of silence are the materials from which Love builds her most stately palaces!

The light in Robert's eyes flickered for an instant, as though a cold wind had blown across this new fire in his heart, when, answering his passionate declaration that she had saved him from that old horror of weakness (he felt himself saved now; the future struggle was nothing, if her hand were in his), Miss Sally said, with quick, uncomprehending pity, "Oh, never mind that; you were sick, — that was all. I never think of it."

Never think of it! All the bitter months rose before him, all the wasted opportunities, all the self-contempt which she had turned to aspiration. Robert seemed to find a violent silence opposing his impetuous words. He did not stay much longer. "I want," he declared, "to tell Alan, and to proclaim my happiness upon the housetops, Miss Sally!" He suddenly realized that it was impossible to say anything but "Miss Sally," and to ask himself painfully, "Why?"

For her part, she said, "Good-by, Mr. Steele," with a little blush and a half-courtesy which went to his heart. There was a solemn moment in Robert's soul, when, with intense consciousness of what he was doing, he kissed her. "Just the way Mortimer did!" she thought, as, with a candle in her hand, she stood that night peering into the looking-glass, almost as though she expected to see some mark upon her forehead. Kisses were rare things in Miss Sally's life; she, to be sure, kissed Sidney night and morning, but that any one should deliberately kiss her! As she stared at her small, old face in the depths of the mirror, where the candle's shifting light gleamed on a silver thread in her hair, she felt that she could never be quite the same again. Happier? Oh, yes, happier, — but how strange it all seemed, how exciting! — and she sighed.

As for Robert Steele, when he left her, it was with a little uncertainty as to his destination. It was strange, but he had no desire to go at once to Alan. Instead, in an aimless way, he wandered out into the country, stopping for a shuddering instant at that spot upon the bridge where he had suffered.

It must have been two hours later that he went, towards dusk, to Katherine Townsend's, and told her that he was the happiest man in the world. Her start of surprise, almost of consternation, as he named Miss Sally Lee, he could not at once forget, although she made haste to congratulate him in that cordial manner which means consideration rather than sincerity.

"I've heard Mr. Paul speak of her, and I've seen her at church; she's a saint, cousin Robert, and I am so glad for you."

He brightened under her interest, and realized how thankful he was for the blessing of Miss Sally's love. "I don't deserve it," he said, "but Kate, I'm going to try to."

"I know you will!" she cried, putting her hands in his, and looking at him with such understanding in her face that he said quickly, "God bless you, Kitty!"

When he went away, there was a mist of tears in Katherine Townsend's frank eyes. "Poor cousin Robert!" she said, but she did not ask herself why she pitied him. She was in that mood where one sympathizes with one's self, under the pretense of sympathizing with some one else. She had been less happy since that walk with John Paul to the birch woods. "I told him only the truth," she assured herself, "and of course he did n't like it, but I can't help that; I am glad I did it." Yet it seemed that this assertion needed frequent repetition; "I was too severe," she began to say; and after a while, "It is all over. At least, there was never anything, but now I know there never will be. Well, I'm glad I did it." It was at this time that Ted observed, one evening at tea, that Kitty looked just as if — she'd been crying!

These reflections of hers were not caused by any diminution of friendship on the part of John Paul, although he came to Red Lane less often than formerly. He still brought jackknives and carpenter outfits with him. In fact, he paid Ted far more attention than he did Ted's sister. He told Miss Townsend, with the gladdest anticipation, that he had gone to the great city of the State to examine into the business of a newspaper — a free-trade journal, of course — with which he hoped to connect himself. It would mean leaving Mercer, but he did not seem to be unhappy at that.

These were bright days to John Paul. That bitter talk on the Perryville Road had told him much; he dared to hope now with all his heart; yet, he said to himself, he must try to grow more worthy of her before he should ask Katherine to make his hope a reality. He began to "answer back," as Davids expressed it, at the tea-table or at the checker-board. Not very often, to be sure, and not very successfully; the attempt to break a habit of years is necessarily experimental. At this time, he was cordial to everybody; even to Mr. Steele, whom he overtook coming home from that call upon Katherine Townsend which had announced his engagement. Alan had been right in saying that John Paul was incapable of appreciating Robert. Still, one's own happiness goes far in blotting out the mistakes of others; so on this occasion he was willing to slacken his pace, and the two men walked on together. Mr. Steele was too tired to talk much, which made his companion think that the fellow was really pleasanter than usual; but when they reached the dreadful place on the bridge, Robert could not pass it without saying how Alan had risked his life there. He told the story heartily, but he did not speak of himself. He could not have displayed the confusion of his soul to John Paul, whose brief and downright expressions of opinion always repelled the man whose mind moved in subtle and inverted lines.

John was enthusiastic. "The boy has something to him! It was splendidly brave in him. Don't you think so?"

"It was human," Robert said, after a moment's pause.

"How do you mean? It was superb! Ice in the river, and such a current as these thaws make!"

"I mean that it was instinct," Robert answered reluctantly; he knew it must appear to Paul that he was cheapening his friend's action. "Alan is superb, but an act like that, instantaneous, without reason, can scarcely be called brave, it seems to me. Alan does brave things always; he is the truest man I know."

"Well," John said coldly, "I suppose we look at it differently. For my part, I'm proud of him."

"Oh, so am I," Robert Steele protested; but his companion did not pursue the subject.

It was not an opportune moment, but they had nearly reached the stone steps that led up the terraces to Mrs. Paul's house, and Robert would not lose this chance. "Mr. Paul," he began, aware of an effort to make his tone match the gladness of his words, — "I — I am to be congratulated! I have become engaged to be married."

John stared at him. "Well, you are the most dejected-looking subject for congratulations, but it's a good thing, I 'm sure." He sighed enviously, and then laughed in a short, good-natured way. "So living in the major's household has not demoralized you? I suppose Miss Sally's ministrations have made you feel you had better get a wife; she is the kindest-hearted little creature in the world when anybody is under the weather, even if she has n't much sense."

After that remark, Robert Steele thanked Heaven that some one stopped to speak to John, and prevented the inevitable question, "Who is she?"

John Paul, however, was so much interested in this curious news — he always thought of Robert as "that queer fellow" — that he actually became communicative, and mentioned it, of course in the briefest way, to his mother; but that he should talk of his own accord surprised her into momentary amiability.

"You say he 's engaged? Now why in the world don't you tell me such things oftener? You know how I like a piece of news."

"Does n't happen every day," John observed.

"Well, to whom, — to whom? Sidney?" They were sitting at the tea-table, and Mrs. Paul rapped the bare mahogany with her stick, to hasten his reply. But he only shook his head. "Don't know? Why, you must know! Do you mean to say you did n't ask?"

John was really abashed. "Somebody interrupted us just then," he explained, wrinkling his forehead.

"Well," Mrs. Paul said, "*really!*" Sometimes stupidity is too great for reproach. "Whom do you think it is? Or perhaps you don't think? That is one thing you've never been accused of, Johnny. Lord! have n't you any idea? It must be Sidney. I'll wager it is. How stupid in you, Johnny, not to have thought of her! Yet I never should have guessed it from her manner to-day."

John Paul looked startled; he had not thought of Sidney, — that was true. But perhaps it was she; yes, very likely. He hoped so, he said to himself; it would be a good thing for the girl; she would be saved from her unnatural life. "But I wish he were a bigger fellow," he thought.

Mrs. Paul was radiant. "Scarlett," she said, when she took the woman's arm to go into the drawing-room, " I do hope it has turned out as I wished about Miss Lee!" The hope began to be a certainty before long, and when she called for the checker-board she nodded to herself once or twice, her lips pressed exultingly together, and her mind so full of plans that she forgot to criticise her son's moves.

"If it's true," she declared, "I'll give her a check on her wedding morning that will make Mortimer Lee open his eyes!"

"She'll need it more if it is n't true," John observed. The clock was almost on the stroke of nine, and it was his habit to say good-night then, so he knew he could escape any railing such a remark might provoke. But Mrs. Paul was too amiable to rail.

"Well, she won't get it! I don't propose to give my money to any silly person; just remember that, Johnny." She was so intent upon her pleasant thoughts that she almost forgot it was her son to whom she spoke, and smiled at him with that arch look which still flashed sometimes from her faded eyes. "If Sidney marries well, I'll make it my business to see that she does n't go to her husband empty-handed. I shall tell Mortimer Lee so. I want to see Mortimer Lee. I want to find out whether I'm right. I know I am! Johnny, just fetch the writing-table here."

John made no comment; if his mother chose to let her curiosity hurry her into such a thing, it was her affair. From this it will be seen that Miss Katherine Townsend had yet something to achieve. He lifted the table to Mrs. Paul's side, and although the brass handles of the drawers rattled upon their square plates, she did not reprove him. She was flushed with interest.

"Fetch a lamp," she cried, "and open that little box for the wax and taper! I shall ask him to come here at once, — to-morrow. And I don't want you about, Johnny; this is not a thing to be discussed before you. I shall ask him to take tea with the others Thursday night. I've decided to ask the people for Thursday night."

She took the feathered pen in her impatient hand, trying the nib upon her thumb-nail, and moving the lamp a little, for a better light upon her paper. Then in her delicate, old-fashioned hand she wrote: "Mrs. Edward Paul presents her compliments to

Major Lee, and begs that he will call upon her, on a matter of mutual interest and importance, on the afternoon of Sunday, January the 30th, at any hour after four." She sealed the note apparently forgetful that she had asked her son to be her messenger; and then John left her, sitting by the fire, with interest and pleasure sparkling in her keen old face. But when he reached the major's he almost forgot the letter in his pleasure at seeing Alan Crossan.

The doctor had no business to go out, Robert had assured him; but there he was, rather white, and with a new look in his eyes whenever they rested upon Sidney.

"Crossan," John began, hardly waiting to bid Sidney good-evening, and looking with a beaming face at Alan, "why did the young woman choose such vicious weather for suicide?"

"Pshaw!" said the doctor, laughing and frowning, "how do you know anything about it? But it was the weather that made her do it."

John was too much interested to drop the subject, and was full of praises for the doctor's courage.

Alan laughed, but with a sudden determination to speak of what Robert had done, or rather failed to do — ("it will come out," he said to himself, "so I 'd better put it in its right light at once.) Talk about bravery!" he said, "Steele displayed a bravery beyond me. He did n't jump in."

"I did n't know he was present," said John Paul, stiffly, looking at Sidney.

"How do you mean, Alan?" Sidney asked; her aunt and Mr. Steele were, as usual, in the parlor across the hall.

"Why, he has a theory," the doctor answered, "that no one has a right to interfere with a moral act."

"Does he call suicide moral?" John inquired.

Alan was eager to explain. "And, Paul," he ended, "surely you see how much finer such hesitation was than mere brute instinct? A dog could have jumped into the river as well as I, but only a human soul would long to save the woman, and yet deny itself, lest it meddled with infinite issues."

John Paul looked bored. "I don't understand that sort of thing. If I were such a fool as to throw myself into a river, I'd dispense with a human soul upon the bank, if there were any brute instinct on hand to pull me out."

"It was noble!" Sidney exclaimed. And for a moment John thought that his mother had been right in her surmise; but as he went on speaking of Robert, he was relieved by the indifference in her face.

"I tell you what it is," he said doggedly, "cold water is not agreeable in any form, and your Steele"—

Alan was almost angry. "You have no idea of the struggle! Steele was wretched! The conflict of the higher duty and the lower duty is anguish to a man like my friend."

"Oh, he regretted it afterwards, did he?" (John was sure now that it was *not* Sidney.) "Pity a man can't foresee his regrets."

"He was in despair," Alan said.

"But," Sidney interposed, "if he did not try to

save the woman because he thought he had no right to, he should not have despaired."

"Where is he?" John asked suddenly, looking about as though he expected to see Mr. Steele.

"He's with aunt Sally," Sidney answered.

John Paul's eyes widened. "Ah!" he said involuntarily; and later, as he lounged home through the garden, he said to himself, "I 'll let the major break it to her!"

XI.

SIDNEY was the last one to know of her aunt's engagement. Miss Sally had longed to tell her, but was incapable of speaking of it to the girl, and so had gone about the house with a confused and absent air, which at last attracted the attention of her niece. But Sidney would not ask what the matter might be, lest she should have to hear some tale of distress about Miss Sally's poor. Nevertheless, the next morning, it was a relief to have her father say, "Sidney, you are probably unaware that your aunt"— He paused; the major was at a loss for words which would properly express this extraordinary event.

"Yes," she answered, "what is it? I know there is something."

They were alone in the major's little study; Miss Sally and her lover had gone to church. "I want to give thanks," Robert had said, with that quiet happiness which always shone in his eyes when he was alone with her. But Miss Sally felt the awkwardness of the unaccustomed in taking possession of this new thing called happiness, and for once in her life would rather have stayed at home. She almost envied her brother and Sidney, reading together in the study, with the pale sunshine streaming into the room, and a green log singing and whispering on the andirons. Sidney was sitting on the broad bench in the window, and had looked up in surprise because her father had not come to her side for the word or two about her book, or the silent resting of his hand upon her head, with which, as though to satisfy himself of the presence of his treasure, he always began the day; instead, he stood by the table, frowning slightly and hesitating. She smiled and waited, and then the astonishing news was told.

"Oh, father!" she said, under her breath. But the incredulity in her face was not like Alan's, or John Paul's, or even the major's. That would be felt later, when she stopped to think that it was Miss Sally to whom love had come; but for a moment it was the thought of love itself which astounded her. Love! "Oh, poor aunt Sally!"

Major Lee sat down at his writing-table, with the air of a man who has done his duty. He began to mend his pen, and appeared to forget Miss Sally's small concerns. "We shall lose part of our afternoon to-day," he observed; "Mrs. Paul has requested me to call upon her."

"But, father," Sidney said, "why is it? Does n't aunt Sally know what she is doing? Oh, father!"

He smiled as she came and knelt down beside him, her face full of confusion and wonder. "You know what she thinks," he explained; "with her peculiar beliefs she is not unreasonable."

"But," Sidney protested, all her young heart in her eyes, "we know her belief cannot really help her; have n't we done wrong not to show her? Oh, he does not love her as — as I should think a person might love, or else he would not try to teach her to love him! Why did n't we save her, father?"

The major hesitated. "Sarah has so few pleasures; her hope of immortality, and all that, was so much to her, I had not the heart to take it from her; I never thought, at least, it did not seem to me probable, that she would wish to marry. But I should have remembered that Sarah is not a thoughtful person. Poor Sally!" The major had not thought so tenderly of his sister for years.

Pity for her aunt made Sidney for a moment almost remorseful that she had had a love to make her wise to escape suffering, and Miss Sally had not; but she would not let her father reproach himself. "No, you were right, — you are always right;" she lifted his hand, that scholarly and delicate right hand, to her lips; "but — poor aunt Sally."

As she went back to her seat in the window, the major followed her with adoring eyes, and then began to write; absently at first, though not because his mind was upon his sister, only that this announcement had turned his thoughts from his work to his daughter's safe and not unhappy future. Sidney, too, dropped the subject, and opened her book. Miss Sally, with her little hopes and fears, or sorrows and joys, had not enough personality to hold her attention. Yet while she read, the mystery which this step of her aunt's suggested burned in her heart; and an hour afterwards, when the major had banished it all and was absorbed in his writing, she looked up and said, "It is the certainty of living after death that makes it possible for her to love him."

"Yes," Major Lee answered; "immortality is the ignis fatuus which Love creates to excuse its own existence."

"How strange it is," she said, "how strange, that people can blind themselves with such a belief, when every day they see that it cannot separate grief from death! But God? I suppose they fall back upon their God, when they find that their hope of heaven does not comfort them." She laughed lightly, and would have picked up her book again, but the major, with a sort of contemptuous anger, repeated her word.

"God! My darling, you would find such persons very quickly dropping their belief in a God if they gave up the desire for eternal life."

"Would they?" she asked slowly. "And yet, do you know, that idea of a God seems to me so much greater than just the hope of prolonged existence. To have Some One who *is*, who *knows*,— that would be enough, it seems to me, without making such a thought minister to little human wishes for immortality. If one were sure of—an Intelligence, then, indeed, one might bear death. But of course it is foolish to talk about it."

"Yes," her father answered. "To limit Force by the idea of personality is indeed foolish."

"There might be something higher than personality," she began doubtfully.

"What?"

She shook her head, and her father smiled.

"It is unlike you, Sidney, to amuse yourself with such reflections? I don't believe you go to church enough; you are idealizing Christianity when you speculate upon the personality of the First Cause. Go to church, my dear." Sidney's face burned. "Or else, do not divert yourself by imagining what a difference it would make if light, heat, and electricity should arrange a heavenly mansion for you."

"But I did not mean a heavenly mansion," she said, with quiet persistence, though her cheeks were hot. "Only that if there were any understanding of life, anywhere, one might be content."

The major shrugged his shoulders. "If?" And she said no more.

His reproof banished Miss Sally's romance from Sidney's mind, and when she saw her aunt for a moment before dinner she had forgotten what the flushed embarrassment of the little face meant. When she recalled it, she kissed Miss Sally, with a hurried look, and said she hoped — and then she kissed her again, for she really did not know what she hoped. "What is the use of wishing people happiness when you know they will find only sorrow?" she thought.

Miss Sally, however, did not attach much meaning to hesitation, and beamed as she told Robert, who fell into sudden silence at her words, that Sidney had congratulated her in such a pretty way. She was wondering if she ought not to announce her engagement to Mrs. Paul, and trembling at the prospect, when the major said, as he opened the door for her after dinner, —

"Sarah, will you be so good as to see that my blue coat is laid out for me?"

"Oh, Mortimer," she said, with sudden inspiration, " will you ?"

" Will I ?" he repeated vaguely.

"I thought," faltered Miss Sally, "that perhaps you were going to see Mrs. Paul ?"

Her brother looked surprised. "Yes, she has sent for me. I do not know why; possibly to consult me upon some business matter."

Even Miss Sally might have smiled at that had she been less agitated, but she only said, " Oh — yes — of course. I only thought — maybe you would tell her."

" Tell her ?" inquired the major, puzzled.

"Yes, about me. You see she sent over a note this morning, inviting us all to take tea with her on Thursday. Perhaps she has guessed, because she said something about 'special occasion,' but I don't know, and I thought she ought to be told."

" Oh — certainly, yes," said the major. "I beg your pardon, Sarah."

Of course he could not know that Miss Sally was full of tremulous haste for him to be off. As soon as he went into the library she brought him his blue coat and even his stick, which she unconsciously dusted. Then she went upstairs and waited in the upper hall to hear him start. Since Robert Steele's departure the yellow parlor had gone back to its holland covers and closed shutters, and Miss Sally, as in the days before she knew what love was, sat alone in her bedroom, or in this open square of the upper hall. She could hear the murmur of voices from the library as, between their pleasant silences,

Sidney and her father talked; and she began to fear that the major had forgotten his appointment, — that he might have forgotten her was of so little importance that she did not think of it. At last she went downstairs, hovering near the library door with a fluttering excuse about books before she dared to remind her brother that the clock in the hall had struck four, with that rattling sigh with which old clocks let the hours slip away.

The major thanked her, but it was with an evident effort that he roused himself from his deep chair and his book, and started out.

Miss Sally did not realize that some one else was as impatient as she. Mrs. Paul had been watching the green door in the garden wall with keen eyes. It did not occur to her, in her excited expectation, that Major Lee would not come in so unconventional a fashion; the lane, and the terraced steps, and the formal waiting at her white front door finally brought him while she was frowning at his delay. She had spent the greater part of the afternoon at her toilet table, and she was still sitting there, in front of the mirror, when Davids at last announced the major.

It was a matter of indifference to Mrs. Paul that her serving-woman should have seen her excitement or understood her anxiety about her dress. Scarlett was useful to her; Mrs. Paul declared that she could not live without Scarlett; but to her mind a servant had no personality, and so she made no more effort to conceal her emotion from the little, silent, shriveled woman than from a chair or table. She was quite aware, and equally indifferent to the fact, that

Scarlett knew why she was made to puff her mistress's soft white hair with such precision, and consulted so sharply upon the black lace scarf which Mrs. Paul pinned about her head to frame her face in softened shadow. The servant heard her sigh as she looked down at her black satin dress. "If I had known a week ago, Scarlett, you could have done another gown?"

"Yes, madam," the woman replied, "but nothing could have become you better."

Mrs. Paul, resting her elbow on the table, looked at herself in the glass; her lip curled, and she struck the floor with her stick. "What difference does it make!" she said, under her breath. Then she leaned back in her chair, absently plucking at the lace about her wrists, and waited.

Major Lee was very long in coming, Scarlett thought. She sat outside the bedroom, in the somewhat chilly upper hall, where she could be within reach of Mrs. Paul's voice and could see her face in the mirror. Scarlett had her own thoughts in that half-hour while she waited in the cold; her thin, stiff fingers were hidden in her sleeves for warmth, and her little dim eyes stared at the faded engraving on the wall beside her, of some long-dead Paul, who, in a silken gown, pointed with the pallid forefinger of his right hand at the roll of manuscripts in his left, and who had a simpering consciousness of the inscription below the portrait, "The Honorable," etc. Scarlett never dreamed of making herself comfortable, but sat upright on the broad, hard seat which ran across the window and was covered with glazed calico. She reflected that Mrs. Paul was annoyed at Major Lee's delay, but she neither rejoiced nor grieved with her, although it seemed to her only right that her mistress should suffer sometimes. In her passionless way, the woman contemplated Life, as it was revealed to her under this roof, with interest; but it never touched Scarlett herself. When at last Davids came to say that the expected guest was in the drawing-room, Scarlett could see in the mirror the sudden quiver of her mistress's face at the major's name. "*That* 'll never grow old, nor her pride," she thought calmly.

Mrs. Paul rose, carrying her head with a certain lofty grace that hinted at lines of her neck and shoulders which must once have been beautiful. She took Davids' arm to the parlor, but discarded it there, and then, handing her stick to Scarlett, she motioned them both back with an imperious gesture. The man and woman looked at each other a moment, as she entered the room without support, and Davids said, under his breath, "Law!" but Scarlett was silent.

The green baize door closed, and the two servants did not see her sweep backwards in a superb courtesy as the major bowed over her hand. "It is a very long time," she said, "since this roof has had the honor of sheltering Mortimer Lee." Her momentary strength was failing, and she needed his arm to reach her chair, into which she sank, trembling beneath the folds of her black satin.

"A recluse, Mrs. Paul," returned the major, regarding her with grave and courteous attention, "does not often permit himself the luxury of pleasure."

"I have not seen you here for nearly four years," she said, with sudden weakness in her voice.

"That must mean," he answered, "that there has been no opportunity for me to be of service to Mrs. Paul for nearly four years. Let me hope to be more fortunate in the future."

She looked up at him, standing at her side, absolutely remote and indifferent, and her face sharpened, but her voice was as even as his own. "I took the liberty, my dear Major Lee, of sending for you, because I wished to say a word to you of Sidney's future."

With a charming gesture and a smile, she begged him to be seated. The major, in his well-brushed blue coat, with his soft felt hat upon his knees and his worn gloves in his left hand, waited in silent patience until this echo of his past, in her mist of lace and hazy sparkle of jewels, should choose to explain why he had been summoned. It was not business, evidently. Sidney's future? That belonged to him; but no doubt she meant well.

"To tell the truth," continued Mrs. Paul, "such a pleasing hint was given me yesterday of Mr. Steele that I felt I must take the liberty of an old friend of Sidney's, — she has, I think, no friend who has loved her so long? — and ask you directly about it. Pray, Major Lee, do you like young Steele?"

The major had looked puzzled, but his face cleared, and there was even a smile for a moment behind the enduring sadness of his eyes. "I scarcely know him well enough to have a personal regard for him," he said, " but his father was my friend."

"Oh, yes, true," returned Mrs. Paul; "and that Sidney's father was once — I am sure I may say is still — my friend, must be an excuse for my questions and interest. You think, I am sure, that he is an admirable young man; one who must be successful some time, even though some youthful theory of honor, which he has doubtless outgrown, made him rather foolish. He will certainly be a successful man?"

"Successful?" The major lifted his eyebrows. "In his particular line he will no doubt be successful. I should think he might achieve a trifle brilliantly."

"Are you not severe?" she said gayly. "But I feared you might have some such impression, and I wished to say — I begged you to come this afternoon that I might say — that if, as I have surmised, he desires the honor of connecting himself with the family of Major Lee?" — the major bowed — " I should like to express my confidence in his ability, and to add, if you will permit me, one word of my intentions concerning Sidney."

"You do my daughter much honor by your kind interest," he answered, still with a slight smile. "I shall be rejoiced to listen to all that you may say of her; but for Mr. Steele my sister must thank you for your very cordial expression of approval."

"*Sally!*" cried Mrs. Paul, sitting upright, grasping the arms of her chair with white jeweled fingers.

"My sister begged me," proceeded the major

calmly, "to ask for your congratulations, and I shall be glad to be the bearer of them to Mr. Steele."

"Sally!" said Mrs. Paul again, faintly; and then falling back into her chair, she looked at her guest's grave face. "I — I beg your pardon, I am — surprised; I had imagined — hoped — that the young man had thought of Sidney."

The putting it into words banished any glimmer of amusement from the major's eyes; he frowned slightly. "My sister is extremely happy."

That he should ignore her allusion to Sidney stung Mrs. Paul into momentary forgetfulness of her disappointment. "I am distressed that it is not Sidney. The child's future, — what is it? Surely — surely — you have not thought of that?"

There was no tenderness in her voice, but the major reproached himself for that. Perhaps he had not been courteous to refuse to speak of Sidney. "You are most kind," he said, with an effort, "but I have no fear for my daughter's future; she will not be unhappy."

"She will not be happy," returned Mrs. Paul quickly, "if you mean that she is never to care for any one, never to marry. Oh, spare Sidney your theories; let her have some happiness in life!"

"If there were such a thing," the major answered simply; "but the best I have been able to do has been to teach her how to escape misery."

"You make it appear," she said, "that there is nothing positive but pain. Is not life worth having?"

"I have not found it so," the major replied; "have you?"

"No!" she cried, with a sharp gesture, "I have not, but — I might."

Mortimer Lee sighed. "Yes? Well, Sidney shall at least not learn its worthlessness through grief, as you have learned it, and as I have."

"Ah!" she said, with a quick indrawn breath; and then, with an inconsequence which made him look at her with sudden attention, "I — I had the greatest respect for Mr. Paul."

"My very slight acquaintance with him," Major Lee replied, relieved to change the subject, "I remember with pleasure. He was a person of most amiable manners."

Mrs. Paul bent her head. "He had not a redeeming vice." The major made no answer, and she, looking steadily into the fire, was silent; they could hear the clock ticking in the hall. "If you do not give her the only thing which makes life endurable," Mrs. Paul began, — "it may not last, or it may not be very great, but it is the best we know, — if you will not let her have the happiness of love, think how empty her life will be! Oh, when she is as old as we are, what will she have?"

"No hopeless pain," he answered briefly, "no bitter memories."

"But what will she have?" insisted the other, leaning forward in her earnestness. "If she has once had love, nothing can take it from her. She need not be afraid of memory, if she has *had* it. It is only when it has been denied that life is bitter."

"Ah, well," said the major, and despite his politeness there was a little weariness in his voice, for the hour was late, "we are old enough to see that it is misery either way. Only the pain remains."

"Oh, that is not true!" she cried with sudden passion. "No, I know it is not true. An instant's happiness, — one would pay for an instant by years of misery! I know it — now! My soul is not old, I am not old, Mortimer, — oh, this miserable body!" She struck her hand fiercely against her breast; anger at the fetters of the years, the extraordinary effort of her soul to break the ice of age, sent a wave of color into her cheeks, her eyes burned and glowed, her whole form dilated, — she was a beautiful woman. It was only for a moment; then she shrank down in her chair, and her lips had the tremulous weakness of age. "Let the child be happy, — let her love some one."

"You are very good," he answered, frowning, and with averted eyes, "you are very kind to take such thought for my daughter, but I merely express her own judgment and inclination in this matter. And to return to the subject for which you were so good as to summon me, I rejoice that you approve of Mr. Steele."

"What I meant to say," she replied, with instant composure, "was connected with him only because I supposed him to be Sidney's lover. Otherwise, I confess, he does not interest me. I was glad to think that she was to marry a rich man." She stopped, wishing that she might fling out some cruel word to wound him. Then, in a flash, she had an inspiration. "To tell the truth, I had been fearful that, with the perversity inherent in young women, she might fall in love with a poor man. Indeed, seeing Alan Crossan's infatuation, I was somewhat anxious; there is no money, and he has, I believe, heart disease. However, as her opinion agrees so entirely with yours, there is perhaps no danger of that?"

"None, I think," the major answered, hot and cold at once; "but I must not intrude my daughter further upon your kindness."

He rose, with a look which was unmistakable, and which acted upon Mrs. Paul as some sharp pain does on a half-stunned and suffering animal. She stood bracing herself by one shaking hand on the back of her chair, and smiling calmly from under the arch of her delicate brows. "You are so very kind to have come," she said, "although, to be sure, I am disappointed to find that it was unnecessary to trouble you, and I cannot be of service to Sidney, as I had hoped; but I must not detain you any longer! The little tea-party which I had proposed for Sidney must turn into one of congratulation for — dear Sally. And you are so much occupied, I fear we must not hope that you will join us?" Her eyes glittered as she spoke, and there was a sting in her voice which would have made acceptance impossible, even had the major wished to come. But nothing was further from his desires, and with an old-fashioned stateliness he "regretted" and "deplored," and, then, bowing over her hand, yet soft and white under its rings, he left her, standing, smiling, in the firelight.

Later, when Scarlett came in to see if she should

fetch the lamps, she found her mistress fallen in a heap back into her chair, her head resting in her hands and her bent shoulders shaken by feeble sobs. "Take me upstairs," she said. "I want to go to bed, Scarlett, you fool! Don't you see I'm sick? Oh, let me go to sleep! I'm so old — so old — so old."

XII.

The Sunday desolation of the streets pressed upon Mortimer Lee, as he went home, like a tangible misery. The working-folk in their best clothes, staring out of the windows in forlorn and unaccustomed leisure, or walking about in the gray, cold dusk as though restless from too much rest, were part of the hopeless dreariness of life to him; and he would have felt that bitter pity for humanity, which is often only intense self-pity, — for each man is to himself the type of humanity, — had not that hint of Mrs. Paul's concerning Alan been burning in his heart. He could not banish it, although it was, he said to himself, absurd, nay, improper, to give it any thought; but he wished Mrs. Paul had not suggested such a thing. It was only in this connection that the sobbing, angry old woman was in his mind.

When, the next morning, he told his sister that the tea-party was to be one of congratulation for her, she turned white with pleasure. "Dear Mrs. Paul, how good and kind she is! If it were Sidney, now; but just me!"

The major frowned. "Sarah, I wish you would be so good as never to refer to Sidney in such a connection."

Miss Sally was very much abashed. "Of course I won't, Mortimer. I only meant" —

"Just so, I understand," said the major hastily. "Pardon me for interrupting you, but we need not discuss it."

Miss Sally had a moment of blankness, but her new interest filled her with such unwonted exhilaration that she forgot the snub in reflecting that she must decide what she should wear, — or rather she must ask Sidney, — for in so important a matter she could not trust her own judgment; so, humming a little song in unaccustomed joyousness, she went to consult her niece in the lumber-room of the east wing, where of late Sidney worked at her carving. It was one of those mild days which sometimes come in winter, when the skies are as blue as June. Little clouds, like foam or flocks of snowy birds, drifted up and across from the west; here and there brown patches of grass, wet from the melting snow, caught the sunshine in a sudden gleam; like a fringe of light the icicles along the eaves sparkled and glittered, and, as they melted in the sun, the flashing instant of each falling drop ended in a bell-like chime upon the wet flagstones below.

This room in the east wing was full of sunshine. Sidney's pots of jonquils on the window-ledge bloomed in white and gold, and filled the air with fine and subtle sweetness. The dusk of the room seemed laced with the sparkle of the sun and the golden burst of blossoms on the sill. Sidney had pushed into the stream of sunshine by the window, a round rosewood table, which was supported by a single rotund leg ending in vicious-looking brass claws; her tools were on it, and a design Alan had drawn for her, and she was intent upon her carving, the sun powdering the soft hair about her forehead, and glittering along the blade of her small, keen knife. Miss Sally, twisting her feather duster nervously between her loosely gloved fingers, slipped into the lumber-room from the hall, closing the door behind her with an elaborate quiet which sent a muffled echo along the lofty ceiling. Sidney looked up, and blushed deeper than did her aunt. It was all so strange! Somehow, instead of the old affectionate indifference, she felt a frightened interest, which was at the same time half repulsion. Her hand shook, and the mid-rib of a curling leaf was notched and bent.

"Sidney," said Miss Sally, going over to the jonquils, and examining their brave green spears, "what do you think I had better wear on Thursday? The major says the party is for me, — just think of that, Sidney! So of course it's only proper that I should pay Mrs. Paul the compliment of looking well, — at least as well as I can."

Sidney listened absently. When her aunt paused, after enumerating her dresses, she made this or that comment upon the modest wardrobe, scarcely knowing what she said.

"After all," continued Miss Sally, with a contented sigh, "a good black silk is the very best thing, don't you think so, love? And you know my bit of thread lace? I washed it out only yesterday, and put it around a bottle to dry, and then pulled it a little so it really does look very well. That in the neck and sleeves, and my mosaic pin, will be nice and neat and in good taste, and Mrs. Paul will like it, I'm sure." She hesitated, wrinkling her forehead anxiously. "I wish my black silk had a little train; but I remember that when I bought it a train did seem too extravagant. I might piece it and let it down in the back, but it has been turned twice, you know, and is so very old I'm afraid it would n't stand that?" Sidney nodded. "It is really a very important occasion," proceeded the other. "I can't get used to being so important. Dear Mrs. Paul, I hope she knows that I appreciate her kindness!" Then it struck her that she had forgotten Sidney, and with remorseful haste she began to talk of what her niece should wear.

"Aunt Sally," said Sidney, leaning back in her chair, but still playing with her little sharp knife, "I suppose you don't have to think of what Mr. Steele would like, because he will be pleased with anything you wear?"

"It's very good in you to think so," responded Miss Sally brightly.

"I meant," Sidney said, — "I wondered" — But she could not put her wonder into words. Love? Was this love? She shook her head silently, and began with a steady hand to curve the petal of a rose. Miss Sally, however, did not stop to speculate upon the nature of love; nor did she know that this new thing in her life had brought a brightness into her timid eyes and a little color into her face which was as though youth had looked back upon her for a moment. Sidney watched her, mystified by it, and by the apparent contradiction of her aunt's thought for small things.

Major Lee also observed Miss Sally closely in those days, but he did not misunderstand her frame of mind. "It is the newness of feeling important," he explained to himself, "and the interest in something quite her own, and the pleasure of being cared for. She does not even trouble herself by the endeavor to suppose that it is love."

And indeed Miss Sally was so happy that she had almost forgotten that she was in love, although she never for a moment forgot that Mr. Steele "cared for her." It was thus she thought of his affection. "She is so happy," Sidney said to her father once, her eyes clouding with a puzzled look, "she never seems afraid?"

"True," the major answered, with half a sigh, "but there are three reasons for that, Sidney. In the first place, she never thinks of his death, — your aunt has no imagination, as you very well know; in the second place, her heaven would console her if she did think of it; but thirdly, she — has a regard for Mr. Steele!"

In fact, Miss Sally had never in the whole course of her devoted and self-effacing life created half so much interest in her own household, and she had never before given so little thought to her brother and Sidney. Afterwards, when the newness of it all had worn off, and she was even wearying a little for the old accustomed round of emotions, she reproached herself for this. But for the present it was all a fluttering and growing joy.

Thursday evening was a climax. Miss Sally scarcely slept the night before for thinking what she should do and say at a tea-party given in her honor. Nor did Mrs. Paul sleep well that night; she was enraged at herself that she had not withdrawn her invitations. "Why in the world," she had cried to her son, sweeping the checkers off the board when she saw defeat approaching, "am I to be bored by these people to-morrow evening? I haven't seen Sally this week; I wouldn't. I sent word by Sidney that I didn't want her to read to me, and what does the fool do but write me a note to thank me for my consideration? And that young Steele! Lord! I can forgive him about the money; vice can be overlooked, but not stupidity!"

She changed her mind about the tea-party twenty times before Thursday morning dawned. "I can say I have a headache, and put it off, even at the last moment, Scarlett, only"— Mrs. Paul closed her lips suddenly. Perhaps Scarlett guessed the rest. Mortimer Lee should not think that his affairs or his daughter's changed her plans. So the tea-party was not postponed, and Thursday evening arrived. At precisely half past six, Miss Sally, breathing quickly with excitement, took Robert Steele's arm, and went with little tripping steps through the garden and up to Mrs. Paul's door.

The path was too narrow for Sidney to walk beside her aunt, and Robert, aware that she was following him, found it strangely difficult to listen to Miss Sally's chatter. Again, as he met the two ladies at the foot of the stairs, he knew with painful consciousness that Sidney's wondering eyes were looking down at him as she stood a step or two above him; one hand was on the twisted rail of the banister, and the other lifted the train of the old brocade, with its gleaming folds of soft blue, and its quaint, stiff bunches of flowers. Miss Sally, fumbling over a glove button, was saying something — he did not know what — with a hysterical little laugh.

Except Alan and the Browns no one had arrived, so Miss Sally breathed more freely as they entered the drawing-room. Mrs. Paul was sitting, as usual, in state beside the fire, and in answer to Miss Sally's bow and outstretched hand she motioned her aside, and cried, " Sidney, you look like Madame la Marquise in that gown and with your hair pompadour ! Let me kiss you, child ! "

Sidney's fleeting color deepened into a smile as she caught Alan's eye, and then, while Miss Sally blushed and trembled against her lover, Mrs. Paul adjusted her glasses, and extended two fingers to the guest of the evening. " Well, Sally, so you 're to be congratulated at last ! "

" I claim your greatest congratulations, Mrs. Paul," said Robert, in a voice which made Miss Sally's heart come up in her throat, but delighted the older woman. She did not much care upon whom she vented the anger which still stung her as she thought of that interview with the major, but her disappointment about Sidney had turned into contempt for Mr. Steele, so she was glad to make him uncomfortable. As for the major's sister, she could scarcely think of her with calmness.

" You may kiss me," she said, turning her cheek

towards Miss Sally, with that peculiar look of endurance with which some people accept a kiss.

"I was afraid we were late, dear Mrs. Paul!" cried Miss Sally, her eyes filling with pleasure at this favor.

"I should never complain of your lateness, Sally," returned the other grimly.

"You are so good to say so!" said Miss Sally.

Robert's face had darkened, but it did not repel Mrs. Paul; she motioned him to draw a chair to her side. "I knew your father so well, I — I had an opportunity of observing his devotion when he was in love, so I can imagine how very happy his son is now. A young man just engaged, and to so estimable a person as our dear Sally, is, of course, in heaven?"

Robert bowed; he could see, without looking at her, that Miss Sally was still guarding her shyness with nervous laughter. His heart glowed with pity. Mrs. Paul was interrupted here by fresh arrivals, and he had a moment in which to reflect how he might seem to be unconscious of the sneer in her words. As soon as she could she turned to him again. "And you are very, very much in love? How charming it is to be young and have enthusiasm! Sally must think so whenever she looks at you."

"We are neither of us very young," said Robert, "but perhaps we are the better able to appreciate happiness, now we have it."

"Oh, of course," returned Mrs. Paul, looking away with scarcely concealed weariness. She lifted her glasses to stare at each guest, but stopped for a longer glance at Alan Crossan and Sidney.

Alan had not looked well since that struggle in the river; he was pale, and there was a luminous intensity in his eyes that was new. Mrs. Paul saw it, and a curious look came into her face.

This was as it should be. It was better that Mortimer Lee had not come; he must not see it too soon; when it had gone so far that opposition would only increase it, then, perhaps, she might be able to forget her humiliation in pointing out to him his own. Mrs. Paul was able to think these thoughts, and yet say pleasant things to her guests. The gleam of many lights, the voices and laughter of her company, the courtly badinage of an old admirer, and more than all, the chance to fling into Robert Steele's quivering soul a truth, tipped and sharpened by a lie, braced her into positive enjoyment of the dreaded tea-party. She would have been glad if Colonel Drayton had seen fit to ignore his cousin Mr. Steele, even though it would have been a rudeness to their hostess; anything to wound the young fool!

There were moments during that evening when she almost forgot her rage at the designing Sally in her contempt for Sally's lover. "One can't blame Sally, at her time of life," she said to Mrs. Brown, " but the young man — Lord!"

When, at half past seven, Davids flung open the doors into the dining-room, Mrs. Paul, leaning on Colonel Drayton's arm, marshaled her guests with charming grace. To be sure, by some oversight, as

Miss Sally explained, there was no one to offer her his arm, until Alan, with a word to Sidney, who had been assigned to him, came to her side.

"Dear Miss Sally," he said, "won't you walk into the dining-room with me?"

Miss Sally hesitated to deprive Sidney of an escort. "And yet, you know, Alan, Mrs. Paul would feel so badly to think she had forgotten me, when the party is for me — perhaps I'd better?"

So Alan placed her at the table, by John's side, and saw her flash one happy look at Robert Steele, who was upon Mrs. Paul's right. Robert's stern expression delighted his hostess and brought a finer cordiality into her face; it also inspired her to make her other guests uncomfortable. She introduced a theological discussion between Mr. Brown and Alan by asking the clergyman if he knew that he had another heathen in his parish. "Fancy," she cried, "how shocked I was (anything irreverent is very shocking to me, Mr. Steele) to hear him say that the church which taught that the Almighty required the blood of Christ as an atonement made Judas Iscariot its chief saint!"

"I merely quoted, Mrs. Paul," the doctor began to say, embarrassed and annoyed, seeing the distress in Miss Sally's eyes, and aware that Colonel Drayton adjusted his glasses for a disapproving look.

Then she turned upon Sidney to regret that Major Lee was not present, ending, with a careless gesture, "But he is so odd — your father. Genius is always taken out of common sense."

These thrusts made, she could devote herself to

Miss Sally. Mrs. Paul was smiling now and very handsome. "You have taken care of Mr. Steele to advantage," she said, bending forward to catch Miss Sally's eye; "to his advantage, I mean, of course."

"He is better," answered Miss Sally proudly, and Robert's face burned.

"I suppose the little pills have done it?" she said, turning to Robert. "Sally's little pills give her so much pleasure, and I suppose they never do any harm,— do they, Alan Crossan? She wanted me to take some once when I was ill," she went on with a shrug. "I told her I preferred death to idiocy. Seriously, I am a loss to understand how persons who believe in the virtues of little pills can be anything but knaves or fools,— I mean the medical men, of course. Don't you agree with me, Mr. Steele?"

"Alan agrees with you, no doubt, Mrs. Paul," he said carelessly; "but I have a great respect for them."

His face was dark with anger. Mrs. Paul was witty at the expense of the woman he loved; yet how ridiculous were the manual and the little pills!

"We must drink to Sally's future," she began again, later; "you young people can stand, but Sally and I may surely think of comfort. Alan Crossan, come, you've been talking to Sidney long enough; propose the toast, and congratulate Sally on the opportunities of life. All things come to one who waits! You might congratulate yourself, too, upon having carried dear Mr. Steele to the house where he was to find his happiness."

By this time, every one at the table, except perhaps Sidney, who was more absent-minded than usual, and Miss Sally, who was incapable of thinking an unkindness intentional, was thoroughly indignant. Alan was tingling with anger. But he rose, and by a happy turn of words said so many true and pretty things of poor scarlet Miss Sally that she sniffed audibly, and very honestly and frankly wiped her eyes. Even Sidney was touched by the gentleness in Alan's cordial young voice, and she looked at the little shrinking figure in the black silk, with a smile which made Miss Sally feel that her cup overflowed with blessings.

"Now," said Mrs. Paul, striking Robert lightly with her fan, "what have you to say? Surely you and Alan have been rivals. Sally, I did n't know you had so many lovers."

"We are all Miss Sally's lovers," observed John Paul; it was his first remark that evening.

Robert was on his feet in an instant, with one quick look of gratitude at Alan, and then a burst of self-congratulation, which in Mrs. Paul's ears told of something beside happiness and hope. She smiled as he proceeded. "He distrusts himself," she thought; and when he sat down, flushed and glad, and with a look at Miss Sally, who was in tears, she smiled again.

"You took no wine," she said, with the solicitude of the hostess; adding, "Not even to drink dear Sally's health?"

"No," he answered, "I do not use wine."

"Mr. Steele does not approve of wine," Miss Sally explained proudly.

The doctor frowned. Was Robert about to assert a temperance which he had not practiced?

"What!" cried Mrs. Paul, holding up her wine glass so that the light sparkling through the claret flashed red upon the starlike cutting about the bowl, "you do not approve of the moderate use of wine? Surely that is one of Sally's theories to which you have submitted? Ah, the head is always the slave of the heart!"

"No," Robert answered miserably, — the discrepancy between his protest and his life was so appalling that he could not stop to think of the impression he was making, — "No, I do not approve of it. I think Miss Lee agrees with me, but I felt that it was wrong, for me, before I knew her views. I have always felt that it was wrong," he added, nervously anxious to say without words that, though he fell short of his principles, he never doubted them. There was no self-consciousness in the distress in his face; only the dismay which every sensitive soul feels in claiming a nobility of thought which his past contradicts. Indeed, it is strange how long after a sin is atoned for, forgotten, even, by all except the sinner, it will thrust a high impulse out of the soul, with a cry of "Unclean, unclean!" Robert's pain was so great that he did not feel Mrs. Paul's significant look, nor care for Alan's annoyance. He was quite silent for the rest of the uncomfortable occasion, which, however, was not prolonged. Mrs. Paul was tired; she was glad to motion Davids to throw open the folding doors again, and once more settle herself in her great chair by the drawing-room fire.

Every one was relieved when the dreary evening came to an end. Miss Sally, to be sure, talked cheerfully all the way home of Mrs. Paul's goodness, looking over her shoulder at Sidney and Alan to say that Mrs. Paul did not mean to be unkind when she spoke sharply.

But there were tears in her eyes, which the darkness hid even from her lover.

XIII.

For days afterwards the tea-party was a nightmare to Robert Steele. It was not that Mrs. Paul's cruelty to Miss Sally hurt him, for it made him tenderer to her, and so, in a certain way, he could almost exult in it; but with terror he found himself examining the quality of his love, and realizing that until that evening at Mrs. Paul's, he had seen Miss Sally only in her relation to himself, and not in relation to life. He could never again be deaf to her foolish laughter or her little fluttering talk, which skirted great subjects without any understanding, though with the same reverence which she gave to all things, both small and great, in a humility that was only humiliation. He saw it all, and despaired at his own perception. "How is it possible," he asked himself, "loving her as I do, honoring her, saved by her, that I can have an instant's thought of what is so small!" He was shamed by his own meanness, and so aware of it that he depended more and more upon Miss Sally's courage and affection. With the consciousness of weakness came greater love. Perhaps this frame of mind was induced by a sharp return of the old pain, and a consequent necessity of morphine with the resulting struggle against that habit, which had become almost dormant. So, thrown more for help upon the woman he loved, the weeks passed not unhappily, although sometimes, when his mind was not filled with her, he was vaguely miserable, because ever since his engagement he had been aware of a subtile estrangement from Alan. It was nothing more than the doctor's unexpressed astonishment at the step he had taken; it was too intangible to question, more a mood than an emotion, and yet enough to make this soul, which marked with quivering exactness every changing expression of its own or of another, fall back into depression. Feeling himself rebuffed, he kept his moods and wonders and vague terrors to himself, or forgot them in Miss Sally's presence and affection. After all, what is redemption but to be healed of self-despisings? Little by little, led by her hand, Robert emerged again from weakness, and looked about him; then, gradually, returned that terror of perception which had followed Mrs. Paul's tea-party. It must have been in March that, one day, depressed beyond the point where words could cheer him, he went drearily out into the country for a long walk.

It was snowing with steady persistency, and there was no wind; only the white cheerfulness of a storm that shut out the world. Robert would have been glad to lose himself at once in its vague comfort, but, with that painstaking kindness which was part of his nature, he stopped in Red Lane to learn how Ted was, for the child had been ill. The inquiry made, he turned, with a sigh of relief, down the lane, crossed an unbroken field, and entered the soft gloom of the woods. The silence closed about him like down. He drew a breath of thankfulness; it was good to be alone. He sat down upon the trunk of a fallen tree, whose twisted and fantastic roots had been plucked long ago from the earth, and spread now in the air like the fretwork of a great rose-window which, on all its curves and ledges, had caught the white outlines of the snow. He could hear, back in the woods, the faint sound of flakes falling on the curled and brittle leaves, which still hung thick upon the branches of the oaks. The vague trouble which he had refused to face was soothed for the moment into forgetfulness and peace. These sounds of nature have a wonderful claim upon consciousness,— both joy and sorrow melt into them: the noise of rain trampling at midnight through a garden, the wind whispering in the dry grass along a hilltop, the rustling haste of hail on frozen snow, — all have a power over the mind, and seem to draw it back into the complete whole from which it has been for the moment separated.

With the weight of snow the underbrush about Robert's feet had bent into wonderful curves, which made a network of low, glittering corridors, vaulted and arched, and so far reaching that when some furry creatures a rod away moved, or nestled softly against each other, a pad of snow from the fretted roof fell with a powdery thud into the white depths at his side. A rabbit bounded past him, turning for one bright, frank glance at the motionless figure upon the log, and leaving small intaglios of his steps upon the surface of the snow. The rustle of the flakes upon the dead leaves, the muffled wood noises about him, his own breathing, were the only sounds which broke the white silence of the woods.

Robert sat with his head resting in his hands; his eyes had but the range of a pile of fresh nutshells dropped at the foot of the big hickory opposite him, and a wild blackberry bush powdered on every thorn and spray with feathery white. Little by little, after that first relief of forgetfulness, he began to come back to his unrecognized pain. There was nothing to distract his mind from Miss Sally, and yet he found himself refusing to think of the treasure of his love, and instead, wondering how long it would be before the snow would cover the shells, and gazing with bated breath at two keen black eyes which watched him with friendly suspicion from a mossy hole between the wrinkled roots of the hickory. He remembered, and then sighed helplessly because he remembered, that Miss Sally had once said she should think it would be dreadful to be alone in the woods. There was something which frightened her about the bare heart of nature. Not that Miss Sally had ever said the "bare heart of nature," but that was her meaning.

After a while, as he sat there on the fallen tree trunk, a tense stillness seemed to take possession of him, which made even the squirrel alert and anxious. The snow settled on his shoulders, and covered the pile of shells at the foot of the hickory. The storm was thickening, and the bending branches of the blackberry bushes were almost hidden by the piling flakes. A whirl of white shut him in upon himself, and in the furious silence of the storm the consternation in his soul clamored to be heard. Beneath the prayer of gratitude for Miss Sally's love, with which he tried to stifle this tumult, one fact asserted itself and insisted upon a hearing.

Robert Steele's heart grew sick. How gray and dark it was here in the woods, under the snow-laden boughs; what an unhuman silence! He looked up through the branches and the driving mist of flakes at the leaden sky. "God?" he said in a whisper. It was the cry of the convict soul which would escape from itself.

The face of Truth had at last confronted him and compelled his horrified eyes; he knew that his self-reproach for perception was an effort to protect what had never existed. He saw that he had called gratitude love, and that he had mistaken pity for passion. No wonder that the hopeless cry trembled on his lips; reproach and despair, and anguish, all at once. God! why had he been born, why had he been thrust into the misery of consciousness? His self-deception was the juggle of Fate, and the very horror of it was his irresponsibility. If he could have blamed himself for having mistaken his emotions, there might have been some comfort for him; but can a man blame himself for the curve of his skull, which decides his character before he is born? Fate? What is it but temperament! Helpless and without hope, he contemplated his own nature. He dropped his head upon his hands without a sound, and his very soul was dumb with dismay.

It must have been an hour before Robert emerged

from the deeper and more selfish terror of self-knowledge, to cry out, with the thought of the wrong to Miss Sally, " What have I done ? "

A long while after that, he rose, the snow falling from his knees and shoulders ; the squirrel darted back into his nest, and far down in the woods there was the skurry and flutter of frightened things.

Robert had a fit of sickness as a result of that morning in the woods; but there was no return to morphine, — the hour was too great for that. Miss Sally did not see him for a fortnight, and when she did she said it was no wonder he had been ill, sitting there in the snow, for Alan had explained that Mr. Steele was fond of the woods, especially in a snow-storm, and had taken cold there ; for her part, she wondered that he escaped with nothing worse than a sore throat.

XIV.

BEFORE Robert was really well, and could go back to the pleasant evenings with Miss Sally in the yellow parlor, April had come, with swallow flights, and sweeping rains, and a hint of greenness on the south slope of the pasture beyond Major Lee's. Miss Sally had missed her lover very much, and welcomed him with timid warmth. She was the more affectionate, perhaps, because his fortnight's absence, apart from her anxiety about him, had been — she was ashamed to acknowledge it to her own heart — a strange relief (it is not always easy to live in the exciting air of happiness; commonplace monotony is really restful); and so she was very remorseful and very kind to her lover. She even told him, with a blush, that she had thought of what he had said of being married in June, but if — if he did n't mind — if he had just as lief, could n't it be in August? The question of living at the major's afterwards had never been settled, because Robert had never thought of it seriously; but Miss Sally made haste to drop the subject of marriage, lest it might have to be discussed. She knew quite well what she wanted, but she knew also, by experience, that it was extremely unlikely that her wishes would govern her circumstances. She began to chatter her small news: Alan had scarcely been to see them since Robert's illness, and she was puzzled to know why; Mrs. Paul had taken Scarlett and gone away for a fortnight's visit (Miss Sally, anxious to be agreeable, did not add that Mrs. Paul had declared that she should die if she had to live among idiots any longer); John Paul had told the major that he was going to leave Mercer by the middle of May, to enter a newspaper office in the city; she had seen Miss Katherine Townsend quite often. "How pleasant she is!" she said, her face beaming. "Once she met John Paul here, and it seems they know each other." It would interest Robert, Miss Sally thought, to talk about his cousin. Katherine had been so cordial and so sweet, and her manner betrayed such pretty deference, that Miss Sally's easily affectionate heart had been quickly won. Of course she could not see what a pathetic little creature she seemed in Miss Townsend's eyes, or know that during the walk home with John Paul, after that meeting at the major's, pity which was almost pain kept the girl in unexplained silence, which caused Mr. Paul much anxiety. Indeed, as he went back to town alone, he became very gloomy, and did not even notice Eliza at the window of the toll-house, so her heart ached also. It is easy to circumscribe a cause, but who can tell how far the effect will travel? · Robert Steele had made the gravest mistake a man can make, and here, in the parlor of the old toll-house, Eliza Jennings cried until she could scarcely see.

Eliza's pain of unrequited love — it was thus she

expressed it, uncomforted by hot muffins and cups of strong tea — had made her pine more than ever to confide in some one. That impulse to confide generally strikes outside the family circle; perhaps one's family sees too clearly the extenuating circumstances, and offers comfort too readily. The easy consolation of those who know us is dishonor to our grief, and it is natural to appeal to a stranger for sympathy.

In this connection, Eliza thought, as she had thought many times before, of Miss Katherine Townsend. Mrs. Jennings might share her joys, but Eliza could not bear to display her sorrows to the maternal eye. It was very well to tell her mother that she had had a talk with Mr. Paul at the toll-house window; or that he had asked her for some crocuses from her garden border (which he had made haste to give to Miss Townsend); or, most beautiful of all, that he had overtaken her at the other end of the bridge, and walked across with her, lifting his hat when he left her. "Oh, ma, if you could 'a' seen the way he lifted his hat!" Upon that occasion, Eliza had been so dazed with happiness that, as she came into the house, she almost tumbled over her mother, who had been peering out of the window at this unusual scene, and she had felt the sharp anger of one who is rudely shaken out of paradise by a blunder of her own. But Eliza's paradise was speedily regained; she seated herself by the stove, and, first carefully turning her skirt back over her knees that it might not be scorched, told her mother every word of Mr.

Paul's conversation. She ended the recital with a sigh, as though aware that one kind of happiness consists in understanding just when to be miserable. She knew exactly what Mrs. Jennings' comment would be, and she knew also, in the bottom of her heart, how groundless were her mother's assertions that it "would all come out right;" but such knowledge did not interfere with her happy imaginings.

It needed something real and tangible to do that, and the reality came the afternoon that Mr. Paul passed the toll-house without giving her a pleasant nod and smile. Eliza treasured this grief for many days. It put a certain life into her sentimentality, and gave her some genuine pain. The entries in violet ink in the diary became shorter as this small reality crept into them. It is not impossible that under such unnatural and artificial conditions a sickly sort of love can actually be created; or rather, as love has no varieties, but many resemblances, a very good imitation can spring from such circumstances. Eliza's round face was really a little pale under her freckles, in those first soft spring days; as the daffydowndillies and hyacinths pushed their green tips through the cold, wet ground in the toll-house borders, her eyes seemed to grow large and her lips took a pitiful droop. She began to spend much time in looking at the river, now very high with the spring rains, or in walking about the winding paths of the garden, stopping to lean her elbows on the white gate and stare down the road or along the bridge; in fact, she was thoroughly enjoying the misery of sentiment.

It is not only the young man's fancy which is affected by the spring; the sunshine and the softly blowing winds, the scudding ripple on the river's breast, the nod of the daffodils and the brimming gold of a crocus cup, touch the young woman's heart, too, and then a confidante becomes absolutely necessary. So it happened, when, on one of these wonderful spring days, Miss Townsend came to give Eliza her music lesson, and noticed with a kindly word the paleness of her pupil's face, that Eliza's misery sprang to her lips.

"Oh, I'm that unhappy!" She swung round on her music-stool, and put her hands up to her eyes. Mrs Jennings chanced to be out, so there was nothing to check the stream of confidences, long restrained and swelling for expression.

"Why, you poor little Eliza!" said Miss Townsend. "Something troubles you very much?"

"Oh, my goodness," sobbed the pupil, "I guess it does!"

"Can't I help you?" Katherine asked. She was distressed to see the little milliner so unhappy, but, as she spoke, she thought, vaguely, how impossible it was to judge by the outside of things. She would never have connected anything so great as grief with the life in the toll-house; it had seemed to her too full of drowsy satisfaction to feel the spur of sorrow. Geraniums were always glowing on the white window-sills of the little sitting-room, and the rippling light, striking up from the river, played in a sleepy rhythm back and forth across the low ceiling; the cheerful warmth which danced out from the isinglass windows of the stove, and shone on the keys of the family organ and on the lithographs upon the walls, told only of content; everything, Katherine had thought, was as comfortable as the big feather cushion in Mrs. Jennings' rocking-chair. Heartache was incongruous in such a room. "Tell me about it," she said, with good-natured amusement, for the sense of incongruity is hostile to reverence.

"I'm — I'm so unhappy!" Eliza answered with a gasp. "I'd — like to ask your advice, Miss Townsend."

"Have you asked your mother's advice?" ("Can it be that Mrs. Jennings does not approve of Job Todd?" Katherine wondered.)

As for Eliza, she was trembling with joyous excitement; the moment had actually come, — she was going to tell Miss Townsend! She rose from the revolving stool, and motioned her teacher to take Mrs. Jennings' big chair, — which, however, Miss Townsend declined, — and then she flung herself down on a hassock, and once more buried her face in her hands. "Ma don't know anything about it," she declared, with filial indifference. "I couldn't tell any one but just you, and I want you to advise me."

"Your mother ought to know whatever troubles you," Katherine said, with kindly sternness, "but tell me, and let me see if I can help you."

"Miss Townsend, I don't know what you'll think of me," Eliza answered, from between her fingers, "but I — I'm in love, Miss Townsend!"

Katherine's smile was like sudden sunshine.

"That ought to make you happy, if he is a good man and your mother approves of him."

"Yes," Eliza quavered, "only he — he don't care anything about me!"

"Oh!" said Katherine blankly. So this was how unhappiness might come to the toll-house. Job was unfaithful! "If he does not love you any longer, you must try not to think of him, my dear." She was really very sorry for her pupil.

"Yes, but," explained Eliza, wiping her eyes and looking up in her earnestness, "he never did, you see."

"Never did?"

"Care, I mean; and I don't know *what* to do. I thought you would advise me."

"But I don't see what advice there can be."

"Oh," the girl cried, wringing her hands, "don't you see? I don't know what to do!"

"I should n't think there was anything to do," Katherine answered, really puzzled. "But if it is Job Todd, I am sure you are mistaken, and it will all come out right; I know that he " —

"'Taint him," interposed Eliza briefly.

"Then," Katherine said, after a moment's pause, "the only thing for you to do, whoever it is, is to put him right out of your mind."

"Do you think it's wrong to love him, if he don't love me?" Eliza persisted, in a broken voice.

Katherine hesitated. It was not wrong; it might even be very great, but not in Eliza. How could she explain it?

"Not wrong, but -- I don't think I would."

The poor little creature on the hassock was really so miserable that Katherine felt like putting her arms around her and bidding her dry her eyes; had she done so, the frightened pleasure of it would probably have banished her romance from Eliza's mind, at least for the moment. "If he cared for Another," she protested, "it would be different. I would — I would tear him from my heart."

"Certainly," Katherine agreed; "but, anyhow, you must try to put it all aside, and " —

" I thought," interrupted the other, — she was so impressed with the importance of the occasion that she actually dared to interrupt Miss Townsend, — "that may be you'd know if — if there was any other young lady. You know him."

" I have no idea whom you mean; but don't you see? — that is his affair, not yours nor mine. All you have to do is just, cheerfully, to make your life richer and better by giving, or else to forget it, and that is far the wiser way."

"But how?" And after all, the question was very pertinent.

"Be a sensible girl, and do your duty, and " —

"It's Mr. John Paul," observed Eliza, in a sort of parenthesis.

Katherine Townsend had risen, meaning, with one or two cheerful, friendly words, to bring this conversation to an end; but she was so absolutely dumfounded that she stood for an instant with parted lips staring at the figure on the hassock.

" I thought," proceeded Eliza, "you'd know if he was waitin' on anybody; for, of course, if he is, I must — tear him from my heart!"

Katherine's impulse to laugh made her face scarlet, but she was conscious of a perfectly unreasonable anger. She sat down again. "I am ashamed of you, Eliza," she said sharply. "Mr. Paul is — you know very well, Mr. Paul is not in your station, and it is absurd and immodest for you to think about him in this way."

At the change in her voice, Eliza looked up, half frightened. "Is — he waitin' on somebody — is he engaged?"

"Not that I know of," Katherine answered, after an instant's pause, "but that has nothing to do with it. Mr. Paul is a gentleman, and you will probably never know him; he would certainly never think of you in any such way. Now, don't be a silly girl. Just put this whole matter out of your mind. I shall not respect you if you give it any more thought."

"I do know him! He's been in an' taken a cup of tea. I know him real well, Miss Townsend. He's walked over the bridge with me, an' he's just as kind" —

"Of course he is kind; but don't you understand? Mr. Paul is kind to every one, and you have no right to think of him — in that way. Try to be sensible, Eliza."

Katherine was aware that she was unjust, and that her lofty thoughts of the greatness of giving were somehow blotted out; so, as she opened the door to go, she tried to throw some sympathy into her voice. "Now, don't cry; just see how foolish you have been. It is n't worthy of you. There! Promise me you 'll not think of it again." She went back, and rested her hand on the girl's shoulder with a kindly touch.

This moved Eliza so much that she gasped out, "I'll try — but it isn't any use — but I'll try " — and she even nodded, with a watery sort of smile, when Miss Townsend looked back at her from the road.

In spite of a curious indignation, the absurdity of which she could not help recognizing, Katherine was so alive to the drollery of the situation that she laughed under her breath; and when she met Mrs. Jennings, a little later, she said "Good-evening" with such smothered gayety that Eliza's mother was stirred to curiosity.

"I'd like to know," Mrs. Jennings reflected, waddling breathlessly towards the toll-house, "what *she's* got to laugh at, poor soul!" But she was to discover the cause of Miss Townsend's mirth. "Law!" she said, standing still in the doorway, as she caught sight of her daughter rocking and sobbing in the big chair, "what is it, 'Liza? You give me such a turn!"

It was some time before Eliza could tell her, and all the while Mrs. Jennings sat in her big fur-trimmed jacket, only loosening her bonnet-strings and taking off her gloves. She was far too excited to think of her own comfort. To see her Eliza crying, and swaying back and forth, and declaring that she wished she were dead, and refusing to say what was the matter, was anguish to Mrs. Jennings.

"Was it your music lesson?" she cried, in despair. "Didn't you know it? Did she scold

That opened the flood-gates; with tears and sobs Eliza confessed that she had told Miss Townsend about Mr. Paul. "An' she said that he'd never look at me —'cause he was rich an' I was poor, an' there wasn't no use to think of him — an' so — an' so" —

She was really incoherent by this time, but Mrs. Jennings could not discriminate between grief and hysterics. She was beside herself with anger.

"So that was what she was laughin' at, the hussy! Not another lesson do you take from her, do you hear that?" In her excitement, she flung her bonnet down upon the floor, and tore her jacket open at the throat for breath; her face was purple. "The like of her to say he wouldn't look at you! She wants him herself, so she does. I'll tell her so to her face, — a miserable music teacher!"

"Ma!" expostulated Eliza. "She was just as kind" —

"The idea of telling her, any way!" burst out Mrs. Jennings. "You ain't got a proper pride, 'Liza, — you don't know your place. Telling such a person as her — I'm ashamed of you! But I'll see to her, just trust me, — trust your mother, lovey, poor lamb, poor dear!"

She lifted her baby in her big trembling arms, to soothe her upon a bosom which held a flame of maternal love as true and tender as though she had been as slight and subtile as any wiser mother. But though she comforted Eliza, and, a little later, still in the heavy jacket, brought her a steaming cup of tea and a wedge of cake, she was raging and doubting at once in her own heart; even while she was assuring her daughter, now able to sit up, and eat and drink, that she " knowed the ways of men — and if she was n't very much mistaken — well ! " she had a vague and awful fear that her first absurd charge was true, and the " hussy " wanted him for herself. Yes, and might get him, too ! " Ain't he always a-walkin' over the bridge with her ? " she groaned, when she went out to the pantry for another piece of cake for her darling ; " though he ain't gentleman 'nough to pay the toll for her ! Well, she 's welcome to such meanness. 'Liza would n't have him. But I 'll see to her ; she sha'n't get him, — so there ! " And then aloud, " Here, lovey, now eat a bit of cake, darlin' ; there, my heart, it 'll be all right, lovey ! "

XV.

As Miss Sally had said, Alan had not come to the major's very often during Robert's illness. The doctor's care for the sick man explained this perfectly to Miss Sally, but there was another reason. Alan, for the first time in his life, was finding decision so difficult that he was deterred from action. He had been uncertain many a time before, and found it hard to make up his mind; but when this had been the case, he had always said gayly, "I'll drift. Fate must decide for me;" and generally he was well content with Fate. But he had come to a point now, when this could not be; he must keep his life in his own hands, he must decide for himself. And these hours with Robert Steele were his opportunity.

"What is the right thing to do?" he asked himself again and again. He knew now, with all his happy heart, that he loved Sidney Lee. The knowledge had come to him in that midnight when he felt that he might die from the strain and shock of his plunge into the river. It is the thought of death, the realization of the poverty of an eternal lull which opens the eyes to the treasures of life. Before this, Alan had been alternately charmed and antagonized by Sidney's attitude towards life. Her father's view he regarded merely as a most interesting expression of the abnormal; it never occurred to him to consider it seriously. An *idée fixe* he had called the major's belief, and had the usual patient, or impatient, amusement with which a doctor regards such a mental condition. But, although the unnaturalness of Sidney's ignorance of life was almost repulsive, her charm became greater every day, even while he realized more forcibly the distance which she placed between herself and the natural human instincts.

With the recognition of his own love, the subtle antagonism departed, and with antagonism his dismay at her tranquil selfishness, and his approbation of that beautiful aloofness which had charmed him. All which had repulsed now attracted him. Even her selfishness seemed natural, for was it not herself that she loved? Perhaps love of the same object often blinds the lover to selfishness. But Alan's anxiety at present had nothing to do with character or with love itself. He was only concerned to know what course of action was demanded of him in view of Mortimer Lee's wishes for his daughter's future, and his own position as the major's friend, or at least as his trusted acquaintance. Over and over the doctor argued with himself that the major's theories were monstrous and unnatural. Sidney had a right to life, — which meant love, — and he, Alan, had a right to offer it to her. Yet to betray her father's trust!

He frowned and whistled in his perplexity. The young man was as confused in his honest desire to see clearly as Robert Steele himself might have been.

"If I tell the major I love her, and ask his permission to tell her so," he said to himself, "it will only give him a chance to stuff a lot more pessimistic nonsense into her mind, and warn her against me; besides, he would probably show me the door. Now, it isn't fair to Sidney to treat her in that way. I think I ought to speak to her first, and then tell the major."

Alan was perfectly aware that this was not his honest opinion, though he continued to assert that it was. As a result, he stayed away from the major's, assuring himself each day that he would go on the next and warn his old friend.

He knew very well — for Alan felt the moods of his friends as truly as a sunny pool reflects cloud shadows, and perhaps no more deeply — that Sidney's father was less cordial to him. The major himself did not recognize any change; he only knew that those words of Mrs. Paul's were a continual but vague discomfort. He watched Alan now very closely, and with a perplexed and anxious look that sometimes turned upon Sidney, but never found any words of question to the one or of warning to the other. Indeed, he did not put what he feared into words even to himself; to combat it in his thoughts would have been to dishonor his convictions by a doubt of the power of truth. But he was depressed, and grew more silent than ever. He fell into a habit of returning from the Bank by way of the great iron-yards of the rolling-mills beside the river, which were deserted after six. Here he walked, his hands clasped behind him, and his worn old face sunk upon his breast, scarcely ever looking up. It pleased him sometimes to stop and glance into the smelting-furnaces, and see the glow of molten metal as it was run into bars of pig-iron in the sand, and note the black figures of the puddlers standing against the fierce glare of red light, or coming out into the gray evening like shapes from the mouth of hell. No one noticed the old man in the blue cloak, and he could brood and dream in his slow walk without fear of interruption. But once, in the keen, sweet dusk of an April evening, Alan Crossan chanced to see him turn from the crowded street towards the river bank and the mill yards, and with a sudden impulse followed him.

It had been in the doctor's mind, as a part of this troublesome question as to whether it was honorable to seek Sidney Lee's love without her father's knowledge, that he would some day discuss these absurd theories of love and life with the major himself. It would probably lead up to a fuller confidence; but in the mean time, merely to plan such a conversation seemed in some intangible way to satisfy his conscience for not having boldly told her father that he meant to win Sidney's love — if he could. A discussion would at least hint the direction of his hopes, he thought; and it was something to let the major know how foolish, nay, how wicked, to his mind, was such a blighting of her life as her father proposed. He had, that very day, concluded to say something like this to Major Lee; and with a decision all his gladness had come back again, and he felt the exhilaration of a man who has done his duty; for the opportunity is a small thing, when the will is ready. But here was the opportunity, and so he made haste to follow the major, his face full of anxious gravity. Mortimer Lee's mind had been of late so occupied with that miserable suggestion of Mrs. Paul's that when he looked up, in answer to Alan's greeting, and saw the earnest expression, he felt a pang of apprehension. A forlorn dismay looked out of his mild eyes. But Alan, as they began to talk, — or rather, as he began to talk, — grew more cheerful. The thought of combat always brought a fresh gayety and boyish confidence to his face, which added to its charm of indolent and sweet good-nature. He scarcely waited for the major's "Good-evening."

"Major Lee," he said, rushing into his subject with all the enthusiasm of a young knight who has never tried his armor, "I have thought so often of that talk we had in your library, one Sunday afternoon in the winter; do you remember? You spoke of the worth of life and the folly of love, and, do you know, I think you were all wrong?"

If Alan had been any less direct, his companion would have quietly turned the subject. The misery of life, as he saw it, was not a thing the major talked about. He had no desire to prove a point; he had felt it. When the grave had closed over his wife, all was said, and life needed no comment. Talk for the sake of talk was impossible, and the fashion of the day to protest that life was not worth living was not honored even by his contempt. The young man's frank declaration that he was wrong would have pleased him, even had there not been something in the young courage of a fool which touched him. Of course he did not mean to enter into a discussion, but he put on his glasses and looked at Alan kindly; he even smiled a little. He had never been so near liking the doctor.

"So?" he said. "You think I am wrong, do you?"

"Yes," Alan answered; "and I've been meaning to ask you how you account for the desire to be alive, even in the greatest pain or misery,— we doctors see that all the time,— if, as you seem to think, life is not worth living; and, also, how it is that those whose love cannot be questioned are yet capable of happiness even after death has robbed them?"

Perhaps because Alan had for a moment drawn his thoughts away from that hint of Mrs. Paul's, and he had the kindly feeling which is a part of relief; perhaps, too, because it was not easy to avoid a direct question, the major found himself saying something about the blind will to live, in the first place, and the belief in immortality, in the second place.

While he was speaking they reached the street, which was parallel to the river, and were about to cross it and enter the mill yard, when Alan felt a detaining hand upon his arm. Drearily along the muddy street came a little funeral procession. Major Lee stood silently, with uncovered head, until it had passed, and then went on with the sentence which it had interrupted.

"How genuine he is!" Alan thought, with sudden compunction. For a moment the young man almost forgot the absurdity of remembering death in one's plans for life.

They walked on, down between the great piles of pig-iron, and reached the high bank of the river, but there the major seemed to hesitate. "Am I not taking you out of your way, sir?" he said. In his own mind he was wondering why in the world the young man should choose this path; it did not occur to Mortimer Lee that it might be for the pleasure of his society. The major would not have walked with any one, save Sidney, for the pleasure of society. Nor did it at that moment strike him that to walk with Sidney's father might be agreeable to a young man.

"Not if you will allow me to accompany you," Alan answered, with that fine deference in his voice which was instinct and training rather than reason, for he was tingling with impatience.

The river, between banks of cinders which had been thrown out of the mills and furnaces, lay black under the falling dusk, but was touched by the wind here and there into a metallic sheen and lustre. On its further side, beyond Little Mercer and the distant hills, the sky was a pale, clear yellow, that melted up into the violet of early night; bars of filmy gray were gathering in the west, but in the upper heavens they rippled into fading fire; a puff of brown smoke from a great chimney drifted like a stain upon the tranquil night. Now and then, from the rolling-mill through the yard of which they had come, a flare of light lifted and quivered and blotted out the tender sky colors, leaving only the gray dusk and the gray river. The very air was a caress, and all the sounds of day came softened into a tired murmur.

The major felt the peace of it, and could have wished that Alan had chosen some other time to convert him; but doubtless the young man's intentions were good. So, in answer to the request to walk with him, he said patiently, "Surely, surely," and began to calculate how soon the doctor would have to turn into the street again to seek his own home.

"This blind will to live, of which you speak," Alan began, "has, it seems to me, a certain reasonableness on the face of it, and that is what concerns us. As you talked of life, that night, you apparently did n't consider any of the pleasures of living, with which the will certainly justifies itself. You did not admit any happiness. Now, Major Lee, there *is* happiness!"

"You are fortunate in thinking so," said Mortimer Lee absently. He had no desire to convert the doctor; he was even glad, in a pathetic way, that any one could be so foolish.

"Surely," Alan persisted, his eager young face aflame with the sunset light, "surely it is not fair, in making one's estimate of life, to leave out the joy of success, and of hope, and of love, the gladness of the senses. Why, this very sky and soft wind, the ripple of the river over that sunken slag, are so beautiful that it is almost pain."

"It is pain," returned the major. He was glad that Alan had not stopped at love, in summing up the happiness of life; he could not have put the reason into words, but he did not care to talk of love to Alan Crossan; and for fear that the doctor might return to it, he began to repeat, with quaint impressiveness: —

> "I know not what they mean:
> Tears from the depths of some divine despair
> Rise in the heart and gather to the eyes,
> In looking on the happy autumn fields."

"Oh, no, no, it is not that!" said the other, "for the 'days that are no more' are not nearly so beautiful as the days which are to come," — his face was radiant at the thought of those coming days. "I think that that pang with which we see beauty or power is only the assertion that we belong to it all, but are not in it; it is the protest of the molecule," he ended, laughing; "the instinct to melt into the current of life, from which we have been for a moment separated. But, Major Lee, I can't be abstract. I think my mind is inquisitive rather than speculative. The concrete attracts me, the real tangible reasons for thinking as you do, or as I do."

The major made no reply.

"You say life is miserable because there is death in it, but it seems to me you don't take belief into consideration. You forget the consolations of religion. Of course I am not stopping to argue for the truth of the belief in immortality, the belief in God; but its comfort cannot be denied. Well, granting that, never mind what is the fact, life is good, and love is wise."

"True," the major agreed mildly, "you would not be apt to consider the fact."

"I consider the peace and happiness," Alan answered; "I do not care to search too deeply. If I am happy, I am satisfied. It is better to have a false belief than none, and with belief loss can be borne."

"Just so," returned his companion, "the truth which makes us free by no means necessitates happiness."

"Whereas," Alan insisted, "your position necessitates unhappiness!"

"I cannot see," observed the major, "that happiness or unhappiness can affect belief; because I should suppose a man must endeavor to believe, not what makes him happy, but what he thinks is true."

"I wonder," Alan said, "whether happiness is not the deepest truth, and so we believe in God, and immortality, and love?"

"Because you prefer to?"

"Because I am a man, because I cannot help it! Yes, and I suppose because I prefer to; at least, I refuse to disbelieve, and I make myself as happy as I can."

Major Lee looked about for escape; this foolish talk was as annoying as a cloud of gnats. But suddenly a thought struck him: he might show the young man, he might prove to him the folly of it all? The boy was a sensible boy in the main, and perhaps he could be taught? The major began to feel a little glow of friendliness.

"If you are in no especial haste, I should be glad to hear your views. May we not stop here and talk for a little time? We shall suffer no interruption if we go down to the river side."

"I shall be delighted to!" cried Alan, really astounded at what he naturally felt to be the result of his logic.

They left the mill yard and the smelting-furnace behind them; the river was banked by slag which had been run into great conical moulds, and then flung out to cool and crumble down by the water. Upon one of these moulds the old man seated himself, drawing his blue cloak around him, and resting his hands upon his stick. He waited a moment, thinking how he might best begin, and looking up at the young man standing against the sunset. Alan had taken off his hat, and threw back his head with a certain beautiful joyousness which made it good to look at him. His voice held the sound of pleasant thoughts. The major's patience exhilarated him. He did not wait for the older man to begin, but hurried on with his arguments.

"Yes; it seems to me you quite leave out this ability of the soul to be satisfied,— this power of belief which makes it possible to bear grief; and there's another thing, which I think prevents a really fair judgment upon the worth of life,— you dwell constantly upon death. Now— I beg your pardon, but the normal and healthy soul does not consider death; it lives in the present, as it was meant to do."

The major did not stop to be amused at one who declared that he understood what the soul was "meant" to do. "Does it really seem to you abnormal to take a certainty into consideration in making your plans for living?" he asked.

"Absolutely so!" Alan answered, and then hesitated. "Perhaps because, while the consideration of such a certainty may be reasonable enough, it simply is not human. And humanity sets the limits of the normal."

"Then you would have a man a fool, just because there are, it must be admitted, more fools than wise men in the world?"

"Hold on! I don't admit that to forget death is folly, — it is merely sane; and I think that the joy of life — I — I mean love, you know, while it lasts, is worth the pain of loss. Beside, I do believe in the goodness of God, — immortality declares that; and if God is good, the purpose of life must be."

"Yet, no doubt, even you go through a process of reasoning?" the major queried thoughtfully; "and when you say that the grief of death can be borne because death does not end all, you prove the reunion in which you say you believe?"

"Yes," Alan answered, "I prove it, at least to my own satisfaction, by saying that God is good."

"Ah, I see," commented the other. "Life, which is one long endurance of sin and misery and exquisite suffering, must be compensated for by an eternity of joy, or else the Creator would be a conception so blastingly cruel that men would die at the very sight of the Frankenstein they had called into their minds; men must be immortal to prove the morality of God?"

"Yes," Alan said again.

"But observe," continued the major, "your belief in the goodness of God rests upon your belief in immortality, and your belief in immortality rests upon your belief in the goodness of God. Admirable logic."

"But"—Alan began to protest, in a confused way.

The major stopped him with a gesture. "Now, if you were not so fortunate as to be able to retain your belief in God and immortality in the face of reason and as dependent upon each other (and there are some persons who are unable to do so), may I inquire whether you would still feel that life is good?"

"I never maintained that it was entirely good," Alan answered; "only that"—

"Goodness is not comparative, I think," interrupted the other.

"Only that it is worth having. It is beautiful and precious because — oh, because, Major Lee, of this very love which you think is an invitation to sorrow!"

The old man had risen, and put one lean white hand on Alan's arm; he was so earnest that his voice shook. "Yes, love," he said,—"love is the greatest curse of all! That is what I wanted to say to you. To the man who cannot go through life with his eyes shut, who cannot summon the dream of immortality to comfort him with the thought of reunion,—and there are few who can do that genuinely,—love is only terror and misery beyond words. Love returns fourfold despair, whatever absence of pain there may be in success, or hope, or the beauty of conduct. Love is hell."

Alan was shocked into silence; the misery in this old face swept the light assertions from his lips. The yellow sunset had faded, and the fog was beginning to steal up the river. Alan shivered.

"This love, in marriage, what is it? Friendliness, perhaps, which commonplace daily living turns almost into indifference; when it is that, it is the profanation of an ideal. Passionate joy, which is the ideal, and with it the blackening, blasting fear of grief, or — grief itself. Then, in either case, the responsibility of bringing new souls into the world, to suffer; such a responsibility is like your God's! But what man shrinks from it? I know that you would say that children make the parting between husband and wife less terrible; it may be so, sometimes; but at what a cost to the child! It must live, it must suffer, it must endure the agony of the fear of death. It is a hideous selfishness that brings another soul here to suffer! You think that I am declaring existence to be a curse. I do so declare it. The only escape from the tragedy of consciousness which the caprice of the motiveless will fastens upon us, is resignation — is the giving up of desire — is the giving up of living. Resignation! even your religion teaches that, disguising it beneath promises of recompense and some future of happiness. Sir, I have studied life as other men study art or nature, and I know — listen to me, young man, I beseech you — I know that the nearest approach to what we call happiness is negation. Believe me, Alan."

The two men stood motionless in the shadows, but

Alan could see the older man's face, and there was a look in it which made him turn away his eyes. There is a brutal indecency in watching a naked soul struggle in an agonized human countenance.

"But to seek only freedom from pain is moral suicide," he stammered, scarcely knowing what he said, "and a woman who is cheated of her right to suffer, of the beauty that there is in pain, has a life deformed and " —

"Ah!" cried the other. "Young man, you talk of the beauty of suffering? Because you know nothing about suffering!"

Mortimer Lee turned away; it was time to go home. Why had he wasted his words? Who can convince a youth? Yet he would have saved him; there had been a point when he had been really disinterested in what he said. He was so absorbed in his own disappointment that for a few moments he was unaware that Alan was still walking at his side. The young man's heart was hot within him, the physician was lost in the lover; he forgot that Major Lee was morbid. The human horror of death and the human instinct of love each entreated him, and he looked at both with that strange simplicity which comes when a man forgets himself in the presence of primal things. For once he could find no words.

It was not until they reached the major's gate and were within the little courtyard that he burst out, "No, no, no! you are wrong. Love is worth while. A man can blind himself, he can cast out fear, he can be divinely happy, with belief or without it. Love is enough; we can shut our eyes to everything else."

"Until the end,—until one is taken, and the other left," the major answered.

As he spoke, the hall door opened, and Sidney stood upon the threshold, looking out into the night. As she saw the two dark figures beneath the ailantus trees, she said under her breath, with that wonderful intonation which was the promise of untouched depths of tenderness in her nature, "Father?"

She came down the steps, and took her father's arm. "You are coming in, Alan?" she said. The major stood as erect and silent as though upon the parade ground, but he glanced at Alan. The young man only shook his head silently, and turned away into the dark.

XVI.

That glimpse of a living grief sobered Alan into patience, almost into reverence, for Mortimer Lee; indeed, he felt a pitying tenderness for the old man's theories which the major would have resented with a pity of his own. But after a while Alan's own hopes claimed him, and he declared that the way was clear. The major knew, he insisted to himself, that he loved Sidney. "I did n't say it in so many words, but he must know it, and so I need not feel like a sneak," and his courage and his hope increased together. There was nothing now to distract his attention, or to prevent him from going to the major's on every possible excuse. He was well aware that Sidney's father did not welcome him, and he guessed, with the compassionate amusement of youth, that the major did not forbid his coming only because that would have seemed to doubt Sidney's convictions. Sidney's convictions! What were they? Thistledown, if the breath of love should touch her lips. It was inconceivable to Alan that there should be any reality in an attitude of mind attained by precept and not experience (he admitted the major's reality since that talk by the river), and he set himself with all his heart to win a conscious look from Sidney's tranquil eyes, a deeper flush on her smooth cheek, or one word that was not as impersonally kind as the April sunshine itself.

Alan's absorption and happiness, but perhaps still more, the absence for the first time in many months, of any anxiety about Robert Steele, shut his friend outside the doctor's life. "Bob is all right," he reflected carelessly, and then had no more thought for him.

Robert was well. There had been a physical rebound after that sore throat which had made Miss Sally so anxious, and he was better than he had been for years; which was of course a great happiness to Miss Sally. But that very health was a humiliation to him. There are times when the body seems to flaunt itself before the sick and cringing soul. Robert was walking in spiritual darkness; he was searching for his duty with blind gropings into his fears. But the blood leaped in his veins, this spring weather; his hand was steady, his eye clear; he was a well man. It is curious how sometimes the soul is outraged by the body. Grief resents hunger as an insult to its dead; anxiety flies from sleep which pursues it with unwelcome comfort; remorse turns its eyes away from the soft impulses which invite it; but how often the body triumphs! Robert Steele felt a deeper shame for his health's sake. And all the while Miss Sally rejoiced.

After that revelation of himself in the woods, there had come to Robert that dogged acceptance of despair which is a sort of peace. His duty to Miss Sally was all he had to live for, and that meant the fulfillment of his engagement. In his eyes, marriage without love was a profanation, and there had been a terrible moment when it seemed that he must tell her of his baseness; but he had flung the thought away from him. It was profanation; but why should he not profane himself if it saved her pain? (Robert honored Miss Sally too truly ever to suspect the quality of her love for him.) To blacken his own soul was a small thing, if she could be spared the grief and humiliation of the truth. Yet he cringed at the thought, and, without being aware of it, beneath his resolution a continual argument was carried on.

There were days when this strange secondary consciousness brought nearly to the surface of his determination, the belief that truth to Miss Sally was his first and only duty. Truth to his ideal walked unrecognized beside that duty. But of late this hidden thought came boldly into his most sacred moments, — came, saying, "Truth is God manifested in the soul. To let silence lie to the woman who thinks you love her is the cruelest wrong you can do her." And Robert, with anguish, admitted to himself that this was so, and the peace of despair was lost in the possibility of greater pain.

But he was, during all this time, as even Mrs. Paul admitted, a most devoted lover; it was she, however, who detected a confession in his devotion. To be sure, she did not witness it, and only knew of it by questioning Sally Lee, and sometimes Sidney, for she scarcely saw Mr. Steele. He had made the proper call after the tea-party; then he had been ill; after that, he was always ready with an excuse when Miss Sally suggested that they should go to call upon dear Mrs. Paul. She never did more than hint that they should go, not having courage enough to reproach her lover for ill manners, but she did hint quite constantly; not because she attached so much importance to the conventionalities of life, but because she was daily reminded of Mr. Steele's shortcomings in this respect by Mrs. Paul.

Indeed, Mrs. Paul's desire to see him was known to everybody except Mr. Steele himself; for the longer he neglected her, the more generally was her annoyance felt; what was really anger at him vented itself in sharp words upon any subject to any person. Unfortunately, it does not follow that the object of one's anger receives its expression; expression is all that is necessary to most people. There was a collateral justice, perhaps, in abusing Miss Sally; but it was hard that Sidney should be scolded, and the girl protested to Mr. Steele, during one of their rare moments of conversation, — for Robert was quite right in feeling that she avoided talking to him. "You must go to see Mrs. Paul, Mr. Steele," she said, with a directness which took away Miss Sally's breath — "she really holds this entire family responsible for your absence." And the next afternoon Robert went.

He had gone to the major's first, and finding Miss Sally out thought that she might be at Mrs. Paul's, and to go to fetch her home would be an excuse for a very short call. But Davids, as he announced him, said that Mrs. Paul was alone, and it was too late then for retreat. It came into his mind, as he saw her alert, keen face, that he had "gone up the winding stair," and here was the spider awaiting him. Her eyes lighted as he entered.

She had long ago decided what she should say to him when he came; yet she approached her subject so delicately, and by that most subtle flattery of friendly silences, that Robert began to be remorseful for having judged her too harshly. It must have been as Miss Sally said, that Mrs. Paul had not been well that dreadful night, and that she was kinder than she seemed. She was entertaining now; she said clever things, but forgot to be bitter. Robert almost enjoyed the twenty minutes before she touched on Miss Sally.

"Oh, you expected to find her here? But you will never be so ill-mannered as to say you did not come to see me?"

"Yes," Robert answered, with instant constraint in his voice, "I came to call upon you, but I hoped to find her here, so that I might walk home with her."

This evident desire to protest his devotion delighted Mrs. Paul; she was almost fond of him, because of what such a desire betrayed, and because of the chance it gave her to wound him. "To be sure, and how sorry she will be not to have waited! She is really, you know, the most lovesick person; and it is n't becoming to a middle-aged woman to be in love! Oh, come, now; if you take offense so quickly, how will you stand the jars of domestic life? And why should you take offense if I merely say that Sally is very much in love."

"Because you do not speak as Miss Lee's friend."

She made a gesture, which meant apologetic amusement. "No, no, you misunderstand me," she said, watching, as though to see how far it was safe to go, the frowning antagonism gather in his face. "I am Sally's friend, her best friend, when I say"— she hesitated, with a look of interest and concern — "that I am sorry with all my heart that she has become engaged to you."

Robert caught his breath. Was she in earnest? Did she really see how despicable he was?

"I am not worthy of her," he began to say, "but"—

"Of course not," she answered, the restraint of temper beginning to show in her voice; "no one is, you know. But what I meant was, — I've known Sally so long, you must let me say just this, — it has been a mistake — of hers, we'll say, not yours. She will not be happy, — I speak for her sake, — she may fancy she's in love now, but she can't be happy. Lord! an old maid can't change her nature." Mrs. Paul lost her patience and her policy together. The young man rose, with compressed lips. "And would n't it be better to release her?" she ended.

Robert was shaken by that tumult of dismay which comes when a man sees what he has thought good, looking at him with a devil's leer, or hears a solemn truth upon lips which turn it into a lie. He does not stop to say that the medium distorts it, and that truth is still true.

"That is for her to say. Whatever she wishes of

me, even my happiness, is hers. But I dare to believe that you are mistaken. I bid you good-afternoon, Mrs. Paul."

He hurried out of the house, tingling with rage and resolution. He would never see that woman again; he would never cross her threshold! And as for her vile suggestion, — a thousand times no! He would be true to Miss Sally, he would make himself love her. He thanked God that that wicked old woman had put his thought into words, the purpose which he had said to himself was honor. He thanked God that she had shown him his own heart, and torn the mask of duty from the face of the hideous selfishness which had insisted that he must tell Miss Sally that he did not love her. Yet how, as that conviction of duty had grown, silently, in his mind, he had weighed his motives to see whether he was honest, — how he had scanned each one in an agony of fear lest he might find a taint of self in it! Over and over again, since he recognized those unseen processes which revealed to him his duty, had he retraced the mental steps which led him to a terrible conclusion, looking for a way of escape, and finding none, — believing all the while that he was honest. He knew better now, he said. Mrs. Paul had confessed him to himself. He had been trying to find his own freedom, he had been hiding behind fine words, he had taken the holy name of honor upon his profane lips. "I have lied unto God!" he groaned.

He was almost blind with terror and pain. He did not know that people looked after him in the street, with a shrug or a half-laugh, and a light word that he was drunk. Mrs. Jennings, toiling across the bridge, shrank away from him as he passed her, and for a moment forgot her own troubles. His loathing of himself was so overpowering that he became indifferent to Mrs. Paul; he had not rage to spare for her. But could he have thought of her, he would have been incapable of imagining that the pleasure of having implanted in his mind the seed of what she must have felt was dishonor, had left her delightfully amiable, — so amiable that when Davids told her there was a person in the hall who wished to see her, she nodded to him in a gracious way, and said, —

"Very well, Davids."

"It is," Davids observed, his eyebrows well lifted and his voice full of condescension, " the bridge person, I believe."

"Very well," Mrs. Paul said again, pleasantly. "She wants some help, no doubt." She smiled archly as the man left her. "Lord! what fools, what fools they are! They can be led about like animals. Of course he was angry, but he'll do it."

She looked up, still smiling, to see Mrs. Jennings entering with heavy awkwardness. Davids, standing flat against the baize door to keep it open, was regarding the woman with an intolerable indifference, which so confused her that she forgot to make the decent bow she had planned, and was filled with the wordless fury of a vulgar woman. "As though I did n't know him 'fore he was in breeches!" she thought. But by the time she had seated herself and said "Good-evening," and made a remark about the weather, she was more composed. She panted a little and swallowed hard before she began to speak, — perhaps because, although she had thought of this scene for days, she really did not know what to say. She hardly knew why she had come. A blind impulse to do something for her little 'Liza had made her resolve that she would "see his mother and stop him breakin' of her girl's heart." Her daughter did not know of her intention. Eliza was too interested in her own grievances to take much thought of the pain her mother suffered for her sake. Mrs. Jennings' rage at Miss Townsend had found an echo in Eliza's soul; she was full of that stinging anger which is really shame, and which follows bursts of unnecessary confidence.

"Oh, *why* did I tell Miss Townsend?" she asked herself a dozen times a day, with a pang of humiliation which sent the tears into her eyes. As is the rule in such cases, the revenge Eliza took caused her as much suffering as she hoped it might cause her victim. She decided to give up her music lessons.

"MISS TOWNSEND," — she wrote, — "I ain't going to take any more lessons. You can send your bill.   MISS JENNINGS."

Mrs. Jennings approved of this note, though she would have been glad if Eliza had said right out that she considered her music teacher a meddlesome hussy. The only relief the poor mother had was to abuse Miss Townsend, which abuse blew up a great flame of wrath out of her almost imperceptible material, — so imperceptible, in fact, there was danger that it would burn out before she could put it into words, here in Mrs. Paul's presence. So Davids' supercilious looks were really most helpful, although for the moment they made her forget how she had intended to tell her story. There was a blown and breathless appearance about her, as she sat upon the edge of her chair, looking at Mrs. Paul. Her small crêpe bonnet was very far back upon her head, and her large and anxious face was mottled with rising color. Her hands, covered with those unpleasant gloves the fingers of which are gathered into a little bag, tied and untied the cord about the waist of an umbrella, which she held between her black bombazine knees.

"Well, my good woman?" Mrs. Paul interrogated, adjusting her glasses and crossing her feet with lazy comfort; her gown rustled, and then fell into soft gleaming folds.

"Ma'am," replied her visitor, swallowing once, "my name is Jennings, — Mrs. Asa H. Jennings."

"Yes?" said Mrs. Paul.

"An' I've come to see you," proceeded the other, her voice growing louder. "I've been meaning to come this long time" —

"Yes?" This enormously stout woman, whose face was quivering with emotion, and who had a chin like the folds of an accordion, was really very droll. Nor, for once, was Mrs. Paul more cruel than the rest of the world. Emotion which tries to express itself through a weight of flesh does not often reach the sympathies of the beholder.

"Yes, I've been meanin' to come, for I've something to say. I'm sorry to be the bearer of bad news. I ain't one that likes to tell unpleasant things; no, nor gossip; no, nor make trouble in families."

"Of course; I think I know exactly how much you would dislike to gossip, Mrs. — What did you say you were called?"

Mrs. Jennings supplied her name, and then, carefully unwinding the cord from around her umbrella, so that its generous folds flapped loosely about the wooden handle, she said, "So it ain't to make mischief I come, only to tell the truth. I'm a mother myself, an' I know how you'll feel havin' some one comin' an' findin' fault. But it's truth, gospel truth, an' my 'Liza, she's suffered enough, so she has! 'T ain't only right but what he'd ought to be made to be different. 'Stead of that, he's goin' to see another young lady; nothin' but a music teacher, too! An' I made out it was my duty to come an' tell his mother."

The lazy amusement had faded out of Mrs. Paul's face.

"You are referring, I suppose, to Mr. John Paul?" she said.

"Yes, ma'am, I am," answered Mrs. Jennings, her eyes roving about the room. "I'm not one to deny it. I am. That's the truth, an' I'm not ashamed to tell it. He's been — he's been — my 'Liza's heart's just broken. An' now he ain't satisfied with sendin' her to her grave, but he's makin' up to some one else. I'd just as lief tell her name, if you want me to?"

"I will not trouble you."

"A poor, miserable music teacher!" burst out Mrs. Jennings, "with two sisters and a brother dependent on her. She thinks he'll marry her; I believe in my soul she thinks he'll marry her. But I told my 'Liza I guessed not, — not if what everybody says about you was true, — I guessed not."

"Well," said Mrs. Paul, tapping her glasses lightly upon the arm of her chair, "and what is your object in coming here?"

Mrs. Jennings stared at her; there was a sudden collapse of all her windy anger. What had been her object? What good would it do, after all? There had been the moment's relief of talking out the pain of her poor old heart, but what now? She opened her lips, but she had nothing to say. There is something pathetic in the struggle of a small soul to grow great with passion. Mrs. Jennings burst into tears, and fumbled in her pocket for her handkerchief; not finding it, she wiped her eyes upon a fold of her umbrella. "My 'Liza" — she sobbed.

"Oh," Mrs. Paul said; "yes, I see." She leaned back in her chair, with delicately knitted brows. "Well?"

"Well?" Mrs. Jennings repeated blankly.

"I suppose you have threatened my son with this visit to me?"

"Ma'am?" said Mrs. Jennings.

"But you have made a mistake. I do not interfere with Mr. Paul. You must go to him for money. I shall not give you any, you may depend upon that."

Mrs. Jennings stared at her. "Why, I ain't a poor person; I ain't in any need," she said. "I don't know what"—

Then it burst upon her. She rose, her lips parted, her broad bosom laboring for breath.

"Shame on you!" she stammered, — "shame, you bad woman! What are you thinking of? Money for my 'Liza that's had her innocent heart broke? An' what kind of a heart have you that you can think such thoughts of your own son?" In her honest and womanly anger her foolish jealousy of Miss Townsend was forgotten. "You think bad thoughts easier than good ones," she cried shrilly, running her hand down the staff of her umbrella, so that it opened and closed with her quickened breathing. "I come here 'cause I was most wild 'bout my 'Liza, an' to warn you 'bout Miss Townsend. Thank the Lord, my 'Liza ain't in any danger of comin' into such a family! An' if it wasn't that I'm a Christian, an' always do as I'd be done by, I'd say I wish 't Miss Townsend would marry Mr. Paul, just to bring your dirty, wicked pride down; but she's too good for a son of yours, if she is poor. Shame on you!" She struck the floor with her mildewed old umbrella as sharply as Mrs. Paul could have done with her gold-headed stick.

"She is poor, is she?" Mrs. Paul inquired, watching the tears course down Mrs. Jennings' quivering cheeks.

"I haven't anything more to say," Mrs. Jennings responded, with a gasp, trying to tie her bonnet-strings into a tighter knot beneath her shaking chin.

"But I have;" returned Mrs. Paul. "Of course I know very well why you came here, and if you had conducted yourself properly no doubt something could have been arranged. But you have chosen to gossip about Mr. Paul. If you had given your attention to your daughter a little sooner, it would have been wiser. As for this Miss Townsend, whoever she is, Mr. Paul has no idea of marrying her, and you will never allude to such a thing again; do you hear me?"

"I will do just exactly what I please!" cried the other, thrusting out her lower lip and flinging her head back. When Mrs. Jennings chose, with her hands upon her broad hips, to make this unpleasant gesture, she was the embodiment of insolence.

Mrs. Paul was furious. She rang her bell wildly, and the savage jangle, echoing through the silent house, brought Davids running to the parlor door.

"Show her out!" said Mrs. Paul. "Show this person out, Davids!"

"Don't trouble yourself, Billy, don't trouble yourself, my dear!" screamed Mrs. Jennings purple and panting. "I would n't stay, I would n't stay, — no, not for all her money; no, nor I would n't let my 'Liza cross his threshold. An' I 'll warn Miss Townsend against him, but I hope he'll get her, poor as she is!"

Mrs. Paul made a motion of her hand which was unmistakable. Davids took Mrs. Jennings' wrist, and before she knew it, still railing and sobbing, she found herself running with the terrifying speed of a large person down the steep steps of the terrace and out through the iron gate. She was hardly able to check her pace by the time she came to the bridge, and, when she reached the toll-house, her knees were still shaking, from such unusual exercise.

Eliza had been watching for her mother, holding back the dimity curtain, so that a wavering line of cheerful light fell across the road; when she saw the familiar figure she hastened to open the door. "The tea-table's set, and the toast is ready, ma," she said, and then broke into a cry of amazement at her mother's face.

"I've been — I've been" — Mrs. Jennings panted, falling into the big rocking-chair, trembling very much, and pressing her hand upon her side — "I've been to his mother's — and that woman, that bad, wicked woman" —

"Whose mother's?" said Eliza faintly. "*His?*" She had run and fetched the toast from the kitchen, but in her agitation she put the plate down among the geraniums on the window-sill.

Mrs. Jennings nodded. She tried, with clumsy gloved fingers, to unfasten her bonnet-strings, and looked appealingly at Eliza for help, but her daughter was too excited to be dutiful.

"Tell me about it, ma, every word, quick!"

Mrs. Jennings, her voice still unsteady, told her story; at least part of it. She could tell Eliza that her mother had been insulted, but she could not soil her daughter's mind with Mrs. Paul's suspicion. When she stopped for breath Eliza burst into tears; in vain Mrs. Jennings tried to soothe her; she had nothing but sobbing reproaches for her mother.

"I don't know what in the world you went for, anyhow," she wailed, " an' I don't see that you said anything, either. Don't seem, somehow, as if there was any point in it, an' I'll never hold up my head again. Oh, mother, how could you do it, — how *could* you?"

"But, 'Liza," quavered Mrs. Jennings, "I did n't mean no harm; I only meant — I only meant" —

"You've disgraced me. She'll tell him, and what'll he think?"

Even as she spoke a vision of Job Todd came into little Eliza's mind: partly because, in this sudden light of common sense, her sentimental fancies showed their real value, and were almost blotted out; and partly because she reflected that if she "took Job, why, then *he*'d never know anything, even if his mother did tell him!"

Of course this was all too confused for words, but Mrs. Jennings was profoundly thankful that Eliza's sobs did not continue very long; and, indeed, she so far recovered that she was soon able to sit up and eat a piece of toast, while shedding a few excited tears into her tea-cup; Mrs. Jennings, all the while, hovered about her like a ponderous butterfly. She was full of small caresses, and tender words, and little clucking sounds of maternal love, but there was a mist of tears in her fierce little eyes. "I was never spoke to so in my life," she was thinking. "I would n't 'a' minded for myself, but to think bad of my 'Liza!"

XVII.

Mrs. Paul's face was white when Mrs. Jennings left her, and her hands shook. She could not bear excitement very well, she admitted, impatient at bodily weakness. She smiled a little, and frowned, and said, tremulously, to herself that it was outrageous that such an affair should have been brought to her ears. But by the time Davids, full of carefully concealed curiosity, returned from ejecting Mrs. Jennings to inquire if his mistress were ready for lights, he found her calm and almost agreeable.

"When Mr. John comes in, say to him that I wish to see him, Davids," she said pleasantly; and Davids, who knew perfectly well that Mrs. Jennings' visit "meant something," pursed up his shaven lips, and went out to the kitchen to say to Scarlett, "She's too polite to be safe,—poor Mr. John!"

But it happened that John Paul was late, and his mother had no opportunity for conversation with him before tea. He found her at the table, and glanced at her with some interest; for Davids had had a word with him before he entered the dining-room.

"If you please, sir," the man had ventured, standing with a napkin over his arm, gravely watching

John pull off his overcoat, "Mrs. Paul wished to speak with you, sir; but that was when she thought you would be in, in good season for tea, Mr. John."

The words were simple enough, but there was a significant look, which John had known from boyhood. However, the threatened storm was not of enough importance to think about, and he merely had a moment of surprise at finding his mother quite good-natured. Indeed, had he come a little earlier, this would have been more striking. She was beginning to remember something that the shocking old woman had said, which was neither amusing nor interesting, — something about a person called Townsend. This hint had begun to assume annoying proportions by the time John arrived. He had been going to see this young woman, had he? Who was she? The name was familiar, but a music teacher? Johnny was always a ploughboy! However, as he entered, she banished all that, and said her clever and unkind things in a really friendly way. Her son took the trouble to be glad of this eccentricity, for he had planned to tell her that night of his intentions for the future. The matter of his interest in a newspaper of the great city of his State had been concluded, and he was to leave Mercer by the middle of May, and, for the first time in his life, go to work. He was full of enthusiasm, and full of hope too, for the step which was to follow this, but of which, of course, no one could know until he had Katherine's promise,

John Paul knew quite well that the breaking his purpose to his mother would not be an agreeable business, so it was a comfort to find her less irritable than usual. He only hoped that her amiability would last until they reached the drawing-room; but it never occurred to him to hurry through his supper, that he might assure himself of her mood. Supper was far too serious a matter to John Paul to be disturbed by anything so unimportant as his mother's temper. Mrs. Paul bore his delay with a patience which confused Davids, who was standing behind her chair, and watching John with an expression of the deepest solicitude.

"There's something pretty bad up," he said to Scarlett, when he went out to the kitchen for another plate of toast,— in his sympathy for his master, his eyebrows quite lost their supercilious arch upon his narrow forehead,— "something pretty bad. Maria Jennings don't come here and talk about *him*, and get put out, for nothing; and *she* ain't so smooth for nothing, either. But, law! I'm glad he can eat. It's hard to stand a woman's tongue on an empty stomach."

"The toast is getting cold," Scarlett observed. As usual, she kept her opinion to herself.

"Like a woman!" Davids thought bitterly, with a man's inconsistency in regard to the mothers of the race. His curiosity was really anguish when, later, he was obliged to shut himself out of the room, leaving the mother and son together. He invented a dozen excuses to go back again, but his common sense stood firmly in the way,— and Scarlett would not hazard a single guess, or even look interested! Davids gnashed his teeth. "Women!"

he said. "The world would be a sight better if there was n't a woman in it!"

Scarlett turned her passive face towards him, and looked at him.

"See the trouble *she* makes for Mr. John," the man hastily explained.

But in spite of Davids' anxiety and sympathy, John Paul was not at all troubled, although towards the close of supper he had begun to feel that there was something unusual in the air. His mother's face had grown harder; she spoke with an increasing sharpness; there seemed to be a deliberate preparation for anger: yet, oddly enough, he could not rid himself of the idea that, beneath it all, she was more than ordinarily good-tempered.

They were no sooner in the drawing-room, where a little fire was burning on the hearth, and where the air was heavy with fragrance from the pots of hyacinths in the south window, than Mrs. Paul began with great bitterness to reproach her son for having been late to tea; John meanwhile silently calculating how soon he could escape into the fresh night, and take a turn in the garden with his cigar. The thought struck him that, according to Katherine's doctrine, he ought, in order to teach his mother a lesson in unselfishness, to refuse to play at draughts in a room which was made insufferable by a fire and by the heavy sweetness of flowers. But he shook his head, and laughed under his breath. Heat, and perfume, and interminable checkers were better than the possibilities in that voice. Yes, very likely he was a coward in such matters, but at least he had no shrinking from greater things. Now that the final moment had come, he did not feel the slightest disinclination to tell his mother of his plans, and he was really glad when Davids, having brought the footstool and arranged the fan-shaped screen, left him alone with his opportunity.

"Now!" said Mrs. Paul. "Davids dawdles so over his work, I really thought he meant to spend the evening with us. No, don't bring the checker-table, — your intolerable lack of punctuality has lost me my game, — for I have something to say to you, and you are too selfish to stay with me later than nine. One would think I had plenty to entertain me, instead of sitting here alone for hours. Though to-day, thanks to you, I have had a diversion, — a most unpleasant, a most shameful interruption. I am astounded, sir, at your conduct!" She struck her clenched hand on the arm of her chair, and John, sitting opposite, noted, lazily, how her rings sparkled. "Of course you know what I mean?"

Her son had been so heedless of her words that his face was quite blank.

"I don't pretend," she said, "that you are a pattern of virtue, though you are a fool; but at least you might keep such affairs from your mother's ears, and not subject me to what I have endured this afternoon."

"What in the world is the matter now?" thought John Paul. He yawned furtively in his beard, and wished that he might begin his own story. If it had not been for a curious feeling that his mother was in a good humor under all this fierceness, he would not have noticed her railing; he observed that she addressed him as "John," with a hint of respect in her voice which he could not understand; he watched her, faintly interested.

Mrs. Paul polished her glasses delicately with her handkerchief, and then put them on and looked at him.

"It is scandalous that I should know of it," (John sat up straight, in sudden attention), "and that you should have permitted that abominable old creature to come here about her daughter." (Her son leaped to his feet, with an unspoken word upon his lips.) "I do not purpose to interfere in such a matter; of course I deplore it, and all that, but it is n't my affair, and I only refer" —

John cried out, with a sharp gesture, "Not your affair? Oh, mother!"

She frowned at his interruption. "Let me proceed, if you please. You should know enough to silence her mother's tongue, and prevent her from coming here — to *me* — to ask for my interference, or aid, I don't know which. It is outrageous."

"What are you talking about?" said John Paul, very quietly.

"You know perfectly well; the girl's mother has been here. It appears that you have made her jealous. And I have to listen to that, too, — *I*, your mother!"

"My mother," John repeated. His face was white. John Paul had borne many things from this handsome woman; he had been railed at, and snubbed, and neglected ever since he was a child. He had never shown her the affection which she apparently despised; perhaps he had never stopped to see whether he felt any affection; but beneath his indifference had been always the instinct of the child for the parent. Once he had rested on her heart, she had carried him in her arms, he had slept in her bosom; she was his mother. And now it was his mother who said that the evil life which she believed he led was no affair of hers. John caught his breath in something like a sob. Then he said, "Who is this person whom you have seen?"

Mrs. Paul shrugged her shoulders. "I do not care to discuss it. I have merely mentioned it to insist that you shall keep such matters from me, and — and to say how your conduct distresses me — of course."

"I must insist upon the name of your informant."

His mother made an impatient gesture. "Be good enough to drop this affectation."

"I have no intention of defending myself to you," John answered. "I only desire to know who has said these things; then I will drop the subject."

"Really?" said Mrs. Paul. "But I certainly shall not tell you, my friend, for you know perfectly well. One thing, however, I will say: it is shameful that you should permit such a creature to gossip about you. You should know better than that, at least. This person who has made her jealous, apparently, this Miss Townsend" —

"Silence!" cried John Paul. "What do you mean? Who has dared to speak her name?"

His calm white face suddenly blazed with passion, and he stammered as he spoke. Mrs. Paul felt as though caught in an unexpected hurricane; she was breathless for a moment.

"You — you — use that tone to me? *I* dare! I accuse you. I say plainly that I am astounded at your stupidity — and your low ways."

"Have you finished?"

"No, sir, I have not! This Townsend girl that" —

"You will leave Miss Townsend's name out of this discussion," interrupted her son. He was standing before her, his arms folded, so that the grip of restraint in his hands was not seen.

"What? There is something in that, is there? You do go to see this person, do you, this — schoolteacher? And perhaps she does think you are going to marry her? The old woman knew what she was talking about, it appears."

"I don't know what you are talking about, and I don't know what you mean by your 'old woman,'" John answered slowly. "I have no idea to what absurd and lying scandal you have listened, nor do I care to inquire further into it, unless some damnable gossip has dared to use Miss Townsend's name without reverence; in which case, she will answer to me. I ask you once more, what is the name of this person?"

Her lip curled into a short laugh. "You may ask me as often as you wish. I shall not tell you; you know perfectly well. Unless, indeed, there are" — ("Oh, hush, hush!" John said. "Oh, mother!")

"As for this Miss Townsend, I want it distinctly understood that I shall not permit such a thing for a moment."

"Permit what?"

Anger and shame had transformed John's face; it seemed to have grown years older.

"You — to marry her. Your friend informed me that the girl had some such expectation; but you had better make her understand that I will not allow it, and that if you choose to disobey me you shall not have one cent of my money. Not one cent! Do you hear me?"

"I hear you perfectly; and now, if you please, you will hear me. I have too much respect for my father's wife to deny to my mother such an accusation as has been made, though I do ask you for the name of the person whom you permit to slander your son. But for this other matter, I have the honor of informing you that Miss Townsend is to be my wife."

"Go on," said Mrs. Paul.

"I had also intended, this evening, to tell you that I shall end my connection with the warehouse on the first of next month."

"Go on."

"I have nothing more to say."

"Then listen to me!" cried his mother. "If you marry a beggar, you can live like a beggar. Do you understand what that means? Answer me."

"Yes, it is what I have done all my life. It is what comes to an end when I cease to eat your bread."

Mrs. Paul choked with rage. "I will not have you marry her!"

John did not speak for a moment; then he said, under his breath, "How terrible, how terrible!"

"Ah, you are coming to your senses, are you? You are wise to reflect upon the husks that the swine do eat, rather than to try them. I warn you that the rôle of the prodigal son shall never be played in my house. If you disobey me once, it ends everything. Forgiveness is weakness. I never forgive."

"We shall be married very soon," John said, looking away from her, almost as if he had not heard her. "You may do what you please with your money; it is nothing to us. But oh, I wish you could see Katherine, — I wish you could see her! It must make a difference." His voice softened as he spoke. "I have been a coward; I see it now. I have helped to make this possible in you. Forgive me. And yet — and yet — I think I shall never forgive you."

Mrs. Paul, staring at him, dumb with anger, and struggling to see some meaning in his words, suddenly shrank back into her chair, and put her hands before her eyes. "You look — like your father!" she said, in a whisper.

John, turning on his heel, glanced back at her. "My poor father!"

He did not stop to call Scarlett or Davids, but went at once out into the heavy darkness of the moonless night. An intent purpose blotted out even the anger in his face, but his hands were clenched, and he breathed quickly between his teeth, in unconscious rage.

When he reached Katherine's door, he stood with

an impatient hand upon the knob, waiting the answer to his ring, and a moment later pushed past the mournful Maria without a word; for he saw Katherine in the parlor, standing by the bookcase, absorbed in the volume in her hand. He was so intent upon his own thoughts that he would scarcely have noticed it had the room been full of people. As it was, there was only Ted, curled up in the big armchair, reading Mother Goose, like a wise baby.

John went at once to Katherine's side, taking the book and her hands in his. "Katherine," he said, "we must be married at once, dear."

"Very well," she answered. She drew a quick breath and bit her lip, and then the tears came into her eyes.

"John," observed Ted, putting down Mother Goose, "why do you and Kitty look at each other so funny? Why don't you do something?"

Katherine laughed tremulously, but John's face was stern with the greatness of the moment. He lifted her hand to his lips. "I will try to be a good man, Katherine. God bless you!"

Ted did not see why he should have been taken in his sister's arms, nor why she should have kept her face hidden so long in his little thin neck; nor did it seem reasonable that he should have been sent to bed just "as John is here, and we could 'a' gone and played with the pups!" It was hard, to be sure, so Mr. Paul promised to come earlier the next time.

After that, there was a very long talk, — very long and very happy. It seemed to John, watching

Katherine with worshiping eyes, as though each moment showed him more clearly how great, and sane, and beautiful life was. He had not meant to do it, but he told her, briefly, that he had had a scene with his mother. "I shall never forgive her, Katherine, and — she is my mother!" he ended.

"Yes, dear, yes," she answered, — he had heard that tenderness in her voice before, but it was always for Ted or her sisters, — "you will. I think you do already, John, in your pity and your own regret."

But John Paul shook his head.

Katherine's eyes had blazed with sudden understanding at the mention of "some old woman and her daughter," but she offered no explanation. How much her silence was kindness towards poor little silly Eliza, and how much that absurd anger which she had felt when she learned the milliner's harmless secret, she did not try to understand.

"When can we be married?" John insisted, after many plans were made and many things explained. "In a week, Kate, surely?"

She laughed, with a rippling gladness on her face that was not a smile, but light in her eyes and tenderness about her lips. "Why, you have never asked me to marry you, John! We've never been engaged. I've just thought of it."

"Have n't we?" John said, frowning, joyously. "It seems as if we had been, always. But that does n't make any difference, you know; only it's queer it did not strike me when I told my mother that we were to be married. I think we take the best things for granted! Now, Katherine, when?"

XVIII.

The next morning, Sidney, pacing between her garden borders, heard her name called, and saw Mr. John Paul coming down the path. These spring mornings filled Sidney Lee with that strange joy which is quite apart from personal experience, and has nothing to do with reason; indeed, it blurs the sense of individuality, for it is but another expression of that life which leaps with the sap in a lily stalk, and guides the frolics of the young sheep in an upland pasture, or brings a prayer upon a man's lip and tears to his eyes.

Sidney forgot the sad world outside her garden walls as easily as she forgot that Miss Sally was busy in the kitchen, and that another pair of hands would make her aunt's work lighter. She was singing softly to herself; singing was like breathing, in this sunshine, and soft wind, and scent of growing things. She stopped when she saw John, and smiled, shielding her eyes from the fresh glitter of the sunshine with one hand, and giving him the other.

"Sidney, my dear," John said, keeping her hand in his big grasp, "look here; will you do me a favor?"

"I'll be glad to." His face was so serious that she added, "Is Mrs. Paul ill?" At which he scowled so blackly that Sidney felt she had said something wrong, and was puzzled, but waited for him to explain; like her father, she did not ask many questions.

"I want you to do me a favor," John began again. "I want you to go and see Katherine Townsend, and ask Miss Sally to go, too. She knows her; Miss Townsend is Robert Steele's cousin, you know. I believe you were n't at home either time she came to call on Miss Sally?"

"No, I have n't seen her," Sidney answered, wondering at the color which had come into Mr. Paul's face. "I'll go with pleasure;" and she waited to be told why.

But John suddenly became aware of the observing windows of his mother's house, and hurried his companion into the evergreen alley that ran across the garden from the green door in the wall on one side, to the fence that shut off the lane, on the other. The alley widened in the middle of the garden into a little circle, where a sun-dial stood; but the path was always in the shade, and the dial did not mark the quiet hours on its stained copper face. The branches were so thick that the alley was quite dark, and the black earth was damp, and faintly green with mould, and powdery with white streaks about the roots of the trees. (There was no danger that Mrs. Paul could see them here; but before they turned into the pleached walk she had a glimpse of her son calmly walking up and down by Sidney's side. That sight was like wind upon a fire; after an instant's breathless silence, she called out to Scarlett with furious fault-finding, and even made as though she would strike the woman with her stick.)

"I'll tell you what it is, Sidney," John was explaining in the evergreen alley. "Miss Townsend, she's — she's going to marry me. And my mother — well, she is n't willing, you see. And though, of course, it does n't make any difference, it is sort of unpleasant for Kate. So I want some of my friends to be nice to her. I knew Miss Sally would go to see her, she's so good; but I thought, perhaps, if you would go — you are nearer her own age — you know?"

Sidney, with parted lips, stood quite still, and looked at him.

John blushed. "I know I seem old to you, Sidney, and I'm sure I wish she'd taken me ten years ago, twenty years ago; only I did n't know her until last fall. Oh, Sidney, she is — really, I don't speak in any personal way — I mean I am unprejudiced, entirely unprejudiced — but, by Jove, Sidney, she's — she's — a very remarkable woman!"

Sidney drew a long breath. "I will go, of course; and aunt Sally will, too; but I — I don't understand!"

"You will love her," John declared, following his own thoughts, and blind to Sidney's confused look. "We are not going to be married until August. Katherine won't have it a day sooner, I'm afraid. Miss Sally is to be married then, too, is n't she?"

Sidney nodded, frowning a little.

"We shall not live in Mercer," John proceeded. "I am going into the office of 'The Independent Press.' The major takes it, does n't he?"

"But Mrs. Paul," Sidney said, scarcely hearing

his reference to the newspaper,— "what will she do?"

John's face darkened savagely. "Sidney, you don't understand these things, more's the pity. But listen to me. If a man and woman care for each other, nothing in heaven, or earth, or the waters under the earth has a right to part them. Do you understand? They belong to one another. See? Why, it would be wicked to let anything interfere. There is," declared John Paul, "no such thing as duty to any one else (even if a — a mother deserved it) that should keep two people apart who — care; at least who care as *we* do. The only thing in the world, Sidney, to be considered, is love, my dear, love!" John lowered his voice, and looked up at the drift of white clouds above the swaying points of the cypresses. Sidney caught her breath. It was wonderful, this illumination in his good-natured face. "And so," he continued cheerfully, "there's nothing to be said about anybody's wishes but just our own." Then he fell to talking in the frankest way of his plans, and economies, and many practical things.

There was gladness in his face, to be sure; but rent? and the size of a house? and whether it were better to be on the line of the steam or horse cars? Sidney felt as though dropped suddenly from a height.

"I will go," she said slowly; "only, if you please, I would like to tell Mrs. Paul."

John looked uneasy. "I don't think it is necessary."

But Sidney was determined. "I shall surely go," she insisted, smiling. "I want to." And with that he had to be contented.

She watched him closely as he spoke again of Katherine; he was certainly very happy. She looked up at the soft blue of the April sky, and at the snowy clouds stretching across the east like a flight of cherubs. She shivered a little and seemed about to speak, but could not. "Does he forget death?" she thought. After he left her, with this new joyousness in his eyes, which made his step lighter and his face younger, Sidney still walked up and down the shadowy alley.

Perhaps, for the moment, John Paul's indifference to his mother and her wishes was the most forcible comment he could have made upon the power of that new emotion which so transformed him. Sidney's very instincts were her father's; disobedience had never been a temptation, because it was an impossibility. Of course she knew that, outwardly, John's relation to his mother was quite different, but — she was his mother. That was the first wonder at what love could do, but the greater wonder came.

There was an old wooden bench near the sun-dial, curved like an irregular crescent; it had stood here so long that its paint had flaked and worn away, and its four thick posts were mossy green and stained with a rust of lichen. In summer the slats of the back were hidden by a tangle of vines, but now only leafless stems and brittle tendrils twisted in and out between them; crocuses grew close about the bench, and, opening their white and purple cups, filled the damp, warm air with that fresh earth-scent which belongs to spring. Sidney sat down here, resting her elbow on one knee, and her chin in her hand.

"Death: death:" she said to herself, — "he can forget it; he never thinks of anything but happiness. Perhaps that is because it is all new; perhaps as soon as he gets used to it he will begin to be afraid?" She watched, with absent eyes, a brown butterfly flicker along the shadows of the path into the open light of the circle; then, with a start, she remembered that she must tell Miss Sally. Did Alan know? she wondered. Sidney's mind was in a tumult. Never in her calm, self-centred life had she been so stirred. Miss Sally's little love affair? She frowned as she thought of it. Yet to stop to talk about rents and steam cars! What did it all mean?

She told her aunt in the briefest way that Mr. Paul was to marry Miss Townsend, but she did not wait to listen to the little spinster's delighted surprise. To have Miss Sally, with a ladle in her hand, fall into a chair, and gasp, and exclaim, and laugh with pleasure through twinkling tears, seemed to the girl profane; she wished she could get away from it all. A strange dislike and passionate interest clamored in her mind.

When she went to see Mrs. Paul, the scolding of the older woman was almost a relief. It was something tangible and easily understood. "I thought I ought to come," she announced in her calm way, "to say that this afternoon I am going to see Miss Townsend. Mr. Paul asked me to."

Mrs. Paul was so angry, so dismayed, so unwilling that Sidney should see her discomfiture at her son's defiance, that for a moment she did not know how to reply.

"I am very sorry to hear it," she said, — "very sorry and disappointed in you. This Miss Townsend has a foolish infatuation for John which I do not at all approve of, — not at all. I am very sure that she is not a proper person for you to know. I suppose, though, like every other young person in these impudent days, you set yourself up to know more than your elders, so I need not expect you to be guided by me when I say that you ought not to see her; but at least I can insist that you do not call upon this very offensive young woman without your father's permission. Your aunt knows you are going? As though Sally had the slightest sense in such matters! I have no doubt she would think it proper to visit her washerwoman!"

"But," said Sidney gently, "Miss Townsend is Mr. Steele's cousin, Mrs. Paul."

Mrs. Paul was astounded, but not for a moment dismayed nor softened. "What, the girl whose mother was a Drayton? I remember; some one told me. More shame to her, then, for her conduct in running after a rich man, — at least a man with a rich mother. I am perfectly disgusted with those Steeles and every one connected with them. I wouldn't have had you look at young Steele for worlds, though it's plain enough why he took Sally. You very properly repulsed him."

Sidney looked at her with faint curiosity.

"This Townsend girl is shockingly forward," continued Mrs. Paul, her voice shrill and her hands unsteady. "No well-brought-up young woman would try to marry a man against his mother's wishes. I should think you would know better than to want to see her. It's this talk of love and marriage that pleases you; you are like all the rest of them, in spite of Mortimer Lee's fine theories. But there shall be no wedding gayeties,—I can tell you that, miss!"

Another girl, with quick consciousness, would have disclaimed interest in such subjects; but Sidney only looked with puzzled surprise at the fierce old woman, whose eyes blurred once as though with terrified tears. Sidney was stinging with interest, and painful interest; it did not occur to her to deny it.

"It shall not be!" cried Mrs. Paul, forgetting that she was betraying her own fear. "Johnny won't throw his bread and butter away, I can tell you!"

But Sidney was too much absorbed in her own wonder to care for Mrs. Paul's dismay. She did not stay very long; she was impatient to see the girl who was going to take love into her life. Perhaps, without being aware of it, this experience of another woman was the greatest reality which Sidney had ever known; for her love for her father was so much a part of herself she was almost unconscious of it.

It was evident, from the confusion of her thoughts, as she walked out to Red Lane this April afternoon, that, whether she knew it or not, the slumber of her mind, which had followed an accepted opinion, had been rudely broken. Life was very bewildering to Sidney Lee. First, her calm and almost beautiful egotism (there is a certain beauty in anything which is perfect) had been touched faintly by Miss Sally's timid happiness. It was as though a hesitating knock had fallen upon the outer gates of a sleeping palace, only loud enough to make the contented dreamer within stir impatiently. But now had come a clamor upon the very door of her heart. She must hear Life! Its importunate gladness banished dreams, even though she barred the door and refused to look upon its glowing face.

She went over in her mind John Paul's words and looks. "It isn't just because he is happy in caring for her," she thought, "but because he has imagined a heaven where his happiness will be continued. And there is no heaven! Oh, that isn't what I should suppose he would imagine, for it doesn't seem to me that heaven would be enough to make up for the years that may come and stand between them. Time is like death, in a way; but if they were sure that their God knew what it all meant, — love and death in the same world, — *why* they lived and *why* they suffered, I should think they could bear to be without their heaven. But it is immortality, not God, apparently, that excuses love. Oh, *I* should imagine — Some One who knows!" Then she fell to thinking of a certain wise man who left a field untilled for many years, that he might observe how it was altered or affected by the earth-worms below the surface. "If the worms could only have known," she thought, intent upon this reality which had pressed upon her dreaming eyes, "if they could have guessed why their field suffered those conditions, and why they were living their poor, dark lives, it would have been worth while. Oh, if there were only any great reason above all the little reasons and ignorances, I could understand that people might be patient to suffer!"

Katherine Townsend saw Sidney coming, and, guessing who it was (for John, taking every opportunity to send a note to Red Lane, had announced that she would call), opened the door herself, and took the girl's hand in her cordial grasp.

"You are Sidney Lee?" she said, leading her into the parlor. "I am so glad to see you." She looked at her with keen, friendly eyes. "John told me you were coming."

Sidney was far more embarrassed than Katherine; but it was not shyness nor any unworldliness, in the sense of what was unaccustomed; only the wonder of the dreamer who has been unaware of any other landscape than the blurred world of sleep.

Katherine's charming tact was for once at a loss. The weather, and the fresh, sweet skies, and the bird singing in the rain under her window the day before; Miss Sally, and Robert Steele's good fortune in winning her, and how kind, and gentle, and unselfish Katherine thought the little spinster; Ted and the pups,— all in vain! Sidney answered quite sweetly and briefly, with a little dignity in her manner which held Katherine very far away. Yet there was an eager, wistful look in her eyes that seemed a shadow of trouble in their placid depths.

Katherine drew a sigh of relief when her guest rose to go, but, with a simplicity which was born of her great content, she held Sidney's hand a moment as she said good-by.

"I wish," she declared, "that everybody could be as happy as I am."

"Oh!" cried Sidney, with a half-sobbing breath.

Katherine looked at her, surprised and not understanding. Long ago John had told her of this young girl's destiny as Major Lee had planned it, but to the very practical and warm-hearted woman it was too absurd to remember.

"Are you happy?" Sidney asked, almost in a whisper.

There was something in the way in which Katherine said, looking frankly at her questioner, " Yes, indeed I am!" that gave Sidney Lee a pang. The tone was too glad. "How can she say it?" would have been her thought, had she known enough to put it into words; it was exactly the same feeling with which she heard when Mr. Paul talked of rent and steam cars.

The question brought back to Katherine the strange thing John had told her, and, with that common sense which hid amusement under the kindliest manner in the world, she added, smiling, "Don't you think I ought to be?"

"But" — Sidney said, and then waited a moment, — "*death?*"

That word touched the glad content upon Katherine's lips, and left her silent.

"Forgive me!" Sidney cried. "I had no right to say that, but oh, I do not understand!"

"Why,"—the other began;—it was towards dusk, and the room was full of shadows, but she could see the strained look in Sidney's face,—"Oh, Miss Lee!" She had no words.

"Are you not afraid—every moment? I have no right to ask you, but it all seems so strange, so terrible."

"No, I am not afraid," Katherine answered. "Death? Yes, of course, but life first; and life is so rich and so beautiful; and after that—heaven."

"If," Sidney protested hurriedly—"if there were not any heaven, then would the beauty and the richness be worth while?"

Katherine was flung into a seriousness which afterwards greatly surprised her. She put her hands up to her eyes for an instant; then she shook her head. Katherine Townsend was too well satisfied with the comfort of her religion ever to have invited any doubts of it by subjecting it to the scrutiny of her intelligence, and therefore she did not feel the dismay which might have shaken some persons with the memory of a forgotten terror. Although not aware of her mental processes, Katherine had curtailed her perceptions to fit her creed, knowing, without having taken the trouble to reason about it, that she could not stretch her creed to contain her perceptions. As a result, she was quite happy, and found the endeavor to live up to her religion far more comfortable than would have been the endeavor to understand it. But Sidney's words showed her a shuddering possibility. "No," she said, "oh, no, it would not be worth while, — not without another life." But her composure was shaken only for a moment. "My dear Miss Lee, I know what you think, — John told me; but you won't feel so when you care for some one. Indeed, indeed, you are all wrong. The good Lord meant us to love each other, and death does not end all, — it only begins it."

Sidney smiled sadly; it seemed to her very pathetic. "Of course you could not love unless you thought that."

"I *know* it!" Katherine declared.

"How?"

The two women looking into each other's faces had forgotten conventionality; the tears were upon Katherine's cheeks, and Sidney's eyes threatened her for an answer. It was a cry for the unknown God.

But Katherine could only tell her of the longing of the human soul for compensation for the pain of life. "Oh," she exclaimed, "because life would be too terrible if it were not true! It must be true!" She sobbed as she spoke; she was very tired, — nervous, she told herself afterwards, not remembering the fierce demand in Sidney's young face, — or this would have been impossible.

"I hope," Sidney said, in a low voice, "that you will not be unhappy."

"I shall be — heavenly happy!" cried Katherine, half terrified. Then she put her hand on the girl's shoulder and kissed her. "I hope you may be, too. And — and, Miss Lee, we have Christ and his promises, — the Resurrection and the Life. Oh, do think of that?"

As for Sidney, she went home with a certain equilibrium of mind asserting itself. This love which could be indifferent to grief, because it hugged a fallacy to its heart, was not beautiful nor great. It deliberately refused to think of the coming of sorrow, or it even forgot sorrow ; and forgetfulness may be another name for cowardice.

" If she had said ' yes, she knew that death would come, and that she had no imagined heaven, but that love was worth while, anyhow,' it might seem great. But that would need — what?" Sidney had no words except that vague *Some One who knows*. Ah, with that! But she shook her head, with a wild instinct of freedom. She exulted, even while she pitied Katherine and felt the terror of life.

"And to talk of promises," she thought, the old contempt coming back, — " promises! Oh, how strange it is that these Christians are not satisfied with their idea of God! Why do they belittle it by their creeds and promises and their non-human man? I should think a God would be enough. But they hang all these little thoughts about the one great thought until they almost hide it. I suppose one could cover a mountain with lace!" She smiled ; perhaps there is no conceit so arrogant as the conceit which follows a conviction of emancipation. Still, the mystery and wonder lingered in her eyes, and did not escape Major Lee. He watched her closely at their silent tea-table, that evening, and later, he asked her what her afternoon had been.

They were sitting by an open window in the

library, for the day had been very warm. The spring twilight, full of the scent of the sun-warmed earth, came in from the garden, and hid their faces from each other as Sidney told her story.

Major Lee's astonishment made him put down his cigar. "John Paul! Is it possible that he found words enough to ask a lady to marry him?"

His face lighted as she told him of Katherine, and of that strange talk, and of her own conclusions. "Yes, it is always so; the young woman has the prodigality of youth in promising what does not belong to her. She can talk about this life, perhaps, although her experience is not large; but her suggestions of another life are pathetic or amusing, as one looks at it. The way in which persons who want to excuse or to explain a position wrench a statement from their imaginations, and then label it a fact, is amazing. But John Paul? He seemed to me a young man of a fair amount of intelligence. Ah, my darling, 'we are the men, and wisdom will die with us'!" He laughed a little; the major felt more cheerful than for many a day. Sidney had seen it for herself.

XIX.

John Paul's engagement produced an astonishment in the small world upon the hill, second only to that felt when Miss Sally and Robert declared their passion; and in this case, as in the other, the most astounded and angry person was Mrs. Paul. John's laconic note announcing that he was to be married in August, and repeating his intention of leaving the warehouse, gave her a pang of more personal pain than she had felt for a very long time; perhaps, indeed, she had never felt that kind of pain before. The smothered and forgotten instinct of maternity was wounded, although not deeply enough to arouse anything but anger.

The major was annoyed that Sidney should have to see more of "this sort of thing," and somewhat disappointed in John Paul, but otherwise indifferent. Miss Sally was frankly delighted; she soon grew very fond of Katherine, and chattered about her incessantly to Robert; repeating the bright and pretty things his cousin had said, and laughing so heartily herself that she scarcely noticed the forced and tired smile on her lover's face. Robert had no heart for Katherine's gayety; he was absorbed in his own perplexities. When that storm of anger and determination in which he had left Mrs. Paul's house had subsided, he was distinctly aware of the ebb of the convictions gained then, and the slow flooding in of the terrible demand of honor; he must tell Miss Sally he did not love her, and be forever a dishonorable man in the eyes of his friends; or fail to tell her, and be dishonorable in his own eyes. How fierce was the alternative: to give her everything he was and hoped to be; to make every day, by tenderness and loyalty, secret reparation for secret robbery; in a word, deceive her so skillfully that she could never detect him, — or, humiliate and wound her!

With this was always the thought of what he owed her, — for surely it had been the will-of-the-wisp of love which had led him out of his slough of despond. He looked back and saw himself holding her hand, — that poor, silly little hand, which believed (had he not taught it so?) that it was a necessity to him, — saw himself struggling to emerge from the terror of weakness; gaining from her his life, his reason, his very honor. The fact that now, standing on firm ground, in clear sunshine, he could see how foolish was the amiable little soul that his imagination had clothed with every power and virtue could not alter the past conditions. Yet again and again returned the simpler and the truer thought. Was he to delude her, to offer her tinsel which she should accept as gold? Was he to let her take, through ignorance, what knowledge might teach her to reject? What answer could there be but No?

With a nature which demanded sympathy and support, Robert was singularly alone; no one knew of his struggle, not even Alan. Once he thought of going to Mr. Brown for advice, but instantly realized that what he wanted was not man to man counsel, but direction which might not be questioned, — the relief of shifting responsibility. It was in this connection that, with blank wonder at his own possibilities, he found himself thinking of the refuge of the confessional. His mother's church beckoned him, offering the allurement of infallible guidance, — the temptation to become as a little child. He said to himself bitterly that when his mother entered the Catholic Church she had left him behind her. He despised his own intelligence, which had deprived him of such peace.

Perhaps, if Alan had been less joyfully absorbed in himself, he might have helped Robert; as it was, the doctor began to be a little impatient with his evident depression. "Steele is perfectly well," he said to himself, "and there is n't any excuse for depression;" so he shrugged his shoulders and silenced his conscience. "It does n't do to notice that sort of thing," he excused himself, with the conviction of the practical man, as well as the instinct of the physician. It is a curious and not a pleasing experience to discover how much real selfishness, and willingness to escape personal annoyance, can be concealed beneath that "conviction of the practical man" that morbidness and supersensitiveness must not be noticed, and to learn how often, in dealing with weak and unhappy souls, a little less sense would have been the greater wisdom. Robert was so alive to the doctor's intentional neglect that he had no impulse to ask his friend's counsel; and yet, one morning, after wandering aimlessly about the streets, he found himself standing miserably at their own door.

"What would Crossan do?" he asked himself.

It was Alan's office hour; a time so free from interruption that the two friends had amused themselves by regarding it as the part of the day to be devoted to pleasant things; they did some translating together; or Alan practiced — quite faithfully for him — while Robert read. So the unhappy man felt sure of finding the doctor alone. He opened the door of their library, not even looking into the department dignified by the name of office. Alan knew the step, and did not turn as he called out, "Hello, Bob!" He was standing by the window with an intent look upon his face, stringing his violin. The room had all the comfortable confusion of a bachelor's lodgings, and much luxury as well. There was the smell of chemicals, to be sure, for Alan made some experiments here, so there was a stand with retorts upon it, and traces of blackened ashes, and bottles of salts, and crystals; but the odor of cigar smoke was stronger, and a great bowl of roses stood upon the table, among the books.

"I want to talk to you," Robert said, throwing himself wearily into a big chair.

"Go ahead," responded the doctor, frowning over the strings of his violin.

Robert lifted an illuminated copy of Italian sonnets from the table beside him, and began, absently, to turn the yellow leaves.

> "Per esser manco almen, signiora, indegnio
> Dell' immensa vostr' alta cortesia,
> Prima, all' incontro a quella, usar la mia
> Con tutto il cor volse 'l mie basso ingegnio.
> Ma visto poi c' ascendere a quel segnio
> Propio valor non è c' apra la via" —

He put the book down, as though the words had stung him.

"Well?" Alan interrogated, suddenly noticing the silence, and glancing over his shoulder at his friend.

"John Paul is fairly started, it appears," Robert said. "I saw his name on the editorial page this morning."

"Is that all you have to say?" inquired the doctor. "Ah, confound it! there goes another string!"

"I wonder if his mother has forgiven him yet?" Robert went on, vaguely.

"I believe not. Sidney told me he did not see her before he started."

The spring wind from the open window blew one trembling chord back into the room. Alan smiled joyously; Sidney's name seemed blended with the music. He drew his bow lightly across the strings, and a burst of sound, like sudden sunshine, flooded the room. Then they talked of many things, in the old pleasant, desultory way; Paul's engagement most of all, with the amused question whether it was the major's theories which had kept him so long unmarried.

"Ah, well," said Alan, with half a sigh, turning round to look at Robert, "the major is right, you know, but not human. Listen; I've set these verses of Henley's to a little air of my own. I want you to hear it." He stopped, and tuned his instrument, and then, lifting his head, began to sing in a musical tenor, which was without that thread of pain that is so often woven into the tenor voice : —

> "'Fill a glass with golden wine,
>   And while yet your lips are wet
> Set their perfume unto mine,
>   And forget
> Every kiss we take or give
> Leaves us less of life to live.
>
> 'Yet again! your whim and mine
>   In a happy while have met.
> All your sweets to me resign.
>   Nor regret
> That we press, with every breath,
> Sighed or singing, nearer death!'

There! is n't that morbid enough for anybody? What do you think of that minor, — 'and forget — forget'?" Robert said something vaguely, but Alan was too pleased with himself to notice his friend's lack of enthusiasm. "Of course," he proceeded, "if there were no love, there would be no sorrow; we all admit that. But what are you going to do about it? Cripple and deform life, to be spared pain? And we can't be spared, anyhow; we're bound to love, no matter how we fear it. There are really only two conditions in life: one is ignorance and the other is misery. Major Lee undertakes to create a third, — indifference. But it can't be done! The thing to do is to be ignorant as long as you can, — that's my belief. Yes, it is the only rational plan: live in the present; forget the future. It is intolerable to think of death and love together. The major's right."

"You are not so great a coward, Crossan," said the other, smiling in spite of his misery.

"My dear fellow," Alan exclaimed gayly, "I am exactly so great a coward. I don't believe I shall have a very long life, with this heart of mine, and shall I refuse to make the most of it?"

"Why do you say that?" Robert protested uneasily. "You are as strong as anybody; you know you are."

Alan shook his head. "Bob, the value of a medical education is, that you can number your days, and apply your heart to whatever seems most worth while. In a word, have a mighty good time, and don't bother with a lot of unnecessary things.

> 'Quid brevi fortes jaculamur ævo
> Multa?'

(I think that line is the extent of my Horace!")

"You — you are not in earnest?" Robert insisted, not noticing the careless words, and his voice breaking with fear.

"I am entirely in earnest, but please don't look so dismayed. I am making the most of to-day, and I mean to make the most of to-morrow, trust me! Why, bless you, I may live to be a hundred; only, I may not. But I assure you I intend to be alive as long as possible."

With his easy sympathy, Alan knew quite well the stunned and horrified dismay in Robert's mind, and so, with a touch that was a caress, he put his face against the violin, and hastened to talk of other things. He was sitting on the arm of a chair, swinging his foot with lazy comfort, intent upon enjoyment of the spring day, and the sunshine, and the soft wind which blew his hair about his forehead.

"There, hang it! don't look at me as though this were my last day. I've a lot of life in me yet, I can tell you, and I mean — I mean to enjoy it."

"But," Robert stammered, forgetting his own pain, "I can't believe it, Alan; it can't be. You must see a specialist, you must" —

"Stuff! Do you doubt my knowledge? And don't I tell you I may live to be a hundred? Drop it, Bob! Don't look so dejected; if there is anything I hate, it is dejection."

All the while, running through his words, was the low and tremulous breathing of the violin; his face, and his careless words, and the ripple of a song somehow blurred this terrible thing he had been saying. Robert drew a long breath of relief. He came back sharply to his own distress.

"Alan," he said suddenly, careful only to protect Miss Sally, and eager to display his shameful uncertainty and weakness, "if you've made a mistake which involves somebody else, what ought you to do?"

"Remedy it. Why?"

Robert got up, and began to walk about the room. The doctor had turned again to the window, and was tightening the strings of his instrument.

"And yet the person might be happier — mistaken?"

"Yes, a delusion is very comfortable once in a while," Alan admitted; "only, unfortunately, we can't delude people to make them comfortable. Look here; ask a straight question, will you? You always go ahead sidewise!"

"I can't," Robert answered hoarsely, "I've no right to; but I'll tell you the sort of thing I mean. Suppose that I had learned, after giving it to you in good faith, that that Corot was not an original. Suppose that you could never discover the cheat for yourself. Should I tell you?"

Alan laughed, glancing at the dark canvas framed in a great oblong of dull gold which made a glimmering brightness on the chimney-breast. "Well, I should be happier to be ignorant, no doubt; but that doesn't help you any. I trust this is only an illustration, Robert?"

"You think I should tell you?"

"Why, I don't see how you could do anything else," Alan said, with that interest in a question of ethics which is often a part of a lazy temperament. "I'm sorry for you if you've got to open anybody's eyes, but I'm sorrier for the other man. You've no choice, so far as I can see. If you give what you think is a jewel to your friend, and afterwards discover that it is paste, you've got to tell him,—all the more, that the friend, just because he is a friend, might never know it (only he would; those things always leak out in time); and as for your picture illustration, which is unpleasantly personal, art would be profaned if you called a spurious thing by its name, to say nothing of the lie of silence! Poor Bob!"

He drew his bow across the strings, and there was a rollicking laugh from the violin.

Robert groaned. "But there are things one cannot do, because they are impossible!"

"That does not follow, Steele," Alan said sympathetically, watching his friend's restless walk about the room. ("What in the world has come into his mind now?" he was asking himself. "I wonder if he means to divide his fortune among the stockholders who were pinched, and is afraid to break it to Miss Sally?")

"I know it! I know it!" cried Robert passionately. "Yes, if there is an impossible thing demanded by duty, by God, the impossibility is God's, the duty is ours. Yes, you are right,—you are right; it is to be done."

"But, my dear fellow," expostulated Alan, "glittering generalities are my forte; you must not make my words particular. The first thing I know, you'll say I have advised you to do — Heaven knows what! And look here; let up on your conscience a little; don't get seedy on conscience! I tell you, Bob, there is a point where concern about right and wrong becomes the subtilest kind of egotism. Yes, sir, you'd be a better man if you weren't so confoundedly good, — if you had a little more of the devil in you!"

Robert was not listening; he shook his head, with a gesture which meant that all was decided. "I *will*," he said to himself; and yet, oddly enough, as he reached the point where he saw himself capable of his duty, a flash of memory brought back the peace of the conquered dreams, the refuge of morphine. He thrust it out of his mind in an instant; but it had come.

Alan looked at him anxiously. "You make too much of this thing, whatever it is. If anybody is mistaken through a mistake of yours, it is n't an unpardonable offense; go and explain, and get the thing off your mind. Man alive! it is n't such a great matter. One would think you were a young woman upon the steps of the altar discovering that she did n't love the man."

A strange look came into Robert's face. Alan had a sudden and terrible thought; so terrible did it seem to him that even as it flashed into his mind he banished it, as an insult to his friend. His face burned at his own meanness.

Robert sat down, bending forward, with his hands clasped between his knees. "Alan, the space between a man's ideal and the man himself is his opportunity. But God help the man who hates his ideal!"

"I don't know what you're driving at?" said Alan cheerfully.

After a pause Robert spoke, and his voice was curiously dull: "I'm going; you have given me good advice, and I shall take it."

"Oh, now," Alan protested again, "I tell you, I object to giving suggestions in the dark!"

Robert smiled a little, but he had nothing more to say. There seemed to be no alternative now, and that brought a sort of peace.

"It would profane love to call a spurious thing by its name," he thought afterward, going over Alan's arguments, "and silence would be a lie." To hear his own convictions put into words by some one else gave him new confidence in his often broken resolution to tell Miss Sally.

The doctor was puzzled by Robert's abrupt departure, as well as by those confused questions. "I swear, there's as much danger of overcultivating one's conscience," he thought, — "as of neglecting it. I wish he was n't so ridiculously good; people don't appreciate it unless they know him well, and it keeps them from liking him, — though it makes them love him!" Then he smiled, and reflected that when Steele saw fit to speak out he would do so, and that it was absurd to feel any anxiety beforehand. Instead, he began to think of Sidney, and later, in the afternoon, he went to Mrs. Paul's, where his hope of finding her was fulfilled. She had come in to read the paper to the fierce old woman, who had grown more bitter and impatient in these last weeks than Sidney had ever seen her. With the new look in Mrs. Paul's face, since her estrangement from her son, had come a new feeling into the girl's heart — that delicate foresight of the imagination, which is called pity. But Sidney only knew it as a vague discomfort in Mrs. Paul's presence, which she resented; so she kept away from her as much as possible. She would not have been here today, had she not been sent for; although Miss Sally was too busy to come, conveniently, and had thought of asking Sidney to take her place. Miss Sally had developed in the last few months a mild self-assertion, which even Sidney noticed, not because of what it was in itself, but because of its contrast with the past. However, as Mrs. Paul's message had come, it was not necessary for Miss Sally to make her request, and Sidney went over to the other house in silent reluctance. She did not look at Mrs. Paul in her usual direct way; the pain and perplexity in the face of the older woman were too unpleasant. She made haste to open the daily paper, that she might begin to read at once, but stopped for a moment of surprise at seeing, instead of the broad head-line of "The Republican," on which she had been brought up, the smaller Roman letters of "The Independent Press." Mrs. Paul actually blushed.

"I'm told that it is a very decent paper. I am not a person who looks only on one side. I was never unjust in my life. And — my — my son is connected with 'The Independent Press.'"

"Yes," Sidney answered, "I heard Mr. Paul talking of it to father, last Sunday."

"Last Sunday? I did not see him on Sunday — I mean I would not see him. I disapprove of this newspaper folly, and he knows it. Though it won't last, — it won't last! But I am willing to overlook it; he may come in, if he wishes to, the next time he is in Mercer. You might tell him so. Only I'll have no talk of — of that Townsend girl! Just let him understand that!" Her hands trembled as she spoke.

"Mrs. Paul," said Sidney tranquilly, "if you knew Miss Townsend, I think you would like her."

"What!" cried Mrs. Paul. "You would dictate my likes and dislikes, would you? And I can tell you, I know quite enough of her. I know that she meditates marrying my son against my wishes. But how long is it that you have been an advocate of marriage, Sidney? This shows what stuff your theories are made of."

"I think," the girl answered, in a low voice, "that it is a pity they should love each other; but since they do, it would be happier for them if you were friendly."

"Well!" said Mrs. Paul. "But I don't know why I should expect you to be different from the rest of the world; of course you are inconsistent. Your father is the only consistent person I ever knew, and that is because he has no soul. There! don't look at me in that manner; I know more about your father than you do, I can tell you! And what does he think of your passion for this Townsend girl?"

"Why, he admires her himself, — he thinks her charming."

"Mortimer Lee has not the slightest idea what *charming* means," returned Mrs. Paul contemptuously. "Now, remember you are to tell John I wish — or at least that I am willing that he should come here at once. I am tired of this folly."

"Shall I not write a little note," Sidney pleaded, "and say that you want to see him?"

"Certainly not! I don't want to see him — unless he can behave himself. Tell him he may come; do you hear me? I am willing that he should come. Put it any way you choose, only don't bother me about it. Just say that he is to come."

It was at this moment that Alan made his appearance, and the subject of John's disobedience was dropped.

Mrs. Paul's past was too vivid a remembrance to her to allow her to feel any surprise that Alan

Crossan came so often to see her; but for once she forgot herself in the purpose which had been growing in her mind since that day when she suggested to Major Lee the possibility which gave him so much discomfort. She was waiting her time to make the same suggestion to Sidney. Indeed, so far as subtile words had gone, she had already done so, but had never yet brought the conscious color into the girl's face. Now, as she saw Alan, she cried out, with a significant look, "She is here, doctor!" Alan's radiant face answered her. That any one should recognize what his heart knew gave it a reality that elated him beyond words. "You are just too late to hear Sidney advocating marriage," she continued. "Did you know that she approves of love?"

Alan dared not look at the young woman at his side; yet he might have done so without giving her an instant's embarrassment.

"No, you misunderstood me, Mrs. Paul. We were speaking of some people who love each other, Alan, and I said it was a pity, — that was all."

Alan walked home with Sidney, tingling with the exhilaration of recognized love, but she was as unconscious of the passion in his eyes as a dreamer is of the sunshine.

XX.

AFTER that talk with Alan, Robert Steele had no doubt as to what he should do. That he still delayed to tell Miss Sally that he did not love her was not from any uncertainty as to his duty, but simply that the crushing misery of it made him incapable of action. He went as usual to see her; listened absently to her gentle and aimless chatter, responded in his kindly way, and — waited. "Just one day more," he told himself, again and again. More than once, while in her presence, he had tried to nerve himself to his duty, but her absolute trust in him made her unconscious of the direction of his thoughts, and overwhelmed Robert with the terror of what he had to do. In this way more than a fortnight passed, until the dawn of a wonderful May morning, whose beauty protested against the lie in his soul.

Alan had started out early, meaning to drop in at the major's and look at Sidney's carving, before he went to visit a patient; so Robert waited yet an hour longer, not caring to encounter the doctor when he went to proclaim his own shame.

Alan, meantime, was walking along in the sunshine towards the major's, absorbed in his own happy imaginings. Soon, he said to himself, surely, soon, something must awake in Sidney Lee's heart to which he might address himself; as yet there had been nothing but meaningless friendship, and to that he was silent.

He found her, that morning, in the garden. She was kneeling, with a trowel in her hand, beside a great bunch of day-lilies, looking at their broad leaves, and wondering what was the promise for August blossoming. When she saw Alan, she took him into her confidence in the frankest way in the world.

"I thought it would be nice if they would bloom when aunt Sally is married,— she is so fond of them."

"Won't she be married until August?" Alan inquired, looking down into her calm, upraised eyes.

"I think," she explained indifferently, pausing to lift the bending blossom of a crown imperial, and look down into its heart at the three misty tears which gather in the scarlet bell,—"I think that she wants to finish most of the preserving first."

"Oh, Sidney!" he said. Her complete selfishness, here among the flowers, shocked him even through the glamour of his love. "Isn't it a pity to interfere with their happiness just for preserves?" he demanded, laughing.

She rose and smiled; then her face sobered. "Miss Townsend and Mr. Paul are to be married then, too."

"I am so glad! But I thought it was to be sooner?"

Sidney looked at him curiously. "Do people

always say that they are glad? Aunt Sally said it when she heard of Mr. Paul and Miss Townsend, and so did Mr. Steele; and Mrs. Brown said it of aunt Sally."

"Well, yes, I think it is a matter of course to say one is glad," Alan answered, lifting his eyebrows a little. "I suppose it is civil to take happiness for granted." Sidney waited. "I mean," he explained, "people may not be happy at all, you know; they may quarrel awfully; but it's civil to suppose they won't."

"Quarrel!"

"Oh, they don't quarrel where they really love each other, Sidney," he declared; "never where there is real love." This was an assertion which Alan would have been the first to find amusing if another man had made it.

"But I thought you were speaking of people who loved each other," she said simply, — "married people?"

What young man in love could resist the temptation to instruct such ignorance? Not, certainly, Alan Crossan. And yet, despite the eloquence with which he explained, Sidney still looked a little puzzled. "Oh," he cried, at last, impatiently, "you are like a person from another world, — you don't understand what I am saying!"

It was one of those perfect spring days, without a breath of wind to ruffle the silence of the sky, or a cloud to blur the sparkling blue in which the world was wrapped. There was the subtle fragrance of sunshine and freshly dug earth; a row of cherry trees in Mrs. Paul's garden stood white against the blue, and now and then a breath of their aromatic sweetness wandered through the still air. The young man and young woman, the young day, the first flowers, the twitter of birds swinging in the vines upon the wall, or whirling in and out among the cherry blossoms, — surely words were hardly needed!

Sidney and Alan had walked along the shadowy path towards the sun-dial in the evergreen circle, and there he begged her to sit down on the crescent-shaped bench. They were silent for a moment, listening to the murmur of the busy town outside the garden walls, and then Alan said, "How strange it is, — this quiet spot in the middle of all that clamor! How shut off we are from it all!" Sidney had taken off her hat, and was leaning back, looking up between the points of the firs at the sky.

"It is like your life," he continued; "it is something apart, — something which does not belong to its time."

"It is very pleasant, — I mean the garden."

"But it is not very great!" cried the young man.

"My life or the garden?" she questioned, with happy indifference in her face.

"Of course — your life. It is neither happy nor unhappy, so it cannot be great."

Sidney shook her head. "I am perfectly happy," she declared. "As for greatness, I don't care for greatness; I only want happiness."

"You will fail of either," he said abruptly; and

then, having gone no further in his love-making than that point where a man falls readily into the vice of quotation, he began to say, his face radiant with the happiness of inexperience, —

> " ' Then welcome each rebuff
> That turns earth's smoothness rough,
> Each sting that bids nor sit nor stand, but go!
> Be our joys three parts pain!
> Strive, and hold cheap the strain.' "

Sidney looked at him with a sparkle of laughter in her eyes. "Now, Alan, what do you know about 'roughness'? For my part, I confess I'm content with peace." She smiled, with that serious sweetness which had always charmed him. The soft air, the sunshine, the flickering white of the cherry trees, Alan's presence, in a word, youth, gave her all she needed, while she was yet unaware that she had need of anything.

"Such content is only ignorance; you must have infinitely more to make life great, to make it worth having!"

"What?" she asked lightly.

Alan drew a quick breath. He had not meant to tell her — yet; he had not meant even to generalize; he still felt lingering doubts about his responsibility to the major; more than all, he had declared that Sidney should not know his deepest life until she had herself begun to live, — he would not startle her into repulsion. But now he did not stop to say, Is it wise? still less, Is it right?

"What?" she asked again, turning to look at him.

Alan's hand tightened upon his knee. "Love," he said.

Sidney Lee started; a slow, fine color burned across her cheek, and was gone. There was a breathless moment between them; for the first time she did not meet his eyes. But when she spoke her voice was as even as his had been shaken.

"Greatness at such a cost? I cannot see how any one can desire it, — greatness that grows out of unhappiness!"

"You are wrong," he said, in a low voice. "It is n't unhappiness, — love."

"It brings unhappiness," she replied calmly.

"It makes life glorious!" he cried. The hope which had been hidden in his face, which had baffled Sidney and tormented Major Lee during these last few months, challenged her from his eyes. Not knowing why, she rose, trembling, breathless.

"Yes — while it lasts; but it does n't last, you know." She wanted to go away; the tumult in her placid soul frightened her; there was a flying terror in her eyes.

"But you don't think of that; the joy"—

"Forgetfulness does not cheat death," she interrupted; "and the joy? I should think that would make the calamity at the end greater for its greatness."

"Sidney," — Alan began, and stopped. Some one was coming along the path towards the sun-dial. Sidney had grown very white, but now suddenly a flood of color mounted to her forehead; her eyes stung with tears. She was conscious only of anger at this extraordinary embarrassment. Why should she want to hide her face as Robert Steele came upon them? Why should her voice tremble when she answered his greeting? She was dumfounded at herself. What did it mean? She could hear, as though at a distance, Alan laughing at Robert's anxious voice, as he asked where Miss Sally was. Alan was entirely himself, and good-naturedly matter of fact. Sidney's confusion gave her a moment of positive faintness.

"Sidney is neglecting her carving," she heard him declare. "I have reproached her so that she vows she won't have me for an instructor. No, I'm sure I don't know where Miss Sally is, Bob; probably delving in a tenement house after somebody's soul."

"I'll — I'll wait, I think," Robert answered; and his voice seemed to grope like a blind man.

"Oh, will you?" said Alan blankly.

Robert sat down beside them in silence. For a moment no one spoke. Then the doctor proposed, gayly, that Sidney should let him see her work. "You must not be discouraged. I'll give you an easier design." He rose. "Come!" he entreated.

"Won't you wait for aunt Sally in the house?" Sidney said, looking at Mr. Steele.

"Yes," he responded miserably. He would have followed them without this invitation; he had the human instinct to seek companionship in suffering. He even went into the lumber-room with them, and glanced with unseeing eyes at Sidney's work, — a curious piece of deep carving, a bitter and evil face under a wreath of laurel leaves.

"Why don't you go and meet Miss Sally, Bob?" Alan suggested, for Sidney had recovered her voice enough to say that her aunt had gone in to Mrs. Paul's.

Robert was incapable of suspecting Alan of diplomacy, so he only repeated dully, "I will wait."

"You need her to cheer you up," Alan commented; "you look awfully down in the mouth."

Sidney, hearing his careless words, was bewildered by her own questions. What had it meant, that thrill in his voice, that wonderful light in his eyes, most of all that sudden storm in her own heart? Yet now Alan was jesting with Mr. Steele, and she, too, was apparently quite composed, although beneath the surface she was stinging with sharp annoyance at herself. She lifted one of her tools, and saw with dismay that her hand was unsteady; she was almost terrified, — her very body was playing her false. Unreasoning anger made her answer Alan, shortly, that she would rather not carve that morning. She put her hands behind her and held her head with a proud indifference; she said to herself that she hated Alan, and she wished he would go away. The doctor, however, had no such intention; he took up a tool, and began to praise and criticise with as much discrimination as though he were not raging at his friend, who stood silently at his elbow. Even in his annoyance he felt vaguely that this silence of Robert's was strange, and he looked at him once or twice keenly. "Poor Bob!" he said to himself. "Confound him!"

When Robert saw Miss Sally push open the door

in the garden wall, he went with a heavy step into the parlor to await her. But by that time a subtile distance had come between Alan and the young woman. Sidney's composure made it impossible to turn the conversation in the direction it had taken out in the sunshine. Those words belonged to the blue sky, and the white gleam of cherry blossoms, and the twitter of birds; here, in the gloom of the lumber-room, with the murmur of voices from the parlor, nothing was possible but the business in hand, and so Alan talked about the carving as long as he could endure the antagonism of Sidney's silence, and then he went away.

Robert Steele only had to wait in the parlor for Miss Sally a moment or two; when he heard her light, quick step in the hall, it seemed to him he could count his heartbeats. Miss Sally had gone to Mrs. Paul's that morning, although Sidney had promised to do so. "But you know I must be out in the garden," the girl pleaded. So Miss Sally read "The Independent Press," and talked, or tried to, until Mrs. Paul's patience gave way over some trifling exactness in her mild little visitor.

"Sally," she cried sharply, "you were an old maid when you were born; and I don't care how often you get married, you'll be an old maid when you die!"

Miss Sally was so earnest in her desire to be agreeable that she laughed tremulously, which annoyed Mrs. Paul so much that she ordered her to go home, and not be a goose. Miss Sally, still anxious to please, said, "Oh, yes, I think I must go," — this to keep Mrs. Paul from any consciousness of rudeness. "I'll get ready at once."

"Oh, pray, Sally, don't get ready; *be* ready, for once in your life!" returned the older woman. Then she watched her impatiently while Miss Sally, with small, trembling fingers, buttoned her cloak, and wrapped her long white nubia round and round her face.

"I've had neuralgia," she explained. Miss Sally was always experimenting with human nature; it seemed to her that Mrs. Paul must be sympathetic. On the contrary, a retort upon the indecency of talking of one's ailments sent the gentle soul home almost in tears. She stopped under the cherry trees to wipe her kind eyes, and then to bend down to smell the lilies of the valley, growing thick in the shadow of the wall; so that by the time she reached the parlor and her lover she was her own cheerful self again.

But Robert's haggard face brought an anxious look into her eyes. "I hope you are very well, Mr. Steele?" she said. Miss Sally had never gone beyond "Mr. Steele."

He lifted her hand to his lips, but made no reply. Her affection ("Love" Robert called it, to himself) seemed to him more than he could bear. Miss Sally did not dream of being hurt or surprised that he had not kissed her. If she had stopped to think of it at all, it would have been to wonder why he should ever kiss her: she could count upon her fingers the number of times that he had done so.

"I am so glad to see you," she said brightly, unwinding her nubia as she spoke. " I want to ask you what you think would be nice to give that sweet Katherine for a wedding present. I know it is pretty far off, — August; but it is so pleasant to plan things. And you know they won't have much money, unless dear Mrs. Paul will forgive John. Dear me, she could n't help it, if she would but consent to see Katherine. I tried to suggest it," said Miss Sally, turning pale at the memory of Mrs. Paul's fury; " but you know she has such a fine mind, she does n't like to be dictated to, though I 'm sure I did n't mean " —

Robert was absently holding her hand, but here he dropped it, and began to walk restlessly about the room. Miss Sally looked puzzled. Then she remembered that she had not removed her overshoes, and, with a little hurried apology, ran out into the hall to take them off. When she came back, she was startled by his face. " Why, is there anything the matter ? "

Robert whitened under her kindly look. "Yes, there is something the matter," he almost groaned. Then he gathered all his manliness together: he must not think of himself, he must not even suffer, — the justice of pain was almost relief, and he did not deserve that; he must only think how to spare her, how to tell her the truth as tenderly and as faithfully as his unworthy lips might utter it. He came and sat down beside her on the yellow satin sofa, but he did not take her hand. There was an empty moment, in which they heard the voices in the room beyond ; and then, through the open window, up out of the sunny street, came a wandering strain from Verdi, trailing off into silence as the itinerant musician moved further away.

"I have come here," Robert said slowly and distinctly, looking all the while at the portrait at the further end of the room, and noting, with that extraordinary faculty of the mind to observe trivial things in the extremest pain, how cruel was the curve of the beautiful lip, and vaguely aware that he was associating it with the white glitter of cherry blossoms and the careless sweetness of Sidney's voice, — "I have come here to tell you that I am an unworthy man; to tell you that my life is yours, that all that I have or hope is yours, but I am not worthy that you should look upon me. I have come here to tell you this." Miss Sally was bewildered; there were tears in Robert's eyes, and his lips were unsteady. "I am unworthy that you should marry me," he said.

"Nonsense!" cried Miss Sally cheerfully. "Of course you are worthy for anybody to marry. But you are not well, or you would not be so low-spirited. I saw that the moment I came in." She looked at him with affectionate concern. His words were merely a symptom, in Miss Sally's mind, — he had taken cold, he was overtired; and her solicitude suggested her manual, or, at the very least, Alan. She put her hand upon his arm, blushing a little at the boldness of a caress. "You must be more careful of yourself."

Robert stared at her blankly; his face was full of helpless despair. As for Miss Sally, she reflected, with comfortable common sense, that when a man was in such a nervous state the only thing to do was to take his mind away from himself; and so, in her pleasant voice, she chattered of half a dozen pleasant things, never waiting for his replies, and ending, with a woman's instinctive and happy interest in a wedding, with the assertion that she and Robert must give Katherine something practical.

"Dear me," declared Miss Sally, "I suppose it's sympathy, but I am perfectly delighted for them!"

Robert had been so flung back upon himself by her failure to understand him that, during all this talk, he could only struggle dumbly towards the point at which he had begun, and when at last he said, "I cannot lie to you; you must know how base I am, how dishonorable," it was evident that he had not heard one word she had been saying. "I want you to know what I am, and then, if you will trust me, if you will tell me that you will marry me, oh, I shall thank God — I" — What else he said he never knew; only that over and over again, after the truth was told, he implored her to let him devote his miserable life to her, to let him atone for his terrible mistake, to be his wife.

He did not look at her, but he felt that she was drawing herself away from him. The changes in the atmosphere of the soul are as unmistakable as they are intangible. The broken and humiliated man knew, before she spoke, that it was the sister of Mortimer Lee who answered him; little kindly Miss Sally had gone out of his life forever. She rose, and stood looking down at him for a moment; when she spoke, her voice was perfectly calm, though her face was pale. Robert felt, although he dared not look at her, that she even smiled slightly.

"Mr. Steele,"— he started, the tone was so like her brother's, —"pray do not be disturbed. Pray do not give it another thought."

"I honor you above any woman I have ever known; your goodness makes it easier to believe in God's goodness. But I could not deceive you; I could not let you think I had given you what it is not in my weak, miserable nature to give any one,— love such as you ought to receive. But take all I can give, Miss Lee; take my life, and loyalty, and gratitude; let things be as they have been."

"There has never been anything," she answered, with such placid dignity that Robert dared not entreat her, "and, don't you see, there never can be? There is nothing more to be said, please." She looked at him, and then all the gentleness came back into her face and her eyes filled. "I am so sorry for you," she said simply. Then, quietly, she left him.

Robert Steele did not move, even to follow her with his eyes; he sat there upon the yellow sofa, his head sunk upon his breast, his hands hanging listlessly between his knees. The shadows from the swinging branches of the ailantus tree in the courtyard fell across a square of sunshine on the carpet at his feet; little by little the bar of light traversed the dusky room, until it reached the portrait and touched the calm eyes of Sidney's mother.

He watched the silent, joyous dance of sun and shadows; he was incapable of thought, but a dull sense of what Sidney's contempt for him would be when she learned what he had done, took the place of remorse and self-reproach.

He saw Alan cross the courtyard, and heard the iron gate creak on its rusty hinges, as the doctor went out into the lane. A little later, Major Lee came up the steps; and then he heard Sidney tell her father, carelessly, that her aunt had a headache, and would not be down to dinner. No one caught sight of him in the darker end of the parlor, half hidden by the open door. It must have been long after noon when he left the house; he did not stay because he hoped to see Miss Sally again, but only because he had not the strength to go away.

It was nearly five o'clock when Alan Crossan entered his house. The day had been a good one to the doctor. The glory of the morning had touched every hour afterwards. He was still elate and joyous, but on the threshold of the library he stopped, appalled. In his absorption, these last few weeks, he had become perfectly accustomed to what he thought of as the meaningless distress in Robert's face, and scarcely any accentuation of that pain could have startled him. But there was no distress in it now; only dull silence. He went over and touched him on the shoulder, in an authoritative way.

"You have taken morphine," he said.

XXI.

Mrs. Paul had not seen her son for nearly six weeks, when, the first Sunday evening that he chanced to be in Mercer after having received Sidney's message, he entered her drawing-room. During that time she passed from rage to contempt, then to indifference, and now she had reached something like fright. Not that she feared losing John's affection, — it was not credible to Mrs. Paul that she could lose the affection of any one; but she had an awful glimpse of a desolate old age. Who would play at draughts with her in the long evenings? Who would listen patiently to her gibes and sneers? Scarlett might do the latter, perhaps, — that was what she was paid for, — but there was no feeling in her silent endurance. Sidney might be summoned for the former, except that of late Mrs. Paul had found Sidney less interesting. Not from any change in the girl, but because her project concerning Mr. Steele had fallen through, and mostly because her own interest of anger at her son pressed upon her and shut Sidney out. She was in a state of tremulous fierceness when at last the night came on which John Paul, with new and leisurely indifference, presented himself at her door.

"Well," she said, rapping the little table at her side sharply, "you are here, are you? I told Sidney that if you were sorry for your conduct you might come home." John raised his eyebrows. "Yes," Mrs. Paul declared, "I'm willing to overlook your behavior. Every man has in him the capacity of absolute idiocy at some time or other in his life, and that was your opportunity. Well, you improved it, Johnny,— you improved it. I'm willing to forgive and forget," she continued. "We'll say no more about it. Just wind up this 'Independent Press' folly as soon as you can. Do you want any money for it?"

But there was something in her son's look that troubled her. In spite of her bold words, her voice shook. In the brief answer that John made, Mrs. Paul heard her defeat announced; heard, but could not realize nor accept it. She grew so angry that her son bent his eyes upon the ground, and refused to look at her.

"You shall not marry that woman!" she cried; "or, if you do, not a cent of my money shall you have,— do you hear me? And she shall never enter my house,— do you understand me? I will not see her."

John had been standing silently all this time, frowning at the jug of lilacs in the fireplace; once he lifted from the mantelpiece a carved and fretted ball of ivory which held another within its circling mystery, and looked at it critically; then he put it down, and waited for his mother to continue; but he glanced at the clock in an absent, indifferent way.

"You are a cruel and unnatural son!" she said, her voice breaking into tears.

John looked at her with attention. " Yes, I think I am unnatural, but I can't help it now ; neither of us can help it now. I am what you have made me ; I suppose I am hard. I am sorry."

" Hard ? You are stone ! My only son ! "

John sighed. Human nature is as helpless to restore as to create love. But had he ever loved his mother ? He had certainly never analyzed his feeling for her. Affection for one's mother is a matter of course ; it is a conventionality, in a way. But now something had snapped, something had broken ; he no longer took his affection for granted.

" No," he thought sadly, looking away from her convulsed face, " I do not love you ; and I shall never forgive you." He knew quite well that, no matter what gloss of reconciliation might cover that awful scene when she had accused and condoned at once, he could never forget it.

Those promises of pardon which we bestow so readily are apt to be given without thought of this terrible and inescapable power of memory. The lover or the husband, the mother or the child, may love as deeply as before the quarrel or the crime, but the remembrance of one bad and cruel word, the color of a tone, the meaning in the glance of an eye, will too often linger in the soul ; such a recollection will start up between two kisses, force itself beneath the hand that blesses, be renewed in vows of renewed tenderness. No assertions of forgiveness or of love can blot it out ; it is as immortal as the soul.

Perhaps Mrs. Paul read the inexorable truth in her son's face ; her anger was drowned in a new emotion. She looked suddenly up at Annette's picture.

"Oh, why did you die?" she said, half aloud. "It is your fault. I would have been different" —

"I must go," John was saying constrainedly. "Should you need me at any time, I will come at once. Mother, I wish you would let Katherine come to see you?"

But she burst out into such bitter insult to the woman he loved, that, without another word, he left her.

She did not even ring for Scarlett when he had gone, and she was wonderfully quiet all that evening. Davids noticed that she left the tea-table without eating, and he hazarded the remark to Scarlett that he believed she cared more for Mr. John than she had ever let on. Scarlett's response of silence made him, as usual, quite angry, but left him with that sense of her wisdom which the mystery of reserve is sure to produce.

"Lord!" said Davids, "if I could hold my tongue like her, she 'd think me something great!"

Mrs. Paul was experiencing this same respect for silence. If John had argued, or attempted to explain, she could have had all the solace of her own rush of angry words. She felt, unanswered, like a flying brig, left suddenly to the waves without the driving force of the hurricane. Her own fury tossed and beat her, but without John's anger she could make no progress.

She did not sleep much that night; she thought persistently of Miss Townsend. She wished, with hot resentment, that she could see her,— at a distance,— so that she might know what sort of a person it was who had wrought this change in her son. Alone in the darkness of her bedroom, the slow and scanty tears burned in her eyes and dropped upon her pillow; the old grief for the dead Annette, the grief which had railed at Heaven, but hidden itself so completely that no one knew that it existed, was sobbed out again in despair and hatred of all the world. "Why did she die? Mortimer is right; it is not worth while to love any one. Oh, I wish she had never been born!" The thought came to her at last,— it was towards dawn, and the furniture was beginning to shape itself out of the shadows as the windows grew into oblongs of gray light,— the thought came to her that she might go to see this young woman; yes, and tell her what she thought of her, and what would be the result if she married John,— which, of course, would end the matter, for all the girl wanted was money. Rage which can be expressed in action is almost pleasure. Mrs. Paul fell asleep when she had thought this all out; but Scarlett was startled by her white face and haggard eyes, when she brought in the coffee the next morning.

"Tell Davids," Mrs. Paul said, as she sat before the oval mirror of her dressing-table, and watched the woman puff her hair with delicate and gentle little fingers,— "tell Davids to go to the major's, and say 'Mrs. Paul's love, and will Miss Lee step over for a few minutes after breakfast?'"

"Miss Sally?" asked Scarlett, whose sense of justice always made this little protest for Miss Sally's dignity.

"Of course not!" cried Mrs. Paul. "I said Miss Lee."

Sidney came, and was asked, in the most casual way in the world, where "that Townsend girl" lived, although the desire for such information was not explained.

Mrs. Paul had ordered the carriage for two o'clock, and she drove towards Red Lane with a face which tried to hide its eagerness beneath the greatest indifference. She had been full of excuses all that morning, explaining to herself that this apparent weakening was only strength. Johnny should see he could not defy her; she would put a stop to his absurdities once for all. No fear that the young woman would want to marry him when she knew the facts of the case.

Miss Katherine Townsend, however, was away from home, and Mrs. Paul's anger was for the moment restrained. "I will wait," she said, sweeping past Maria, who was very much overcome by the caller's rustling silks, as well as by her impatient and disdainful eyes. It was curious that the servant's vacant face and the plainness of the house should have aroused in Mrs. Paul, not anger at John, but the old indignation at what, long ago, she had called the "low tastes" of her husband. "He gets it from his father," she thought, her lip curling as she looked about at the severe but cheerful room.

The walls between the windows and doors were covered with bookshelves, so that there was no room for pictures; the piano was open, and sheets of music were scattered beside it; there was no carpet on the painted floor, "only," said Mrs. Paul to herself, "those detestable slippery rugs." On the table was a great India china bowl full of locust blossoms. The shutters were bowed, for the day was warm, and one ray of sunshine fell between them, striking white upon the flowers, but the rest of the room was shadowy; so dusky, indeed, that Mrs. Paul did not observe Ted standing in the doorway, his grave little head on one side and his hands behind him.

"Who," he observed at last, "are you?"

"Oh," thought Mrs. Paul, "this is the brother. Of course the child is pert and forward."

"Kitty says," said Ted gently, "'at it's polite to speak when you are spoken to."

"You are an impertinent boy!" Mrs. Paul assured him. She put her glasses on and inspected him.

"No," Ted corrected her, "I'm not an impertinent boy. I'm Kitty's big brother."

"I am Mrs. Paul," explained his auditor,— "now you can run away, please."

"Oh," cried Ted, with evident delight, "are you John's sister? We love John, Kitty and Carrie, Louisa and me."

Little Ted knew of no other relationship than that of brother and sister, so his remark had no flattery in it, but Mrs. Paul smiled involuntarily. "I am his mother," she said. ("A scheming, ill-bred person," she added, in her own mind, "teaching the children to talk about Johnny in such a way, to please him, of course.")

"Should you like to see the pups?" Ted asked, anxious to be agreeable. "John gave 'em to me."

"Oh, pray be quiet!" returned Mrs. Paul impatiently. "When is your sister coming home?"

"Do you mean Kitty?" The child leaned his elbow confidingly on Mrs. Paul's knee, and looked into her face. "You haven't got such pretty eyes as John."

There was no reply.

"Kitty thinks his eyes are beautiful," declared Ted calmly, "an' she's coming home 'most any time. Kitty does just as she pleases, you know."

Mrs. Paul's face expressed only silent endurance.

"Does John love you the same as I love Kitty?" Ted continued, after a pause, during which he inspected the lace upon Mrs. Paul's wrap. A moment later, he exclaimed gayly, "There she is! Kitty, there's somebody here!"

For once Katherine scarcely noticed him. She had guessed whose was the carriage at the door, and she had summoned all her happiness and her courage to her aid. She entered with a smile, in which there was the faintest gleam of amusement.

"You are Mrs. Paul," she said, with an outstretched hand, which, as Mrs. Paul did not notice it, began to wheel an easier chair forward. "How good of you to come to see me! But pray take a more comfortable seat."

Words fluttered upon Mrs. Paul's lips, and left her silent. This dignified young woman was so different from her expectations that it was necessary to take a moment to adjust her anger to her circumstances.

Katherine, meanwhile, had drawn her little brother to her side. The old sofa upon which she sat, with its uncomfortable mahogany arms and its faded damask covering, had an air of past grandeur about it which impressed Mrs. Paul, although she did not know it. All the furniture in the room had this same suggestiveness, as well as the rows of leather-covered books upon the shelves.

"She comes of People," Mrs. Paul thought angrily. "Her conduct is inexcusable!"

"I trust you have not waited very long?" Katherine was saying. "And, Ted, you have not been a bore, have you?"

"Indeed," said Mrs. Paul, "he has been quite — talkative." She was furious at herself for ending her sentence so mildly.

"Had I known that you were coming, I should have been at home," said Katherine.

But Mrs. Paul was not to be drawn into commonplace civilities. "Miss Townsend, will you be so kind as to send this child away? What I wish to say perhaps he had better not hear."

"Certainly," answered Katherine gravely. But when Ted, with his usual reluctance, had left them, she said, with quiet dignity, that had in it a curious condescension, "Mrs. Paul, I know very well that your son's engagement to me is a disappointment to you, and I appreciate with all my heart your coming here to see me."

"You are quite right," returned Mrs. Paul; "it is a disappointment. It is for that reason that I am here. Of course my son will do what he wishes with his future, but at the same time it is only proper that you should know what that future will be if — he displeases me." Katherine's slight, waiting smile, full of courteous and decent deference for her age, confounded Mrs. Paul. She was perhaps more puzzled than angry, and the sensation was so new that she was at a loss for words. Those which she had prepared for the upstart music teacher were not to be spoken to this young woman. "Yes," she ended, "his engagement is a very great disappointment. I regret that I am obliged to say this."

"I hope you will believe," Katherine Townsend answered, "that I have realized perfectly that it might be so. I do not mean because I am poor, — that is something which neither you nor I could consider, — but I have the care of my brother and sisters, and it is a very serious thing for a man to marry when he must assume such responsibilities."

"I am glad to see that you appreciate this," said Mrs. Paul. "I — "

"Yes," interposed Miss Townsend quietly, "of course I know it. And yet I have felt that this very assumption would give John the strength which your strength has really withheld from him. He has had no responsibility in life, I think, has he? I am sure you understand me. I do not mean to reproach your love for him, which has spared him, but surely responsibility will help him, too?"

"It is, however, scarcely necessary that he should marry, in order to find responsibility," Mrs. Paul answered; she leaned back in her chair, glancing at Katherine from under slightly lifted brows; Miss Townsend sustained the look with a calm, direct gaze.

"True;" she admitted.

"My son has, of course, told you that he has no means of support other than my — "

"Other," Katherine finished, "than your too great kindness." "Yes, of course, I know that; — and I know, too, that it must end now. To continue it would be quite wrong; indeed, I should be entirely unwilling that John should accept it when we are married. He must make his own way in the world, and I am sure I need not say to you how confident I am, that your son will make his own way." The little gesture with which she said this was subtly flattering; she felt the color come into her face as she spoke. ("It is true," she assured herself, "the son of so clever a woman must succeed.")

"Yes — I have no fears," she continued, aloud, — "but I am talking too much of my own concerns!" She stopped, smiling in half apology. "It is such a tiresome drive over from the hill; will you not excuse me for one moment, and let me bring you a cup of tea?" She rose, ignoring Mrs. Paul's quick negative. "Pray let me," she said, and left the room.

In the hall she drew a long breath and set her lips; then she went into the kitchen, and with an intent haste, which silenced Maria, she made the tea herself and arranged the small tray upon which she was to carry it to her guest. It was a bold stroke, she reflected, and the risk was great in leaving Mrs. Paul alone to collect her thoughts and her objections; but it had been the only thing that had suggested itself to Katherine. The excitement and restraint made her eyes bright, and there was a little color in her cheeks; and when, tranquilly and without haste, she came back to the parlor, she was almost handsome. Mrs. Paul could not help seeing that, nor the quiet way in which Katherine seemed to dismiss the subject of John and his engagement. She began, as she poured the tea, to talk lightly, with cutting words, of this person or of that. Had Mrs. Paul heard of that absurd affair in Ashurst? What a painful thing for the family such a scandal must be! And what did she think of that ridiculous love-story which, just now, every one was reading?

It was the mention of love which gave Katherine Townsend the chance to say things as bitter and as untrue as even her guest might have done.

"A book," Mrs. Paul was constrained to say, "which tries to denounce second marriage is silly, is immoral."

"Who is it that says a second marriage is the triumph of hope over experience?" queried Katherine gayly. "Truly, I don't like the idea myself, but it's better than Major Lee's theory." This with a slight shrug. Even as she spoke, she was excusing herself by saying she would confess to Sidney Lee what she had said, never for a moment realizing how incapable Sidney was of understanding the situation, or approving of that temporary insincerity which is a weapon of society, and rarely implies a moral quality.

At that suggestion of a sneer, Mrs. Paul saw her anger slipping away from her. She made an effort to recover herself. "At least, absurd as it is, Mortimer Lee's view would prevent many unhappy marriages; and I am sure you will agree with me that no marriages are so unhappy as those which are unequal in any way. It is of this, Miss Townsend, that I wish to speak to you."

Then Katherine, who had given away her warm and honest heart as loyally as any woman ever did, lifted her eyebrows a little and seemed to consider. "Yes," she said cynically, "of course; except that the reasons for an unequal marrirge are always so apparent. No one ought to be deceived. Regard has very little to do with it. It is invariably personal advantage which is considered; happiness is not expected." She held her breath after that; perhaps she had gone too far? Yet if it made Mrs. Paul feel that, in her own case, she acknowledged no inequality, much was gained, even at the expense of a slur upon love. ("This is bowing in the house of Rimmon," she thought, with shame and elation together.)

But Mrs. Paul smiled. At least this young woman was no fool, — there was to be no love-talk, no tears; and yet, as she again tried to turn to that subject which she was here to discuss, she found such a discussion as difficult, although not as disagreeable, as if she had been answered by tears and protestations. She could not make her threat about money to this young person who treated money with such high-handed indifference. Indeed, so skillfully did Katherine parry the slightest hint of the disapprobation Mrs. Paul wished to express that the older woman became aware that, although she was not allowed to say what was in her mind, Miss Townsend knew quite well all she desired to say.

There are few who are not more or less impressed by cleverness; but Mrs. Paul respected it, even when it was to her cost. As for Katherine, she was exhilarated by her opportunity; to anticipate Mrs. Paul's sneers was like a game. That she was not sincere she was aware, but she silenced her conscience by a promise to repent as soon as her wrongdoing was ended. It could not, however, end with its recognition; she was not yet victorious, although she saw victory ahead. So, for the present, she must not lose the chance of assuring Mrs. Paul, that, for her part, she believed that vanity was the beginning of most of the virtues, and expediency of the rest, — or any such flippant untruth as Mrs. Paul's conversation might suggest; and Mrs. Paul's conversation never lacked suggestion.

At last, the older woman's final reserve broke down. "My dear," she cried, "you are delightful. The Providence that takes care of children and fools has guided Johnny. As for your brother and sisters, no doubt we can find a proper boarding-school" — She ignored Miss Townsend's laughing negative. Mrs. Paul was never half-way in anything; she was as charmed as she had been enraged.

"But I am afraid," Katherine said, — "I am afraid that I must beg you to excuse me. I have a lesson to give in just twenty minutes, and I must go. I am so sorry!" She rose as she spoke, extending her hand in very courteous and calm dismissal. "It has been a pleasure to see you," she said, with no more enthusiasm than politeness demanded.

Mrs. Paul was beaming. She glanced at Katherine keenly for a moment, as she took her arm. "Where have you learned to walk?" she demanded. "One does not expect deportment from Little Mercer. But what am I thinking of? Your mother was a Drayton, of course! I remember now: young Steele told me so, and Sidney, but I had forgotten it. So foolish in Johnny not to remind me! How could I suppose that anybody he would care for could have antecedents?"

"But poor John," said Katherine lightly, — "he was more concerned with living than with dead relatives. Four Townsends are bad enough, without a dozen Draytons too."

"Oh," Mrs. Paul assured her, "I have no doubt that they are very well, — the children; I assure you I sha'n't mind them much." They had reached the carriage, and a thought struck her. "You are going out to give a lesson? (Nonsense, all nonsense; we'll stop that at once!) Then just get right in with me, and I'll take you wherever you want to go. It has begun to rain, you see."

"That will be delightful!" Katherine assented. She had not removed her bonnet when she entered the parlor, so without any delay she took the place by Mrs. Paul's side. The enjoyment of leaning back among the carriage cushions, and directing the coachman to drive to one of those cheap suburban villas, which irritate the eyes and look as though they had been made with a jig-saw, was something Katherine never forgot.

"You are to come to see me to-morrow morning,"

commanded Mrs. Paul, more pleasantly excited and interested than she had been for many a day. "I shall send for Johnny, and we will wind up this nonsense of the paper."

Katherine laughed and shook her head. "I am so sorry, but I am occupied to-morrow morning. I must not disappoint a pupil for my own pleasure, you know." Under all her calm, Katherine was flushed with victory. She had triumphed, yet it was at the cost of her self-respect. She realized this when she stood at the carriage door saying good-by.

"My dear, you are a clever woman, and I congratulate you. (No one can say I have not always appreciated cleverness.) You don't make any sentimental pretenses, — I like that. As for Johnny, I dare say you will make the best of him; he's stupid, — but that's all."

Katherine grew hot with shame; she could scarcely control her voice to thank Mrs. Paul for having carried her to her pupil's door. She had succeeded too well.

Mrs. Paul, when she drove away, was in that state of radiant satisfaction which demands a spectator. So it was something to come across Miss Sally trudging home in the rain, and to stop and insist that she should get into the carriage.

"Why in the world," she cried, "did n't you tell me about Katherine Townsend?" She would not drive home immediately, "for I want to talk to you," she said. And so Miss Sally, sitting opposite, shivering a little in her damp skirts, listened with genuine pleasure to Mrs. Paul's praises of

Katherine. "It is really a pleasure to talk to such a young woman; and a great relief, after what I have endured these last few years. Why did nobody tell me what she was like? Of course I could not know; the fact that Johnny was in love with her made me think she could not amount to much. Johnny has no sense about women. I was always afraid he might think he was in love with you. But, thank the Lord, he never reached that state! So it was natural that I should object to her, not having seen her, and neither you nor Sidney having the sense to tell me what kind of a woman she was."

"I should think," ventured Miss Sally, shivering a good deal, "that you would have known she must be a sweet, good girl, just because John cared for her."

"Sweet? good?" repeated Mrs. Paul contemptuously. "That's like you, Sally. And it's like you to say I must have known, *because* — Now that you are engaged yourself, you really are too silly."

Miss Sally swallowed once or twice, and then looked out of the window. "I am not engaged, Mrs. Paul."

Mrs. Paul's "What?" was explosive. "When did you break it off? What an idiot you were, Sally, to let him go! You will never get the chance again. Why did you do it?"

"I — I didn't break it off," said the other simply; "he told me he had made a mistake. So there wasn't anything to break off, you see."

XXII.

If Mrs. Paul had not been so absorbed in Katherine, she would have felt in Miss Sally's broken engagement the collapse of a person who has lost a grievance. As it was, she thought of it only to repeat the news, two or three days later, to Robert's astounded and dismayed friend, and to rail at Sally for a fool to have let young Steele slip through her fingers. When Alan Crossan really grasped the fact that Robert had thrown Miss Sally over, — it was thus Mrs. Paul expressed it, — he stood in shocked silence for a moment; it was too tremendous for comment. Then came the instant rebound: it was impossible; it simply could not be; by believing such a slander he again had wronged his friend. Why, it was only a week ago that Robert had come to look for Miss Sally in the garden — Then, like a blow, came the remembrance of the evident return to morphine in the afternoon of that day, and since then Robert had been away from home.

The doctor scarcely heard Mrs. Paul's triumphant talk of Katherine; he only waited for a pause to say good-by, and then he went at once, not knowing why, to the major's. There, at first, it seemed as though this terrible news was confirmed. Sidney met him, looking puzzled and half annoyed.

"Aunt Sally is ill, I think. She has a cold. I was going to send for you, Alan, though you won't mind if she keeps on taking her little pills too, will you?"

"Is — is anything else wrong, Sidney?" he said. "Does Mr. Steele know she is ill? Has he been here to-day?"

Sidney shook her head. "There is nothing wrong; what could be wrong? Aunt Sally is ill, and I can't tell what she wants done downstairs. She is sleepy all the time." She frowned; she was troubled, and she was impatient of all trouble.

It was no time to ask questions; Alan had to forget Robert. A physician's private anxieties are out of place by the bedside of a patient, and Miss Sally was really sick. That walk in the rain, and then the long, shivering ride with Mrs. Paul, had come upon a little body which the new emotions of the last few months, and especially of the last week, had greatly taxed. Miss Sally was exhausted. Her pathetic desire to appear stronger and wiser than she was had been a continual strain; that desire was at an end now, and she felt instead the old content, the old enjoyment of a narrow life. Yet such content was a mysterious pain to Miss Sally.

In the night of that day upon which Mr. Steele told her that he did not love her, she had cried as though her heart would break. She knew, vaguely, that her grief was not because she had lost her lover, yet she knew no more than that. She was incapable of finding a reason for her tears, or of understanding that there is a bitter pain, which recognizes its

There, in the dark, kneeling at the side of her high bed, she cried until, from weariness, she fell asleep; sinking down upon the floor, her head resting against the carved bedpost. In the morning she awoke, stiff and chilled, and in a dazed way groped about in her mind to find her sorrow. She caught a glimpse in the mirror of her small anxious face, stained with last night's tears, and pressed into wrinkles and creases where it had rested on the gathers of the valance. The tears were still very near the surface. She drew a little sobbing breath of pity for herself. But perhaps at that moment she dimly understood that it was relief which had come to her, not sorrow; and that the dear and commonplace little life was hers again. There would be no more effort, no new emotions. She cried as she smoothed her hair and bathed her tired eyes, because, without understanding it, she knew vaguely, that her tears would soon be dried. It was a little soul's appreciation of how impossible for it is greatness. But no one could have guessed this cause of grief, least of all Robert Steele, drowning his misery in the old familiar dreams of opium. He had shut himself up in a hotel in the city, and given all his thoughts to the contemplation of his own baseness; and when that grew too terrible to be borne, taking up that strange little instrument of heaven and hell, and by a prick in his arm forgetting. There was a fitness in such sinning, he said to himself, deliberately yielding to temptation. He had flung Miss Sally's saving love away, so he had best fall back into the misery from which she had rescued him. Perhaps no one, not even Alan, could have appreciated the sincerity of a man allowing himself to sin, as a punishment to himself.

But the doctor, on that day, a week later, when he found Miss Sally ill, had no knowledge of Robert or his condition, and he could not spare a thought for him in concern for her. Alan looked worried when he rejoined Sidney in the library.

She was reading, and it was evidently not easy for her to leave her book.

"Yes," he said, "Miss Sally is ill; but don't be alarmed." Sidney looked surprised; evidently, nothing was further from her thoughts than the annoyance of alarm. "So far as I can see, she has n't anything on her mind. (Mrs. Paul was wrong; I knew she was.) But I don't like that room for her: there is no sunshine, and too much draught. The room across the hall would be better. I think she ought to be moved at once."

"But," said Sidney, in consternation, and putting her book down, "that is — is" —

"Your room?" Alan finished. "Why, Sidney!" The selfishness which could admit of such a thought startled him for a moment.

Sidney did not speak. To put some one else before herself required an adjustment of ideas; but when that was done, the resulting consciousness was not altogether unpleasant.

"Miss Sally ought not to be alone," Alan began, — he must not pause to give a lesson in ethics, with his patient's pulse over a hundred, — "some one ought to be with her."

"Oh!" Sidney answered blankly, so plainly distressed at her duty, that Alan forgot his.

"Sidney, don't you care for Miss Sally?" he protested.

"Yes, of course I care," she said; but there was no offended affection in her face, nor did she say "love." In such matters the major had taught her to call things by their right names.

"Then," cried Alan, "why don't you want to be with her, and to give up your room to her?"

"Because," she explained, "it isn't pleasant, Alan."

The doctor looked at her. "But is this sort of thing pleasant, — this selfishly refusing to see what is painful?"

"It isn't unpleasant," she replied. But she was troubled; Alan seemed to disapprove of her, she thought.

"Oh, Sidney," he said, "it distresses me to have you unwomanly and selfish. I cannot bear to see you selfish." (This was the first time that they had been alone since that morning in the garden.)

She smiled. "But look; why do you want me to be different? Because it is unpleasant to see what you call selfishness?"

"And it is not right," added the doctor.

"What is 'right'?" she asked. "Oh, Alan, you and I act from the same motive, — *comfort;* only you are more subtle about it than I. You call 'comfort' 'right;' it's expedient to be good, you know." She laughed, and looked at him so frankly, with such entire absence of that beautiful consciousness which had filled him with hope, that Alan's heart sank.

"Sidney," he said passionately, "I told you that you needed love to make you really live. It is regeneration, as well as beauty! Do you remember what I told you? Oh, you could not be selfish if — you had love in your heart!"

He stood close beside her; it seemed as though a wave of light quivered across his face as his eyes sought hers. Miss Sally, right and wrong, the subtleties of altruism and selfishness, were forgotten; the woman he loved was looking into his face.

"Oh, begin to live, Sidney, — begin to live, *now!*"

It was an extraordinary moment, which seemed to Alan an eternity, as, with her hand crushed in his, he demanded life from the frightened silence of her face. The scene stamped itself upon his brain: the sunshine streaming in through the long, open windows; the murmurs of the busy street; the Virginia creeper swaying from the eaves of the west wing; the sudden sparkle of a crystal ball upon the writing-table; and through all a wandering breath of mignonette, and the ripple of a song from little Susan, singing in the kitchen.

Alan's voice sounded strangely in his ears. His individuality was swept into that Power of which each individual is but the fleeting expression. It was Life which called to Sidney; it was the Past, it was Humanity, it was all Nature, — nay, it was her own soul which entreated her from Alan's lips.

"Love is more than death; it is life itself. I love you."

She did not take her hand from his, nor turn her eyes away; she looked at him in absolute silence, dazed and uncomprehending. Alan had one moment of blankness, which was so intense that it seemed a physical shock; it was as though he had uttered that "Come forth!" into the ears of the dead.

"Do you love me?" His tone compelled an answer.

Sidney, looking at him as though she could not take her eyes away from his, slowly shook her head. The spell of the moment was lifted; the sense of power was gone. The young man was no longer the creator, summoning life, but the lover, pleading, fearing, scarcely daring to hope.

"Oh, you are not in earnest? Think! Don't you, — a little?"

"No."

Her voice was as the voice of one who dreams; but she knew, keenly and intensely, what she was doing and saying. It was this knowledge which brought the absorbed vacancy into her eyes. This, then, was love? — this look in Alan's face; this strange earnestness, which was, she thought vaguely, like anger; this breathless pain in his voice. How terrible was love! "Alan, Alan," she said, "please do not be so unhappy, please do not love me."

"Not love you? Why, I should not be alive if I did not love you, Sidney. It seems as if it were my very soul, this love. Don't you care for me at all?"

But already he despaired; it did not need that she should answer him, trembling, "Indeed, I do not; truly I do not," to assure him that his entreaties fell upon ears which could not understand them. He felt, watching the dismay growing in her calm face, as though he had been telling his love to a marble woman. For a moment he did not feel the despair of a rejected lover. It seemed to him, looking at her passionless pity, as though the girl were incapable of emotion; there was something unhuman about it, which gave him, at the heart of his love, a curious sense of repulsion.

"I am so sorry for you, Sidney," he heard himself say; and then he burst out once more: "Sidney, you don't know what I am trying to tell you, you don't know what love means! But you must learn; let me teach you?" He took her hand again, with a gentleness which may come when love is great enough to forget itself.

Sidney looked away, and sighed. "Alan, don't say anything more." Her voice was so ultimate that the young man was silenced for a moment; then he said simply, —

"Don't you think you could learn to love me, Sidney?"

"Truly I don't," she answered. There were tears in her eyes. Alan turned sharply away.

He went over to the window, and stood with his hands behind him, staring into the garden.

The crystal ball in its ebony circle still flashed in the sunshine; the murmur of the bees and the scent of flowers came in through the windows. Life and the day went on; little Susan was still singing in the kitchen, and, like a green and flowing arras, the woodbine wavered in the wind. All was the same, and yet, to this young man and woman, how infinitely and eternally different!

"Alan?" Sidney said at last.

"Yes?" he answered quietly, but he did not look at her.

"I — I think I must go to aunt Sally," — she began, her voice unsteady.

He turned quickly. "Wait one moment," he said. "I want to write a prescription for her."

He sat down, and began to make queer cabalistic marks upon his prescription paper. He did not lift his eyes to hers; the repression of the moment made his face stern. "Will you have this filled, please?" he said.

Sidney did not answer. A soul had revealed itself to her in this last half hour; all her twenty-five years had brought her no such wisdom as had come in these quick moments. What had been a word to her, flashed before her eyes, a living creature. Love had looked at her, had implored her. Sidney had that feeling of escape which comes to one who has seen another overwhelmed by a danger which he fears. Alan left her with a very brief farewell; but she sat there by the window with the prescription paper in her hand, until long after the time her aunt should have taken her medicine, — sat there, in fact, until Katherine Townsend, entering, with an anxious look upon her face, asked her how Miss Sally was.

Katherine had seen Alan, and when she heard that Miss Sally was ill she said she would go to her at once. "For I am afraid," she added good-naturedly, "that Miss Sidney Lee is too dreamy to be of much use in a sick-room?"

Alan was apparently too absorbed to express an opinion. "Doctors think of nothing but their patients," Katherine complained to herself. She would have been glad to talk of Sidney, who interested her extremely, but Alan did not encourage her to pursue the subject, and so she turned to an interest and anxiety of her own.

"Dr. Crossan, I want to ask you something. Mrs. Paul told me that — that cousin Robert had broken his engagement, and now you say Miss Sally is ill; and it almost seems — But I would not believe Mrs. Paul!"

Alan came back with a start; he had forgotten Robert and Miss Sally too. "Mrs. Paul told me the same thing, but it cannot be true. Miss Sally's illness has nothing to do with any nervous condition. She has a cold, and she is feverish; pneumonia is what I fear. Miss Townsend, I would not believe such a thing of Robert, if he told me so himself!"

Katherine's face brightened. "I thank you for saying that. I don't think I really believed it, only Mrs. Paul said — But never mind that. Then it is not broken off, you think?"

"I don't know," Alan answered. "It may be at an end; Miss Sally may have broken it, you know. I haven't seen Robert for a week. But Mrs. Paul insinuated — if you will pardon the word — that Steele had asked to be released, and of course that is impossible. I wonder why Mrs. Paul always puts the worst construction upon everything?"

Then, with a comment upon the weather, he left her. It is odd what attention one can pay to the commonplace, with one's soul in a tumult of pain. He thought of Robert again, only to declare to himself, briefly, that this thing Mrs. Paul had said was obviously false; and then he forgot him until later in the afternoon when he reached home.

Robert Steele was waiting for him in their library. He was resting his elbows on the table, and his face was hidden in his hands. "Alan," he said, "how is Miss Sally? I called there, and they told me she was ill."

His manner confessed him. The doctor was flung out of his trust and confidence. "She is ill," he said sternly. "She is very much prostrated, also. I suppose you know why that is?"

"Yes, I know," answered the wretched man before him.

Alan stared at him with dismay. "Steele, tell me what this means. Is your engagement broken?"

"Yes."

"But it is not true that you did it? That is what is said,—but of course it's a lie!"

"It is true," returned Robert, running his finger along the carving on the edge of the table, and not lifting his head.

"Good heavens, Steele, what are you saying? I don't believe it! You are an honorable man. It is some piece of insane folly that you have fastened upon yourself which has made her dismiss you.

But then, why are you so miserable? Did you" — he lowered his voice — " did you love her, after all?"

"No," answered the other, "I never loved her, and I told her so. I told her that it had been a mistake from the beginning."

Alan did not speak.

Robert raised his head. " Do you want me to go away?"

Alan looked at him speechlessly. Robert did not love Miss Sally? He realized that he had made a mistake? The doctor could easily believe all that, but — tell her! Was it not a sufficient injury to fail in love without adding the insult of telling her so? His face grew darkly red. "I am done with him," he thought.

" Do you want me to go away?" Robert repeated, in a dull, hopeless voice.

" I do," said the doctor.

Without a word, Robert Steele rose and left the room.

XXIII.

"Oh, pray, Sidney," said Mrs. Paul, "don't look so forlorn; I have no patience with people who look forlorn. Sally will do well enough. I don't know why in the world she should keep Katherine with her all the time. It's just like Sally to monopolize any one. You do very well, my dear, but you are not Katherine."

Mrs. Paul was in Scarlett's hands, sitting before her mirror, holding her head very straight, and looking sidewise at Sidney.

"Alan said aunt Sally was not so well this morning," Sidney answered, with persistent anxiety in her face.

"Well, never mind! Scarlett, have you no sense? That puff is crooked. She'll be all right in a day or two; don't be foolish, Sidney. Now, can't you persuade Katherine to come over? I don't want you, if she can come. Besides, there is nothing of any consequence the matter with Sally; so cheer up at once; do you hear me?" It was unpleasant to have Sidney low-spirited, and so she took the trouble to administer comfort: "I tell you she will be well in a day or two, child. So go and see if you can't induce Katherine to come in for a while."

Sidney's life was too full of real things, just now, for her to be hurt, or indeed aware that Mrs. Paul had very decidedly and completely dropped her. The fact was, the older woman found an absorbing interest in Katherine Townsend, who told her bitter truths with a charming air, and refused to do as she was bid with a high-handed indifference as perfect as her own. Katherine had captured all her affection and her pride. Sidney was stupid, Mrs. Paul declared; and instead of making herself miserable over the failure of her plan to marry the girl to Mr. Steele, or furthering the project of bringing dismay to Major Lee by encouraging Alan's suit, she gave herself up to the thoughts of John's marriage. Her one desire was to put an end to the folly of "The Independent Press," and make her son bring his wife home.

"He never can support you, my dear," she told Katherine; "and though I love you, I won't be dictated to by Johnny. He has got to come to his senses, if he wants me to continue his income."

Outwardly, Mrs. Paul had made a truce with her son, and, by many contemptuous allusions to himself and his plans, she tried to restore her old supremacy; but things were not the same. During his dutiful weekly visits he listened silently, as of old, to her sneers, but there was a new look in his face, which made her always conscious of that dreadful scene between them. Even her praise of Katherine did not move him to any friendliness, and he scarcely replied to the entreaty, disguised as a command, that he should live at home after his marriage. Indeed, Mrs. Paul could think of nothing but this home-coming, and took every opportunity to urge it upon Katherine as well as John. So it was really very annoying to have Sally Lee take it into her head to fall ill at such a time, and claim Kate so constantly.

"I am tired to death of hearing about Sally," she announced, as Katherine, on Sunday afternoon, was about to leave her, to go over to the other house. "I wish she would get well, or — or do without you!"

John looked at his mother with that interested and impersonal curiosity which struck upon her heart afresh each time she saw him, but Katherine was ready with a reply.

"How frank you are, dear Mrs. Paul! As for me, I am afraid I try to hide my selfishness; I am such a coward that I assume a virtue. But I shall have you for an example now."

"My dear," returned Mrs. Paul, with a wicked smile, "do not be discouraged: you are very much like me; we may even be mistaken for each other."

"Do you think," cried Katherine, with a laugh, "that the recording angel can make any such mistake? *You* should warn him, really."

"Lord, Kate!" said John, as they left the house, and Katherine's impertinence sobered into anxiety, and a little self-contempt as well, "how you do talk to her!"

"The worst of it is," she confessed, "that what she said is true. I am like her. Oh, dear! why am I not good, like Miss Sally, or true, like Sidney? John, Sidney is so strange. She spoke to me yesterday of love and death; I suppose anxiety about her aunt put it into her mind. She said there would be no sorrow in the world, if there were no love. Just think — no love! It is dreadful that she should be so morbid. Why can't she take life as we do, and let the future alone?"

"Yes," he answered, looking at her with simple and honest tenderness, "life is a first-rate thing, and the major — I'm fond of him, you know, Kate, but really he is an old fool? And for him to have taught Sidney all that trash — it's too bad!"

"Besides," Katherine went on, "there is heaven. I never think of death unless I think of heaven?"

John nodded. "Of course," he said, in his comfortable, matter-of-fact way; "but I never do think of death, anyhow, — unless I have a fit of indigestion, — though I'm sure I hope I'm prepared for it; but it is morbid to think about it."

Nevertheless, with that word they fell into silence, as though the inevitable shadow laid a solemn finger upon their happy lips.

Sidney was indeed anxious about Miss Sally, but there had been no thought of her aunt in the one or two troubled words of death and love which she ventured to say to Katherine. Her mind was dwelling constantly upon those words of Alan's. She felt a trembling exultation as of escape from a great calamity, but there was a consciousness in her face that declared that at last the calm of her life was broken.

Major Lee saw a change in her, and was quick, although Sidney told him nothing, to connect it with Alan. The little reserve in the doctor's manner gave the old man a sense of relief and assurance, but he wished that Sidney saw fit to confide in him; and yet he felt, regretfully, that it would scarcely be proper for her to do so. In his absorption in his daughter, he was the last person to be affected by Miss Sally's illness. To him it meant, for the most part, that Alan seemed to find it necessary to make a great many visits, and that his own meals had not the punctuality to which he was accustomed. With scrupulous exactness he asked Sidney every day about her aunt, but her knowledge was almost as vague as his. This was partly because it pained her to hear bad news, and so she did not often inquire of Katherine or of the doctor; but mostly because she kept out of Alan's way as much as she possibly could. Once he met her in the library, and told her briefly of Robert's broken engagement. "I thought," he ended, "that you ought to know about it. Miss Sally wishes, when she gets well, to explain to the major the real reason that the engagement is broken; she told me so the other day. I am only to tell him now that it is at an end. But you ought to know the truth, so that you need not see Mr. Steele when he comes to ask for her. Susan says he comes two or three times a day."

His face puzzled her. "Why do you speak so fiercely? Are you angry with Mr. Steele?"

"Angry?" cried Alan. "I despise him! I am done with him!"

"But why?"

"Why did he do it, do you mean? Because he — I can hardly speak of him! — he felt that he did not love her."

"Well?" she questioned gravely.

"He did a dishonorable thing, Sidney; to break his engagement was dishonorable."

"Was it?" with a doubtful look. "Why, Alan, I should call it dishonorable not to have told aunt Sally?"

"I despair of making you understand life," he said, love so impatient in his eyes — for hope had grown again, after that first dismay — that the young woman, in sudden terror, left him, without the question she wanted to ask of Miss Sally's condition.

Alan's pity and tenderness were giving Miss Sally a joy which she had never known before, and her small confidences came as naturally to her lips as though the young man were her brother. "Alan understands," she said to herself, with a sigh of comfort and relief. He never made her feel how foolish she was, she thought, although, of course, he was so much wiser than she. To her timid suggestion that for such symptoms as hers her manual prescribed coffea, the two hundredth potency, he listened with "as much respect as if she had been — Mrs. Paul!" He never even smiled, when she said, looking up at him with wistful entreaty that he would be patient with her, that the little pills in the vial labeled 1 were for certain disorders of the left side of the body, and those in the vial labeled 2 for indispositions of the right side. It was curious to see with what gentle pertinacity she clung to her belief in the manual, although admitting, with a contradiction which in its entire unconsciousness was distinctively feminine, that Alan knew far more than did the writer of her beloved volume. It was on the third or fourth day after she was taken ill that she had said to the young man in a hoarse voice, that she had something to tell him when they were alone. So the doctor was instant to send Katherine out of the room, upon some excuse, and then to take Miss Sally's little hot hand and wait for whatever she might have to say. She looked up at him appealingly, and with a face upon which a veil of years seemed suddenly to have fallen.

"Where is Mr. Steele?" she said.

Alan flushed. "I do not know, Miss Sally."

"I'm afraid he is not happy," she went on, apparently taking for granted the doctor's knowledge of the broken engagement; "but he was so good, Alan, so good and kind to me. And he did just what was right. It would have been cruel to have deceived me, when I trusted him." Alan was silent. "But what I wanted to say was, that I'm afraid Mortimer would n't understand, and — and I don't want him to know that it was Mr. Steele who — who did it. You know what I mean, Alan. I'll explain, when I get well; but will you just tell Mortimer now that I — that I did n't want to get married? He won't blame me. He 'll think I am — *wise.*" She smiled a little as she spoke, and closed her eyes, as though she were tired; but in a moment she looked up brightly. "Will you please give Mr. Steele my love, Alan?"

If Miss Sally had been able to think, she must have had enough worldly wisdom to see the apparent connection between her illness and her broken engagement, and to have explained her honest and mortifying relief. As it was, she concerned herself only with facts ; and the little plea made for her old lover, she fell asleep.

Alan, with a brevity which concealed the truth, told the major that Miss Sally desired him to know she had felt it best that her engagement with Mr. Steele should come to an end, and the major received it as briefly. " I have no doubt my sister acts wisely in this matter." He would not let Alan fancy that he could blame a woman of his own house, but he was annoyed at what he thought of as Miss Sally's changeableness. He made up his mind that he would speak of this to Sarah as soon as she was about again.

There are some persons whose place in the world is so small that it is not easy to fancy they may die, and Major Lee never thought of his sister in connection with anything so great as death. It was only Alan who saw how seriously ill she was.

One day, — Miss Sally had been sick for more than a week, and the household had fallen into that acceptance of discomfort which comes with an illness which promises to be long, — Sidney met the doctor on the staircase, just after he had left her aunt's room. He looked troubled, and for a moment did not seem to notice her ; then his face brightened, in spite of his anxiety.

" I want to see you a moment, Sidney. Come into the library, won't you ? "

" I am just going to aunt Sally," she answered quickly. She was on the first landing, where the great square window with a fan-light over its many little leaded panes, opened outwards and let a flood of June scents and sunshine pour down into the dusky silence of the hall. She did not look up at him, as he stood on the step above her, his hand resting on the stair rail, and his serious eyes searching her face.

"Then sit down here." He pointed to the broad cushioned seat that ran across the window. "I want to ask you about Miss Sally."

Sidney sat down, reluctantly; but she looked away from him at a trailing spray of woodbine which crept along the window-sill. One hand, with upturned palm, lay idly in her lap, and the other plucked at the leaves of the vine.

"I am really alarmed about Miss Sally," said Alan. "I want to ask the major to let me bring in some other doctor, so that we may consult. I don't know whom he would prefer, and I must not wait until evening to see him. I thought you might tell me whom he would like to have me call in?"

Sidney had had no experience with sickness, and she did not have the heart-sinking with which one hears that a consultation must be called. On the contrary, she was so much relieved that Alan chose this, instead of that other subject, that she looked directly at him. "I am sure she is better, Alan: she does not talk so much; you said she talked because she was feverish."

"She is a good deal worse," he answered decidedly; "to tell you the truth, I am very anxious about her."

Sidney's face whitened. "Is she going to die?" she said, almost in a whisper.

"I hope not, — I hope not!" cried the young man. "But we must do all we can; and so I want to call in some one else."

Sidney nodded; she could not speak. Alan looked up and down the stairs, and over his shoulder into the garden. Then, leaning forward, he took her hand in a quick grasp.

"Sidney, have you thought, — have you thought again?" The speechless reproach in her eyes could not silence him. "I had not meant to say anything just now; but — oh, Sidney?" He felt the protest of her silence. "I can't help it. I — I love you, and I can't help telling you about it; perhaps it will teach you to care — a little?"

"Alan," said the girl, her voice trembling, "won't you please let go of my hand?"

He released it, but he lifted it to his lips and kissed her soft white wrist with sudden passion and instant compunction. "Oh, Sidney, I ought not to have done that. I won't do it again" —

A kiss is a wonderful thing. Sidney turned white and red; her eyes filled, and her breath came in a sob in her round throat. For a moment neither of them had any words. The sun, pouring in through the great window, fell in a pool of gold at the foot of the bare, dark staircase, where a jug of roses stood on a spindle-legged table; the tarnished gilt of the picture-frames along the wall showed in straight glimmering lines; all was so still down in the dusky hall, one could see the motes floating in the long bar of sunshine.

"Sidney?" he entreated softly.

She glanced at him hurriedly, and then out at the fragrant tangle of the garden.

"I've been thinking ever since," she said, with simple directness, "and it has seemed to me that you didn't know what you were saying, and I felt as though I wanted to tell you how foolish you were, Alan." She was so earnest that he smiled. "I felt as though you did not understand, you had not thought, how dreadful it is to care for any one. And I — I thought I would explain to you. Oh, listen to me, — don't interrupt me! Oh, Alan, love is so terrible!"

"No, you mean that grief is terrible," he protested. "Love is only good and beautiful."

"There would be no grief if there were no love. Love means grief; it means fear. Oh, truly, I do not see how sane people can deliberately invite suffering by loving each other."

"But, Sidney," he interposed, "we don't keep thinking of death all the time; it isn't natural — it isn't" —

"Oh, but, Alan," she cried, her voice breaking, "death is coming, whether we think of it or not. Why, it seems to me, if some being from another world could look down at us, and see us actually *planning* our grief and misery, arranging for it by loving each other, it would be horrible; but it would be — it would be almost something to laugh at! And yet — that is just what you would do."

The young man looked at her in despair; he knew not how to oppose to this unhuman reasonableness and calm reality (a reality life studiously ignores), that passion of unreason called love.

"To teach any one to love," Sidney went on, "seems to me selfish; indeed, it does. How could I, *if* I cared for you, — how could I let you love me, when I know that it would mean, some time, sorrow or fear for you? We are such friends, you and I, I can't bear to think that you might suffer, I can't bear to make you unhappy." She had risen, and stood looking down at him, her face quivering with tears. "Oh, how can people bear life? Father is the only person in the world I love, and when I think, when I remember, that perhaps he will — he will — Oh, I cannot say it! When I know that I fear *that*, then I say to myself, I will suffer only *once;* sorrow shall never come to me again. Alan, Alan, I do not love you, and I never will love you; and I would not, for anything this world could offer me!"

Even as he listened, he knew in his soul that this terrified, entreating woman loved him; he knew it with a sudden pain about his heart that made his face gray. He could not speak, except to say, brokenly, "It is nothing; do not be alarmed."

Sidney, in the terror of ignorance, knew not what to say or do. "What is it? Oh — Alan! what is the matter?"

He caught his breath, and tried to speak, to reassure her, but could only motion with his hand, as though to say again, "It is nothing;" and then, almost before Sidney realized that it had come, the attack was ended, although his breath was still labored and his face haggard.

In that instant, Alan Crossan came face to face with great realities. The physician claimed the consciousness of the lover. He thought, in a sudden flash of intelligence, that he knew what this increasing pain and hurrying breath foretold. It meant that he had asked Sidney to give him what might be only a few months of happiness, and at the cost of lasting grief to her. He could not collect his thoughts enough to reply to her, with this horrible spasm still lingering at his heart, yet he knew that he exulted and resigned at once.

A moment later, he answered her, his beautiful dark eyes radiant with gladness: "My own Sidney, you are not right, not right; love is worth the cost. One does not think of the end with the hope of many years together. But if there may not be many years, then it is not for you to withhold it; it is for me to resign it. So don't grieve; I will not let you love me, Sidney."

XXIV.

Until that day when he promised Sidney that she should not love him, Alan had felt incapable of delivering Miss Sally's message to Robert. He had seen his old friend once or twice in the street, or coming out of the major's gate, and had given him some stern, brief greeting, but nothing more; no encouragement, no reproof, no reproach. He knew where Robert was staying, and was careful to avoid that part of the town. Such avoidance was really, although the doctor did not know it, the protest of a possibility, the fear that he might forgive him. But after those moments with Sidney upon the landing of the stairs, after his glimpse of death and life and love together, Alan entered into that exalted silence which accompanies the glory of renunciation, and in which a man girds himself with joy for any duty.

So, towards evening, still very much weakened by that terrible pain about his heart, he went to find Mr. Steele, that he might tell him what Miss Sally had said. When he reached Robert's door, a new, or rather a very old, tenderness began to assert itself in his heart. "Poor Bob!" he said to himself once; adding fiercely, "He deserves all he gets!"

Robert was sitting listlessly at his desk. He looked up, as the doctor entered, with a terrified question in his eyes. "No," said Alan curtly, "but she's worse. I am here — she sent me here to say that you did right, that you were 'always kind and good,'"— Robert dropped his head into his hands, and Alan, with satisfaction, observed that at every word the iron entered deeper into his soul, — "'kind and good,' she said; and she sent her love to you."

"She is going to die?" the other asked, at last.

"Probably." And then silence.

After a while Robert looked up. "I thank you for coming." His face was so changed and strained, so haggard, and, worse than all, so stamped by the relief which he had sought, that something blurred Alan's eyes for one quick instant.

"My God, Steele! *why* did you do it?" he demanded.

"I had no right to deceive her," Robert answered. "She was going to marry me because she thought I loved her. I did not love her. I had to tell her so." There was no question in his voice; only dull despair that the inevitable should have fallen upon him.

"I cannot grasp it!" Alan cried; and then, remembering, "So this is what you asked my advice about, and I spoke of the picture or the jewel?"

The other assented, absently. He had no thought of sharing his responsibility.

Alan struggled with instinct and affection. Robert had been dishonorable, but — he was Robert! "Bob, I know you meant what was right; I — I understand, old fellow, but I can't forget it, ever, nor forgive it. You must have a friend who is greater than I. You must let me go, Bob."

Robert Steele's lack-lustre eyes stared blankly at the emotion in the doctor's face. "Very well," he said.

It was a comment upon the power of that moment which had so shaken Alan's soul, that he felt no repulsion as he saw this betrayal of the return to weakness and vice. He grasped the listless hand of the miserable man before him, and held it hard in his. "I will trust your motives so long as I live, but I detest the expression of them."

He turned as though to leave him; he was too much moved even to warn or entreat his friend to shake off the habit which was fastening upon him again. Alan's hand was on the door, when Robert, smiling dully, spoke: "I've gone back to hell, Alan. It is retribution; it is just."

"You shall not go back to hell!" cried the other. "I will not let you go!"

He turned, and came again to Robert's side. Neither of the men spoke: Alan because he could not; but the other, his head bowed upon his hands, was apparently as indifferent to silence as he had been to words. At last the doctor began to speak, and told him, pitifully and truly, all about Miss Sally, and how little hope there was. Yet Alan had to learn, as many another eager and forgiving soul has learned, with tears, that forgiveness may not sweep away the fact; a good deed and a bad deed have, equally, the permanence of the past. His friend seemed to listen, but made no comment.

Alan's tenderness, even his remorse for his harshness, could make no difference to Robert in this stress of fate. He had wounded, insulted, humiliated, the woman who trusted him: and now she was dying. He scarcely noticed when Alan left him, with that speechless sympathy of the grasp of a hand which is better than brave words.

The drift of circumstances in these June days brought Miss Sally into the very centre of her small world; and when her patient feet went down into the valley of death every one's thoughts were upon her. Perhaps it is the possibilities of the Great Silence which so dignify the most insignificant living thing. Miss Sally had never, in all her useful life, commanded such respect as now when her usefulness was drawing to an end. Her dignity silenced even Mrs. Paul, sitting alone in her big drawing-room, and forgetting to rail at neglect which once would have infuriated her; for of course Sidney could not leave her aunt, and Katherine was always at the major's when not giving a lesson. Once Mrs. Paul had cried out impatiently at Sally's selfishness in keeping her; but Katherine's quick indignation had silenced, even while it delighted, the old woman.

Katherine still kept up her teaching, to the annoyance of Mrs. Paul, and the great but protesting admiration of Mrs. Paul's son. To be sure, there was one pupil less, as Eliza Jennings had ceased to experiment upon the organ with twenty-two stops. Katherine told John that Eliza had dropped her, but she did not see fit to add why. Indeed, it would have needed a more subtle mind than Katherine Townsend's to have understood why it was that, under all her amusement at the silly little milliner, under her laughter at having been dismissed "without a character," there was a feeling very much like anger when she reflected that Eliza had said she was "in love with Mr. Paul." This was far below the surface. Katherine's mind and heart were too full, while Miss Sally lay dying, to give way to such folly; whereas Eliza had nothing to keep her thoughts from preying upon her own humiliation. Her little freckled face tingled whenever her eyes rested on her organ, which she absolutely refused to open. In vain did her mother implore her to play the hymns with which it was their custom to end every Sunday evening, or to practice "just a bit, to keep your hand in, 'Liza."

"No, ma'am," returned her daughter sternly. "I ain't got any music in me, nowadays."

She said this with such a bitter look that Mrs. Jennings almost wept. Indeed, Eliza's disappointment, which expressed itself by filial disapproval, wore so upon her mother that Mrs. Jennings' face really looked thinner; her small, twinkling eyes, rimmed with red, grew larger, and their short lashes held very often a glitter of tears. Both mother and daughter had heard that Mr. Paul was to marry Miss Townsend. Mrs. Jennings did not attempt to conceal her anger and spite, but the little milliner set her lips and fell into stony silences, which terrified her mother. Everything had come to an end, Eliza told herself. To be sure, she still occasionally saw John Paul's burly figure lounging across the bridge and hurrying towards Red Lane; but what was that to her, if he loved " Another "? So she let her mother take the toll, and turned her eyes away, lest she might have to say good-afternoon. She had nothing now — this in the diary in violet ink and underlined — " to live for." So, as one will fill a vacant life with anything, she thought much of Job Todd.

One day, — it was towards the end of June, — Mrs. Jennings was more than usually unhappy about her daughter. Eliza had been very morose for two days. That morning she ate her breakfast in silence, and then started out for a walk, — at least so her mother supposed; but Eliza vouchsafed no information concerning her plans, although Mrs. Jennings hinted timidly that the gooseberries and black currants ought to be picked, and she did n't know but what Eliza would like to do it? Eliza, however, ignored the veiled entreaty that she should help her mother in the tiresome task. So Mrs. Jennings, when she was alone, with a sigh which seemed to struggle up from the soles of her feet, took her shining tin bucket, and went out into the garden to do the work herself. The black currant bushes stood in a row along one of the winding paths, and although it was inconvenient to peer through the leaves, Mrs. Jennings, sitting on the ground and holding the pail between her knees, could still keep an eye on the toll-house window, in case any one wanted to change a nickel. Again she sighed; she wished Eliza could have stayed at home just this once. The soft roughness of the musky leaves was

still gleaming with dew, and when she began to
pluck the black shining clusters, her hand and
sleeve were wet. There was a bush beside her, of
big pink flowers, with the pungent scent of peach
kernels. Mrs. Jennings called them "piano-roses;"
and she glanced at them as one regards, listlessly,
an outgrown interest; then she stopped to smell a
spray of lad's love, and stick it in her bosom, but it
was from habit rather than any enjoyment of summer sights and scents. On her fat left hand the
narrow thread of her wedding ring was sunk deep
into the flesh. Mrs. Jennings' eyes filled as she
looked at it. "I do believe I'll get thin," she
thought; looking as unhappy as a very stout woman
may. (It is strange what poignant misery this
thought of lessening weight indicates in a large person.) But her self-pity never reproached Eliza.

The hot sunshine and the glitter of the river below, the glow of her poppies and lady's-slippers, and
even the loaded branches of the black currants failed
to cheer her. She picked the fruit with dreary
steadiness, winking away her tears now and then,
and thinking all the while of Eliza.

The hour among the currant bushes seemed very
long to Mrs. Jennings, and she was glad at last to
go back to the house, and begin to make her jam
and jelly. Still Eliza did not come home. Mrs.
Jennings was not an imaginative person, but her
anxiety during the last two months because of her
daughter's trouble, and her forlorn dismay at being
disapproved of, had made her really quite nervous;
that is, if nerves are ever found in such depths of

flesh. At all events, she began to be tremulous and
frightened; she glanced often out of the window,
along the footpath of the bridge, and once or twice
she walked to the little gate, and, shading her eyes
with her hands, looked up and down the dusty white
road. But there was no sign of Eliza. She found
herself remembering with cruel persistency that
winter afternoon when the handsome gentleman
jumped from the bridge into the river, because a poor
girl had tried to take her own life. Mrs. Jennings
shivered and gasped, and went back into her spot-
lessly clean little kitchen to stir the black currant
jam. Once she heard a noise upon the bridge, and
rushed breathless to the toll window, with a horrible
vision of her Eliza being borne home, drowned!
Her slow, unused imagination showed her the dripping,
clinging garments, the loosened hair, even that
strange sneer with which, through their half-closed
eyes, the dead sometimes regard the living. She
was experiencing that quickening of the mind which
comes under the spur of terror or grief; indeed, her
anxiety had brought a sort of refinement into her
face. The noise, however, was only because a flock
of sheep was being driven to the shambles. She
stood and watched them, staring into the gloom of
the covered bridge. Dusky lines of sunshine
stretched down into the darkness from the small
barred windows in the roof; they were so clearly de-
fined that the poor silly sheep, trampling and running, leaped over them, one after another. In the
past this had often diverted Mrs. Jennings, but it
could not divert her now.

The drove of sheep came out into the glare of sunshine, a cloud of dust following them up the road; and then all was still again, — only the splash of the river and the slow bubble of the jam in the kitchen.

Mrs. Jennings could not stand the strain. She dropped into the big rocking-chair, and burst into tears. Rocking and sobbing, she did not hear Eliza enter; but when the little milliner spoke, the change in her voice electrified her mother.

"Ma," said Eliza; then she put her hand behind her, and thrust forward, bashful and uncomfortable, Job Todd.

"La!" gasped Mrs. Jennings.

"Yes," returned Eliza gleefully. "Job's building 'way up at the end of Red Lane, an' I was walking up there; an'— an' then I coaxed him to come here to dinner."

"Thank the Lord!" said Mrs. Jennings devoutly. "That's just right. An' he shall have the best dinner he ever had in his life."

Job protested, but suffered her to put him in the chair she promptly vacated for him; he then accepted Eliza's offer of cake, and received a fan from Mrs. Jennings' hand. The two women said nothing to each other, but both beamed with happiness, and seemed to consider Job Todd an object of the tenderest solicitude. Apparently, they thought that he had been through such an exhausting morning that he needed refreshment and repose. Eliza told her mother to hurry and get dinner, "and," she added, "I'll play the organ, so Job can rest." Eliza blushed so prettily as she assumed this air of proprietorship that Mrs. Jennings, before she prepared the dinner, even before she removed the kettles of jam and jelly from the stove, knelt slowly and heavily down by the dresser in the kitchen, and, hiding her face in her hands, breathed a very humble and grateful prayer.

That was a great day at the toll-house. Job spent the whole afternoon in the sitting-room, rocking vehemently in the big chair, or sitting on the horsehair sofa, at Eliza's side. Once or twice, Mrs. Jennings, first coughing outside the door, ventured to enter, just to see her darling's happiness and to assure herself that she was forgiven. In Mrs. Jennings' circle, the formality of asking and receiving pardon is not often observed.

In Eliza's mind, however, the end for which this whole blissful day had been created was the manner in which the evening was to be spent. By dint of entreaties and a little pouting, she persuaded Job to go with her to tell Miss Katherine Townsend the great news. "I want her to know it first of all," she confessed, sitting on Job's knee and hiding her face in his shoulder. Of course she did not explain why she wished Miss Townsend to be told, nor did she yield to Job's suggestion that it would be just as well to go the next night. She was shrewd enough to be perfectly certain that her plan must be carried out on this especial evening, or not at all. This first day was an occasion so solemn, so important, so uncomfortable, that Job could be induced to bear almost anything. To-morrow it would be quite different. So when, at Miss Townsend's door, Maria told them that her mistress was not at home, Eliza had one moment of blank dismay, while Job's honest face began to brighten. But the milliner was equal to the occasion.

"Where is she?" she demanded, and Mr. Todd's jaw dropped.

Maria mournfully directed her to Major Lee's house, adding that somebody was sick there, and —

"Never mind," said Eliza; "we're just going to the door," and, taking Job's arm, she marched off triumphantly.

"Well, now, do ye know, really, it seems to me," observed her lover, "I ain't sure but what it would be as well to just fetch up with a walk, 'stead of making a call, 'Liza?" This with a tender look; but Eliza was firm.

It was quite dark when they reached Major Lee's, and under the heavy shadows of the ailantus the unlighted house looked blank and forbidding. There had been no thought of lights in the library, that night, or in the hall; only in the dining-room, where the little group about the table spoke in hushed voices, and fell into long silences.

Miss Sally was very ill; Miss Sally was dying. Alan had told Major Lee so, and Katherine. He could not tell Sidney yet; he would not let her give up hope. He had come down from Miss Sally's room for a cup of tea, and Sidney slipped upstairs to her aunt as he entered. Major Lee was pacing restlessly up and down. Katherine and John sat silently watching Alan, as he hurriedly ate and drank.

It was just then that little Susan, trembling in a way that told her terror as well as her grief, pushed the door open and looked into the room. It was a comfort to see the people, Susan thought, now, while Miss Sally lay dying upstairs, even if it were only to say there was somebody waiting at the door. "If it had been any one else that was — that was — dyin', Miss Sally would n't 'a' let a girl sit all alone in that big kitchen," she thought, with a sob, looking fearfully over her shoulder at the shadows on the staircase.

"Miss Townsend," she said, "there's a lady and gentleman to see you, but they won't come in."

"To see me?" Katherine answered, surprised, and rising.

"Shall I not go for you?" John asked, with that lowered voice which is the tribute of life to death; but she shook her head.

She waited for Susan to follow her with a lamp, and then went to the front door, which the servant, uncertain of the character of these callers, had closed, leaving them standing on the porch.

Neither Job nor Eliza could see the anxiety in Katherine's face, for taking the lamp from Susan, she held it so that the light fell only upon her visitors; but the man was more sensitive than the woman, and felt instinctively that they had made a mistake in coming. He shifted from one foot to the other, and would have shrunk behind his sweetheart, had she permitted it. But Eliza had no intention of permitting it. She put her little rough hand upon his arm and pulled him forward.

"Miss Townsend," she said, an unusual glitter in her eyes and a hint of boldness in her voice, "we came. Job and me, to tell you — to tell you"— Eliza hung her head.

"Yes, Eliza?" Katherine answered, guessing the news at once, but too sad and too absorbed to express the pleasure she really felt.

"We are engaged!" burst out Eliza. "Miss Townsend, we're engaged, and we expect to be married."

"'Liza would come to tell you," Job objected feebly.

"She knew I would be glad to hear it," said Katherine; and then she added some kind and pleasant things, and Eliza, to her great surprise, felt all the old love and respect come back with a rush.

"You are real good, Miss Townsend," she declared, and squeezed her teacher's hand between her own. "Ain't she good, Job?"

"I was always saying that," Job answered gallantly, feeling really very happy.

Katherine was honestly glad of little Eliza's happiness, but she was astounded to find something beside gladness in her heart; was it possible that it was relief? "Well," she thought, listening to Job's clumsy praises of his betrothed, "after all, there is nothing which can surprise one so much as to discover one's own possibilities. Heaven knows what crime I may be capable of, if I have resented Eliza's nonsense!"

She smiled at the lovers in the kindest way, and then, with a word of there being sickness in the house, dismissed them; for it was evident that Eliza was willing to linger for further display of her joy.

Katherine stood in the doorway a moment, holding the lamp high above her head, so that her guests might see their way across the courtyard to the gate; but as she turned to go into the house, she was startled to see a dark figure approach her from the distant end of the piazza.

"Who is it?" she said quickly; and then, "Cousin Robert!"

"How is she now?" he said hoarsely. His face was wrung and torn by suffering, and the tears sprang to Katherine's eyes.

"Oh, have you been out here all alone? Come in, — come in."

He shook his head. "Is it over? Is she dead?"

"No, — oh, no!" cried Katherine.

"She is dying, — I know that; Alan told me."

Katherine could not answer him, for tears.

"I have killed her, Kate," he said dully.

"Dear cousin Robert," she entreated, "don't stay here in the darkness; come in, and wait and pray with us. We all love her, and while there is life, you know" — She forgot that John Paul was within, — John Paul, who had called this agonized soul "a man too contemptible for contempt."

"Come in, — come in; don't stay out here by yourself. *She* would be grieved to know that you suffered so."

"She would be grieved?" His voice broke into a cry. "At least she does not know it — at least she is spared that!"

And then he turned back into the night.

XXV.

SIDNEY said, very quietly, that she would sit up with Miss Sally that night. Heretofore, Katherine and Scarlett had divided the watching between them, and for the last two nights Alan had not left the house; but it was a matter of course to every one that Sidney should rest, and, so far as the others knew, she had done so. At least, she had gone to her room. But Sidney was living too intensely, easily to lose herself in sleep. She was leaving her old life to go out into a wider living, and she found Death standing on the threshold. Love did not oppose him, but human instinct did. Her neglect of her aunt, of the pitiful little love which was drifting away from her, stung her with intolerable impatience. She felt that helpless impulse to go back into the past which comes with the sense of duty left undone.; and the consciousness of the futility of such an impulse is almost anger. It *could* not be too late. She must do something, say something *now!* Yet, there being no love in her heart, this effort was, although she was not aware of it, for her own relief rather than for Miss Sally's happiness. Again and again, before the dull stupor drowned her aunt's unfailing tenderness, Sidney had tried, in broken, hesitating words, to say, "I am sorry — forgive me." But Miss Sally never seemed to understand; she was only feebly concerned that her darling should be sorry about anything. That Sidney could blame herself because she had neglected her aunt was not credible to Miss Sally, whose life had been too full of the gladness of giving to realize that there had been no receiving in it.

As Sidney watched the relentless days carry her opportunity away from her, the pain of self-knowledge grew unbearable. Alan had told her she was selfish? Oh, he did not know how selfish she was; no one knew it but herself. The burden of a human soul fell upon her,— the knowledge of good and evil.

Her remorse filled her with a mysterious fear. It was something outside herself, terrible, inescapable; with it was an insistent suggestion of some different line of conduct, which confused her by its contradiction of all which had been the purpose of her life. What was this impulse to self-sacrifice against which she had always opposed herself, as one who beats against an unseen wind? To turn and advance with it might be peace, for setting herself against it had brought dismay; but the recognition of such an impulse filled her with the terror of the Unknown.

She saw the unloveliness of selfishness, and was quick to turn away from it, with an æsthetic perception of the beauty of holiness. Goodness commended itself to her; she would be good, she would be unselfish. She could not comprehend why, this resolution made, pain should still dominate her consciousness. Anger and fear lifted her out of herself; it was the same tumult of emotion which had clamored in her soul when Love had first whispered to her.

Miss Sally's dim realization of Sidney's pain was too indistinct even for her sweet forgiveness, which would have protested that there was nothing to forgive. She liked just to rest, she said, and let Sidney read the daily chapter in the Bible to her; or, sometimes, to listen to a word or two from Mr. Brown, who came often, in these last few days, to see her. It was Mr. Brown's presence which pointed out the future to Miss Sally.

"Why, am I very sick, Alan?" she said, in her little weak voice.

"We are anxious, dear Miss Sally," the young man answered tenderly.

She looked up at him and smiled. "Don't be worried," she said, with the old instinct to make other people comfortable; and then, later, as though half asleep, "I thought — that I had all the world, Alan — but I seem — I seem to have eternity, instead." And with great content Miss Sally went down into the shadows.

All that last day, except in the paroxysms of coughing, she had seemed to Sidney to sleep. But it was a strange sleep; and when she roused a little from it, there was no loving look, no murmur of thanks, even when Alan gave her medicine, or when Katherine slipped a bit of ice between her lips.

John Paul stayed very late that night. Little Susan sat trembling in the kitchen until twelve.

The major walked softly and restlessly through the halls, and up and down stairs. Katherine, worn out with watching, had fallen asleep on the broad seat of the first landing, her head resting on a cushion the major had brought her from the library. Alan, quite without hope, sat outside Miss Sally's door; Sidney was within. Everything was tingling with the intensest life to the girl; the dark silence of the stately old house was palpitating with the thoughts of birth and death; the procession of the years had left luminous touches upon the very walls. Everything thrilled with life; the house was alive, and this drama of death was its soul. Sidney was living as she had never lived before; every nerve was tense with terror, not of death, but of life.

As she sat by Miss Sally's bedside, she watched the yellow blur of the night-lamp in the darkness of the further corner, or glanced at the terrible whiteness of the face upon the pillow; and to each — to darkness, and to death, and to her own stress of life — her soul cried out, *What are you?* The slow hours drifted into each other, marked only by Alan entering or departing, or by Major Lee pausing in the doorway to glance silently, first at his daughter, and then at the small, motionless figure upon the bed.

It had rained early in the night, and now the breath of the wet flowers down in the garden was fresh and cool. Sidney went over to the window, and looked out at the distant darkness of the dawn. The silent night was a hush of breathless expectancy. The gray sky, the stars fading as the east lifted and whitened, the misty outlines of sleeping houses, were all waiting; and for what? Death! She knelt down by the window, resting her face upon her folded arms. Alan was in the next room. What if it were Alan lying there upon the bed, without words, or motion, or remembrance; Alan who was waiting death; Alan who would be — nothing? Down below, the wall between the two gardens began to loom out of the crystal dark; one by one, as though to some unheard call, the trees shaped themselves in the mist. How strangely one were night and day; how all life grew out of death! Human existence, like an endless spiral touching light and darkness, life and death, stretches into eternity: a blossom falls; a seed ripens; another flower blows — to die! Over and over, the pastime of eternity enacts itself, and the heartbreak of the world gathers into one word, "Why?" Yet with the majesty of an inevitable certainty proceeds the universe. Men's cries and wonders echo far into the past, and accompany the present; yet all the while the perfection of detail never falters, — seedtime and harvest, night and day, life and death.

A Lombardy poplar, close to the house, swayed and shivered in the night wind. Sidney felt rather than saw that flying quiver of its leaves which is a voice made visible. Each smallest leaf obeyed in beauty the same law that orders star systems, scattered thick as dust in the vast silences of space. How all things are only one thing!

What were those words she had read to her aunt?

"*All things work together for good.*" What if that were true? What if one could believe it not only for the leaf and star, but for life and death? They do work together, surely, — each grows out of the other; but suppose it were for good, suppose it were with some sort of purpose? "Working together for good?" They would be part of a plan, then; there would be a meaning somewhere. It would not matter whether the meaning were understood. The good need not be a human good; it might be an infinite and unknowable good, one which needed men's pain, nay, men's sin for its perfection; but to think that there was a good somewhere! To feel *that* would make up, perhaps, for grief and for death; one's own death, — yes, surely, a thousand times! "*The Eternal God is thy refuge.*" A purpose, — if there were such a thing, — seen or unseen, would be a refuge. But the Dominant Will which enacts forever its own tragedy is caprice, — traveling without motive, in the circle of eternity! Yet if it were true, — just suppose it were true, and all things did work together for good, all things did have some purpose and meaning, — then one could be content to cease, just as that star dropped out of darkness into the growing brightness behind the edge of the world. But if one loved the star? Would it be enough that it were swallowed up in light, swallowed up in what was itself, if it should not dawn again? Suppose it were Alan lying there, would it be enough to say, The Eternal God is my refuge? That is, there is an Eternal Meaning in it all — if it were Alan?

The bank of mist in the east melted into filmy bars; they throbbed as though they hung before some beating heart of light; the bushes in the garden grew out of the shadows like soft balls of darkness, and the Virginia creeper, hanging from the lintel of the window, showed in wavering streamers black against the sky. Sidney strained her eyes down into the gloom; surely, over against the evergreen hedge, where the tall lilies stood, there was a gleam of white? The garden was very still; not a tremor of air stirred the motionless leaves, or the roses on the lattice below the window; a bird twittered in the poplar tree, and another answered it over by the lilies, and then another and another. There was a wandering perfume from the white trumpets of the petunias in Miss Sally's border, and then a breath of the keen sweetness of mignonette brushed her cheek, and she seemed to hear Alan's voice, as she heard it once before in the fragrance of mignonette: "Do you love me, Sidney?" What if it were Alan?

Oh, if there were a refuge! But is there anything that is eternal? Endless desire, endless restlessness, or call it the pain of life, — for is not life desire? Oh, weariness of longing which is the expression of the universe, which is eternal! And the deepest longing is for a meaning. Conduct is not everlasting; conduct is only expediency, the deepest and most subtile selfishness; her father had shown her that beyond a doubt. But expediency is necessity, in one way; or call it Right. "All things work together." Is not conduct part of all? — conduct, and the perception of right, and the pain of sin, and the mystery of love, and that demand of the soul for *Something* which would explain all things, the Eternal Meaning of all. To see a meaning would be to find a refuge; yes, it would be like arms in which one rested and trusted.

What is this which beckons to the stars, or lifts the sweetness from the flowers? What is this which makes the thought of Alan flash into her brain? What is it which moulds the rain into a drop in the heart of that rose, and brings the instant remembrance of Miss Sally's love of roses to burn Sidney's eyes with tears and lay upon her heart the burden of regret? All working together; all one; an eternal — what? Force? All these were force, and force is *one*, and "force is the energy of a cause." Who said that? Never mind, now; Sidney could not stop for verification, with her hand upon a fact.

Like a person walking in the dark, through perilous places, she had touched something firm and sure; she knew not what, but she clung to it. If Miss Sally had spoken to her at that moment, Sidney would not have heard her.

After all, it was this oneness, this cause, — her father stopped at the energy, — which people called eternal, which they chose to name God; that was all. They might as well have named it anything, or left it without a name. It meant nothing; there is no such thing as justice or pity behind phenomena; so how could it help her, how could it comfort her, to admit the unity of the force which produces at once pity and the suffering which calls it forth? But if there were a Purpose, a Meaning, in the expression of this Force, — and phenomena is its expression? Ah, if? Surely then we might be content not to speak of it as it affected humanity; we might be content to leave out such definitions and limitations as "pity" and "justice." That it *was* would be enough. But why should such a Meaning seem so much to her? Only that her soul claimed it; was not this very claiming an expression of it? Might not Death belong to it, and life belong to it; would not love be in it; would not all things be *It?* If this were so, then it was the explanation and the mystery, the certainty and the doubt, the meaning of all things, the refuge and the Eternal God!

The clouds across the east had caught the light upon their rippling gray, and turned to fire. It seemed as though, far up above the world, a wind without noise was blowing across flames. She turned to look at Miss Sally. All was still; the sick woman was sleeping in the profoundest quiet. "That is good for her," Sidney thought, with a strange reverence for her own tenderness, which was not hers, except as she was part of the Eternal Meaning, as she was one with her aunt herself.

The dawn had transfigured Miss Sally's face with a light which thrilled Sidney like a touch out of the darkness. Outside, the brightness in the east widened and spread until the whole sky was a luminous shadow, which began to flush and glow, and along the eastern hills a film of gold rose like a mist across the flames. The Cause; the Meaning; which was always; which was strong; which was right, — at least inevitable. If it were Alan going out into blankness, that is going back into this mystery, or Cause, to be part of it forever, as he had been part of it always, but not to be Alan always, would it seem right? No, "right" was not the word; she could find no word. But the pain would be part of the mystery, part of the Eternal Purpose, and so, bearable. Sorrow worked together with joy in the Meaning of all things, and therefore could be borne. But one could not use little words, little human words like "right" and "justice," to make it seem worth while to suffer. Oh, just to rest upon a certain Purpose! — that would be enough. A Refuge. Yes, yes, but what terror! It did not make life less terrible; it only filled it with confidence and peace. It made it worth living, if it were lived struggling for oneness with the Eternal Purpose, of which sorrow was as much a part as joy, death as life.

Back over the evergreens there was a rim of gold. Sidney held her breath and looked. How quickly, how greatly, it grew, pushed up from the darkness into the wide spaces of the endless air, fuller and rounder, the whole generous, beautiful soul of light! The birds, twittering over by the white lilies with joyous expectancy of waiting, fell into silence with the fulfillment of desire. The Eternal: for the sun, for the birds, for her. The Eternal was that exquisite pain of joy in the beauty of the dawn; it was the passion of desire for itself; it was the instinct of unselfishness, the terror of remorse; it was her Refuge. "I don't know how," she heard herself saying in a sobbing breath; "but that I want a Meaning proves it. — it is the *want!*"

Does not the hunger of the body declare that there is bread? Even so the hunger of the soul implies immortal food! She did not speak of love, for love was swallowed up in that of which it is only one single expression.

Outside, the world was waking to its old story of disappointment and continual hope, but Sidney, standing in the golden light, saw a new heaven and a new earth. A thread of smoke went up from one of the chimneys of the tenements beyond Mrs. Paul's house. The salutation of the dawn smote like a finger of flame upon countless windows, gray a moment before, and beckoned men out to their labor. The splendor of the dawn, the small needs of living, the swaying and murmuring of far-off seas, the flute in a bird's throat, the melting back into It all which we call death, the consciousness of Itself which we call life, — all were one. Sidney looked down at the smile of her garden, and then at the silent, smiling face upon the pillow; as she did so, her father entered. He stopped an instant at Miss Sally's side, and touched her hand; the look upon his face turned Sidney white. "Father?"

"My darling," he said in a whisper, "she is dead."

He would have taken Sidney in his arms, but she put her hands upon his breast and breathed rather than spoke. "No, not dead, — there is no death. Life and death are one; the Eternal Purpose holds us all, always. Father — I have found God."

XXVI.

Sidney Lee came out from that experience of death and dawn with an absolute conviction. She did not attempt to justify herself by reasons. She *knew.* That was all, but it was enough.

She had left Miss Sally's room with a face which shone; even the grief which veiled it — while yet that silent Presence dominated the household — could not hide the solemn light in her eyes. Grief and pity and regret moved across the peace which she had found, but did not disturb it; even as the winds, engraving themselves upon the sensitive sea in a thousand intricate and flying paths, do not stir the quiet of the deeps below.

With Sidney, there was perhaps less grief than regret. She was feeling, even in her exaltation, the misery of the lost opportunity; she was realizing that it is impossible to atone to the dead for indifference to their small interests, carelessness of their daily cares, — in a word, for unexpressed love; that such a realization is always pain Sidney had never known before. But it was that pain, mingling with her strange gladness, which brought into her face a new look, — at once wistful anxiety and calm desire. Major Lee saw it, and, remembering his daughter's words on the night when Miss Sally died, — " Father, I have found God," — said to himself that this changed expression was part of the same nervous excitement. Sidney had come to him that next day, and tried to tell him, briefly, what those words had meant; not that she courted discussion, — only that, with the gladness of the woman of old, who, after lighting her candle and searching diligently, called in her friends and neighbors and said, "Rejoice with me," Sidney desired to share her certainty. But her broken words, with no attempt at argument, indicated only a physical condition to her father. As soon as this strain was over, her common sense would assert itself; he was sorry and perhaps a little disappointed, — Sidney had been so different from the ordinary hysterical young woman, but he would let it pass; it was of no importance.

Even Mrs. Paul noticed the change in the girl, and she was annoyed by it; it made her uncomfortable, as anything which she did not understand was apt to do. "Poor, dear Sally is dead and buried," she said to Katherine, "and crying won't bring her back again. Sidney should look pleasanter, or keep her room. Red eyes belong to one's bed-chamber; they are too personal to be modest. You never see me with red eyes."

"Because you are too modest?" said Katherine, with great simplicity. She was sitting in the drawing-room with her prospective mother-in-law, behind bowed shutters. It was very hot; all the sounds which crept into the shadowy room were hot, — the droning of the bees in the honeysuckle around the west window, the rattle of heavy drays down in the scorching street, and the pant of a steam-drill a block away.

Katherine looked white and languid, but Mrs. Paul, fresh from Scarlett's cool fingers, was alert and comfortable. Her thin black silk had a frost of delicate lace about the neck and wrists, and she swung lightly, back and forth upon her arm, a green taffeta fan. On a table by her side was an India china bowl crowded with roses, and near it a tall silver tumbler full of sangaree, which was so cold that the polish of the silver was dimmed with beaded mist. Katherine had declined the claret and the fan, and everything, in fact, except a little cushion in a white lavender-scented linen cover, which Scarlett placed behind her head.

"Still," Mrs. Paul conceded, "I have no objection to your declining things, because you don't annoy me by looking uncomfortable. Poor Sally used to distract me by declining, — I suppose out of some foolish idea of politeness, — and then looking like a martyr. Really, you know, Kate, not that I would talk against the dead, — I don't approve of it, — but poor Sally was very trying at times?"

"I never found her so," Katherine answered. "I think it was the instinct of unselfishness which made her decline a pleasure. Oh, how good she was! (It is strange how quickly we learn to say 'was' instead of 'is'!")

"Of course she was good," returned Mrs. Paul. "I never said she wasn't good. But really, you can't say she was entertaining. Now, I never pretended to any remarkable goodness, but I am not uninteresting, I think?"

"Oh, far from it," said Katherine. "You are

interesting, most interesting. And Miss Sally, as you say, was not; but she was good and lovable."

Mrs. Paul looked blank for a moment, but Katherine's frank and confidential air reassured her.

"It was her goodness," she announced, clinking the bits of ice in the silver tumbler, "which made your cousin propose to her. Katherine, my dear, the only thing I don't like about you is your cousin."

"Poor cousin Robert!" said Katherine sadly. "Yet I am sure, I am quite sure, that he did not realize that he was dishonorable."

"He was only dishonorable because he was a fool," returned Mrs. Paul, with a shrug. "He should have made Sally break the engagement. A man of the world engaged to a prude would easily have arranged that. It was hard, though, that Sally should die. It was merely coincidence, of course, but the young man gets the credit of it, and people think she died of a broken heart. (As though Sally could die of a broken heart! Between ourselves, my dear, a good woman is not capable of a great passion. Did that ever occur to you?) No, to my mind, your Steele is unpleasant rather than dishonorable, — most unpleasant. And what do you think I heard yesterday? That the very day of the funeral he was found in his hotel drunk! Now, I am not a temperance fanatic. I have seen a gentleman overcome after a dinner, for instance, and thought none the worse of him; but — after a funeral! Really, the occasion should be considered."

"*Oh!*" said Katherine, the tears starting to her eyes.

"He is a mass of inconsistencies," Mrs. Paul continued, tapping her fan thoughtfully upon the edge of the table. "Some one told me — Scarlett, I believe it was — that those last nights he hung about the house all night long. He gave Scarlett quite a start, when she came upon him in the darkness. Yes, I have no doubt he was unhappy; and yet — to be intoxicated! Did you know Alan had taken him back to live with him again? Alan has not very much backbone. Men with faces like his have no depth nor persistency. I only hope his passion for Sidney will last."

"But if she does not return it, that is hard upon him."

"I was not thinking of Alan," Mrs. Paul answered. "I was thinking — of Mortimer Lee!"

Katherine looked at her with wondering interest. "You really have no heart, have you, Mrs. Paul?" she said.

"My dear," explained the older woman, "I am all heart. But I believe in justice. Mortimer Lee has been a wicked atheist, and he ought to be punished. And you know — ridiculous as it is — what it would be to him if Sidney fell in love with any one. But of course my chief desire is to benefit Sidney. It has always been my habit to try to help others. Lord! how annoyed I was that your cousin did not fall in love with Sidney! I could forgive his conduct about his mother's money and the breaking of his engagement, but — to propose to Sally! I can forgive wickedness; but that was worse than wickedness, — it was stupidity."

"It seems to me a matter of imagination," Katherine observed. "We can forgive a condition which we can imagine for ourselves; but what we can't fancy ourselves capable of, we despise."

"Exactly; you have a great deal of sense, Kate. Now, I could not be a fool."

"No, indeed," Katherine assured her, warmly. "But what an inference you make one draw!"

"Very true!" cried the other, in high good humor. She was distinctly flattered, and loved Katherine more than ever. "As for Sidney and Alan," she continued, " unless I am very much mistaken, — and I never am mistaken in such matters; I've lived myself, — Sidney has come to her senses at last, and Mortimer Lee is to learn a lesson."

"What do you mean?"

"I mean that Sidney is in love with Alan. Such a change does not come into a woman's face as has come into hers, for nothing."

"Mrs. Paul," said Katherine, sitting up and looking at her with sudden attention, " there is a change, but "—

"Well?" demanded Mrs. Paul. "Don't grow commonplace, Kate, and hesitate over a sentence."

"It is not because of Dr. Crossan, — I am sure of that. It is because (yes, I don't see why I should not speak of it. Sidney told me, and I think she would be glad to have it known), — it is because Sidney is not what she was."

"Go on," said Mrs. Paul.

"I think the change in her face is from some deeper reason than that she has fallen in love. (If she has, which does n't seem to me probable.) But she told me — that she believed."

"Believed?" repeated the other, frowning. "Believed what?"

"She said she had 'found God.'" Katherine lowered her voice. "I tell you only because I am sure that as we all knew what her old thought was, she would wish us to know her new thought."

"What!" cried Mrs. Paul. "Sidney says she's 'found God'? (though I am sure I think the expression very irreverent. I suppose she means she's been converted?) Lord! what does Mortimer Lee say? Well, I am glad!"

"Oh, Mrs. Paul!" said Katherine, shocked into remonstrance.

"But how has it come about?" persisted the older woman. "Has Mr. Brown seen her? I did n't suppose Sidney had been to church for years." She paused, lifting in her delicate old hand a little silver vinaigrette, made like a fish, with glittering scales, and curiously flexible. Her face was full of the keenest interest and pleasure. "Mr. Brown was never allowed to try to convert her, you know. Well, I am very thankful, of course. It has always been a grief to me to have Sidney out of the Church. She was never even baptized, — did you know that? I expected to be her godmother; but Mortimer Lee would not have the child christened. Shocking, was n't it?"

"How careful you are of your creed!" commented Katherine, with delightful deference; "and yet I notice you do not often intrude your religion?"

"I hope not, indeed! Conversation about religion leads to horrible self-consciousness; and thank Heaven, I never had any need to talk about my spiritual condition. I never had a doubt in my life."

"You mastered the eternal verities with your catechism, I suppose?" said Katherine.

But Mrs. Paul did not notice the remark. "As for Sidney, with her antecedents her unbelief did not reflect upon her socially, although it was unbecoming,— most unbecoming. I'm sure I'm rejoiced that she has come to her senses. I suppose she'll be confirmed at Easter?"

Katherine shook her head. "I don't know, but think not. I spoke of it, but she looked at me in the blankest way; and when I said something about seeing Miss Sally again, you know, and all that, she apparently did n't understand for a moment, and then she said, ' *That* expression of the Eternal is gone, but *He* remains.' I don't know what she meant," proceeded Katherine doubtfully. "I asked her if she did not believe in immortality, and she said she did not know anything about it, but ' God was.'"

"She does n't know what she is talking about!" cried Mrs. Paul impatiently.

"At least she is convinced," Katherine answered.

"Convinced!" returned the other. "My dear Kate, anything so positive as a conviction is scarcely modest in a well-bred young woman. And there is too much talk about convictions in these days, and too little good behavior. Sidney should have been confirmed ten years ago, with convictions or without them, if I had had my way."

"I wonder if her — change of opinion will make any difference in Major Lee?" Katherine asked.

"Certainly not. The day when the infant converts his grandfather is past, my friend; and as for saying she *believes*, but not in immortality, and that she won't be confirmed, — I never heard such nonsense! Really, Kate, I wouldn't encourage her to talk in that way; it is quite improper. I hoped, when you first spoke, that she had become — well — you know what I mean — a change of heart, you know — a Churchwoman."

Katherine did not pursue the subject; she had been awed by Sidney's uplifted look, and she had vaguely understood it; but as she tried to explain it the idea melted away.

Sidney had chosen to name "*God*," that tireless, eternal activity which constitutes the universe; that energy which is in all and through all, pulsing in every atom, recognizing itself in the conscious instant of a man's life, creating and destroying, working towards its own infinite end. With this naming (or let us say this perception), and the devout submission to and trust in the laws of nature which it implies, there had come to her, not happiness, but blessedness, and that peace which, truly, the world can neither give nor take away. But the process by which she had reached peace must be personal before it can commend itself to the understanding, and for that reason she could not show it to Katherine.

In a direct and simple way, Katherine felt that

Sidney would wish that others might know her present attitude, and so told Mrs. Paul, whose absolute inability to understand the situation made her uncertain as to her own grasp of it. She did not want to speak of it any further, and she was glad that at that moment Sidney entered; not that she meant to question the girl, but she wanted to watch her.

Mrs. Paul looked up impatiently. Sidney, in her black gown, her face marked by some deeper pain and meaning than merely grief for Miss Sally's death, confused and annoyed the older woman; beside, with that curious vanity which leads one to confess a fault, she had been just about to tell Kate a story — Lord! why could not Sidney have stayed at home? Innocence is a great nuisance at times.

"Well? What? Dear me, Sidney, the heat has made you white; pray go and ask Scarlett for some rose-water, and bathe your face. It is very unpleasant to see any one look fagged."

"I came over," Sidney answered, with an absent air, which did not acknowledge the fault-finding, "to ask you — I was putting away her things, and I thought you might like something which belonged to her — and I came to ask you if you would care to have this piece of lace?"

"Do sit down, and don't look so white. Lace? Let me see it. Yes, I'll take it; but I am sure I don't see why in the world you should bring *me* lace. I have more now than I know what to do with. I mean to give Katherine some superb lace when she is married. Do you hear that, Kate?"

Katherine was looking anxiously at Sidney. "My

dear," she said gently, "you really are worn out; you should not have crossed the garden in this blazing sun. I shall have to ask Dr. Crossan about you."

In an instant Sidney's face flushed to the forehead. Katherine smiled and glanced at Mrs. Paul, who asked, "Does Alan still call every day? Really, poor, dear Sally's sickness was an opportunity for Alan! I saw him yesterday," she continued, swinging her fan lazily. "He is looking shockingly. I don't believe he will live long." Katherine gave her a warning look, but Mrs Paul ended her sentence. "He is really ill, you know."

Sidney drew a quivering breath; her eyes dimmed with a flying terror. "Is Alan going to die?"

"Well, some time, I suppose," returned Mrs. Paul. ("You see, Kate? I said so!")

"Is he?" Sidney repeated, standing before Mrs. Paul, and trembling very much.

"Oh, Lord, Sidney, don't glare so! No, of course not. But he was ill a little while ago, you remember; and poor Sally told me that Mr. Steele had told her— But what is it to you, my dear?"

Sidney did not answer. She scarcely heard Mrs. Paul say, in a perfunctory manner, that Katherine had told her something she was very glad to hear, and she hoped Sidney would try to live a consistent life, and be sensible about confirmation; and then,—

"Just arrange, will you, to come in when Katherine is n't here? I don't need anybody else if she is here. Oh, and give the lace to Scarlett, will you?"

Sidney would not let Katherine go home with

her; she shut herself out of the cool darkness of the hall, and then went slowly back through the blazing garden. She had left that inevitable task of "putting away" to bring Mrs. Paul the piece of lace, but she forgot how much yet remained to be done. Alan had been ill! She walked over to the evergreen circle, where the sun-dial stood among the shadows, and sat down on the curved bench. It was here Alan had told her that she needed love in her life,— it seemed to Sidney that her life dated from that day; then, afterwards, he had said he loved her, and she had declared that she did not, and never would, love him. "Oh, but I do," she said quietly, aloud. "I do." She looked up between the dark points of the firs into the cloudless and dazzling sky; her eyes overflowed with tears, but her lips smiled.

She forgot everything but joy. She was as entirely glad as the soul can be which has one moment without memory. She put out her hands as though to meet the hands she loved; her face was wet with tears, but it was illumined. Suddenly it changed. Love? No, she must not love him. Her heart was bounding, her lips breaking into smiles, her joy overflowing in words, when this old habit of thought asserted itself. With it came the memory of that experience of dawn and death; the strange unreasoning conviction, the solemn instinct, that her life was to be an expression of the Eternal Life. Yes, that was all true, all true; and she would be good; and it was well to be alive, though she did not know why. She would do her work; she would try to help any one who needed her,— but she would not know sorrow; why need she? She could do her part in the world as well, and better, unhampered by the horrible fear of death; she would not love Alan. Yet inescapable joy shone in her eyes; she only knew that she loved, while, mechanically, she asserted that she would escape from love. The long z-z-ing of insects stabbed the silence of noon; the hot scent of flowers wandered in among the shadows; and on the old sun-dial a bird perched, and plumed itself, looking at her with fearless interest.

In a numb, helpless way Sidney was struggling to be obedient to the heavenly vision, and yet to save herself. At last it seemed to her that she was incapable of meeting this crisis, and, with that power which comes at rare moments into every life, she put aside the truth which had been revealed to her, and took up again the small details of death and life. "I will finish putting the things away, and then I will think," she said to herself.

She went into the house, so intent upon thrusting this new greatness aside, until she could find an hour which should be all its own, that she was really only aware of the work she at once began to do; she did not think of Alan. Her eyes blurred again and again as she folded Miss Sally's little wardrobe away: the pathos of the small darns, of carefully brushed, and turned, and turned again gowns, of bits of ribbon, and treasured pieces of lace, struck upon Sidney's heart with a pain which was part of her new experience of life. "Oh, if I had only been kinder!" she said over and over to herself.

If we could but take our possessions with us when

we leave this world, life would be less terrible to those who love us, whom we leave. The many small things, which are so useless to every one except the owner, suddenly become sacred. They cannot be destroyed; to give them away is a confession that they are cumbersome, and is another unkindness to the dead. This thought came to Sidney, on her knees before the lower drawer of Miss Sally's bureau. Of what use to any one was the little ugly mosaic pin? But Miss Sally's fingers had touched it; it was her pride and joy; it must be kept. The black silk aprons which Sidney had always disliked, the small bags of rose leaves which would so soon crumble into dust,— none of these could be thrown away. The collection grew as the girl's tenderness and remorse grew. There was a little faded pincushion, which with a pang she recognized as one of her youthful gifts to her aunt, which Miss Sally had cherished through Sidney's indifferent years. There were daguerreotypes; and some photographs of Sidney, on which were written, "My darling Sidney," and "Dear little Sidney," and the child's age. One thin, square book gave her a shock of memory, as she unfolded the white paper in which it was wrapped, and saw the familiar gilt cherubs on the brown cover of "Reading without Tears." Sidney sat down on the floor, and leaned her head against the old dressing-case, with the book open in her lap. How it all came back to her!—the time when she learned her letters standing at Miss Sally's knee, while her aunt's gentle voice alternately implored and encouraged her, as might be the condition of Sidney's temper. Never out of patience, never unjust, what matter if sometimes unwise? "Oh, if I had only been kinder!" she sobbed. It was not reading without tears now. And so the book was added to the "things to be kept;" memory of that old tenderness made it sacred. Almost all these forlorn little treasures were connected with Sidney or her father, in some way, and so made the sting of her remorse sharper.

These voiceless possessions of Miss Sally's raised such an outcry of regret and self-abasement in Sidney's mind that, at last, she could not bear it, and rose, the pathetic task still unfinished. Her conscience clamored that she must do some kind act. Miss Sally's poor seemed to entreat her, and it was to them she fled: down, in the fading afternoon, to one miserable tenement after another; then coming shuddering back again. "No, it is all too awful! Oh, I cannot live! I cannot bear it. It is not enough to know that there is a Meaning, and I will not love Alan."

XXVII.

The blue July day grew sullen with heat towards evening, and the skies blackened along the west. There was no wind, but the trees shivered. That night the major's tea-table was very quiet; Sidney could not talk, and her father desired only to listen. He knew that she was troubled, and longed for deeper understanding of her pain, but he asked no questions; he waited for her to know that she needed him before he should try to help her. Unless, indeed, she did not need him? The remembrance of that hysterical experience might now be only a painful mortification, and she would prefer that they should both forget it.

But as they sat at tea, in the half darkness of the long, octagonal room, — it was too hot for lights, — he was aware of a hopeless depression in her face that filled him with an aching pity. "If Sarah had not died!" he said to himself. The major had never recognized his affection for his sister until she was dead; but it was not of his own loss that he thought, as he saw Sidney's pain. He was almost angry at Miss Sally because she had died, and so his darling suffered. He spoke only of commonplace things, however: of the mutter of thunder, retreating and retreating, in the west; of the heavy sweetness of the white phlox beneath the window; or some query concerning Katherine and John.

Sidney scarcely heard him; the tumult in her mind shut out everything else; it seemed to her almost as though her father must hear it, too. Once she lifted her eyes and found him looking at her with a face full of troubled love. She started, and smiled. "Did you speak to me?"

"No," he answered; and then, as they rose to leave the room, he rested his hand for a moment upon her shoulder. "Sidney, what is it?"

She put her hands up to her face. "Oh," she said sharply, "I do not know — I thought I knew — and yet — and yet" —

"Yes?" the major queried, in a mild voice. He was already less anxious; she was going to tell him, and it was inconceivable to him that his child could have any trouble that he could not lighten. He already saw himself explaining that of course he had attached no meaning to those confused words of hers, and she must not feel the slightest embarrassment; that such a nervous condition was most natural under the circumstances. The major readily appreciated that she suffered as she remembered her foolish excitement. The patience and sweetness in his worn old face made the tears spring to Sidney's eyes. "Oh, I have not even thought of him! He wants to help me, and I have shut him out for fear he would not understand."

"I cannot seem to make it right," she said; "what shall I do?" They had come into the library, and the major, sitting down in his big leather chair, still kept her hand in his.

"Make what right?" he asked.

"That there should be suffering," she answered, with a cry in her voice. She dropped her head upon her father's knee, and he felt her tears against his hand. "I thought God was enough; but when I see pain, when I feel it, myself, then it seems to me that the Meaning must be understood before the pain can be borne; and yet a Meaning ought to be enough."

"Sidney," he said, "my darling, I had not meant to refer to this; I hoped that you were better, if I may be allowed the expression. Surely, you are not serious in speaking as though this were a reasonable subject?"

She lifted her head, but still knelt beside him, looking at him with miserable eyes. "It is the only subject there is, it seems to me; there is nothing but the Eternal. Suffering and death are part of it; only — only I do not want pain, father?"

For a moment Major Lee was too amazed for words; then he said gently, "Let me understand you. I fear I have not followed you intelligently, — the fault is mine. But do I understand that you have " — he stopped and smiled — " have become a Christian?" He was troubled at the condition which this conversation indicated, but he was amused. He wondered if it were worth while to treat it seriously.

"A Christian?" the girl repeated vaguely. "Oh, no, I am not that. That means to believe that Christ is — God?" She paused; then she added, eagerly, "Except as God is in all things, in every one; in Him preëminently. And, father,

He felt that it was worth while to suffer, to lend His life to the End."

"I beg that you will be more clear," the major said. "I still do not follow you?"

Sidney had risen, and was sitting near him; she had an open fan in her hand, and in the dusk it looked like a great white moth swaying upon a flower. Her face had grown clearer as she spoke, but her voice was unsteady. "Oh, it is not that my truth is not true, and that it is not *enough;* it is only that I do not want to suffer. But," she ended with a hopeless sigh, "that is equivalent to saying that I do not want to do my part!"

"You will have to explain what you mean, Sidney," said her father patiently. "What is enough?"

"The — the Meaning," she answered, almost in a whisper. "*Eternal*, I call it to myself."

The major leaned forward in his chair and looked at her. "If you were quite strong, my darling, instead of being worn out by your aunt's illness, it would be worth while to discuss this with you; but, for the present, had we not better put it aside?"

"No," she entreated, "oh, no, let me tell you about it now;" and then began to speak with the deliberation of one who fears to lose the thread of his discourse, as, step by step, he advances along some intricate path of argument. She did not even look at her father; she pressed her lips together once or twice as she proceeded, as though to insist upon calmness. It had been so real to her, that one great moment of her life, that she could not understand, as she tried to tell the story of Miss

Sally's death and the beginning of her own life, how impossible it is to bound an experience by words, or by an explanation define the unutterable God. Once the major made an impatient movement, and said something under his breath, but she did not seem to hear him.

"And so," she ended, "the Meaning in the universe is the Refuge,— is what aunt Sally called God; and oneness with that, it seems to me, makes life bearable,— and it ought to make it beautiful."

"Is that all?" said the major.

"Yes."

He looked at her with puzzled tenderness; he was so grieved that she should suffer, so anxious because of her white face, so incapable of treating her convictions seriously or entering into an argument upon this fantastic idea which she chose to regard as the solution of life, that he did not know what to say. It occurred to him to beg her to go and rest, and yet he would not hurt her by dismissing her convictions lightly.

"Your proposition," he began with the gentlest courtesy, "is of course gained without the assistance of reason. And you will forgive me if I say that I am sure your calmer thought will show you its inadequacy." Sidney did not answer. "And its inevitable conclusion: you now call the universe God, just as one creates a name for a hitherto unapprehended fact; but you might as well have called it Devil. You invest it with no personality, I observe, but you regard it with that poetic fervor which is, I am inclined to think, a phase of intellectual growth that expresses itself in art, or religion, or love. Do you mean "— he smiled, with tender amusement — " do you mean to have a garland of roses and a goat with gilded horns, and to sing hymns to the great god Pan ? For you see just what you have evolved, — pantheism."

She tried to say that her conviction was without a name; that terms, it seemed to her, were limitations.

" If I were not assured of your intelligence," her father said, "I should fear lest you might go a step further, and say that this 'Meaning' was good, and that it was Love " (" Love is God," Sidney said, under her breath), " and then all the rest of it," proceeded the major lightly, but with that sweet concern for her in his voice that would spare her the pang of mortification, — " the coming down to the earth, the vicarious atonement, heaven, hell, even prayer, perhaps."

Sidney leaned forward, resting her cheek in her hand. " Why not prayer ? " she said slowly. " That impulse is the Eternal. Is not prayer just claiming one's self, in a way ? Oh, father, everything is of Him." She was so absorbed that, for the first time, her father felt a thrill of anxiety. " But to call the Eternal good," she went on, " why, it seems to me it would be almost presumption ! or to say that I love — It. But still — good ? Yes, I suppose so, if that means the process by which an end is attained. What the end may be we may not know; but that there *is* an end, a meaning, is enough."

"So, then," questioned the major, " you construe

that sin, misery,— in a word, life,— is for your good?"

"My good? Oh, no, not mine; only they must be for good, in some way. I don't think it need make any difference to us what the good is, do you? See, father, the clay in the brickyard: it is pounded, and burned, and made into bricks, and houses are built and streets paved. Well, that is good, is n't it? Not the clay's good,— but what of that? There is a reason why the clay should be tortured, and if it could only just dimly know that there was a *cause* for its pain, it would be content; yes, and do its part. Well, I've seen that there is a meaning, for us. I don't know what, but that does not matter."

Major Lee looked at his daughter, in silence. Was this the result of twenty-four years' training to exact thought,— the poetical fancy of a tired girl!

"Yes," Sidney proceeded, "life is worth while when one sees that the Eternal Purpose is a refuge! Do you remember that little church we saw the summer we went to the seashore, made of stones from the beach,— stones covered with barnacles? Well, the barnacles were killed, but the church was built. Oh, father, life is surely less hard to bear if there is a meaning in it!" She rose as she spoke, her face radiant, and with an uplifted look in her eyes.

The major took her hands in his, and drew her down beside him. "Come, be your reasonable self, Sidney! My dear, I detect traces of the Calvinism of your maternal grandfather. You have practically announced your willingness to be damned for the glory of God! But, seriously, you have nothing more than you had before; you have not even personified the Unknowable, as an attempt at comfort."

"No, I trust Him, — that is all," she answered eagerly; "and I don't say Unknowable any more. Unknown, perhaps, but, oh, in my soul I *know* God! It limits Him to say Unknowable, and have we a right to do that? One has but to give one's self to the purpose of life, I think, — so far as one can see it, — and then, wait."

"For heaven?" inquired the major. He was torn between derision and anxiety, but tenderness dominated each.

"Waiting means trust, it seems to me," she said slowly. "No, I have not thought we were immortal. Somehow, that seems unimportant, father. But have we any right to dogmatize either way? It may be so. We used to say love needed the illusion of immortality as an excuse for being. But" — she stopped — "but the Eternal is enough."

"Sidney," said Major Lee, "has Alan Crossan told you that he loves you?"

"Yes," she said, in a whisper.

"Well?" questioned her father, sternly.

"I told him I did not love him." Major Lee breathed again. "But I do. Only I — cannot!"

It must have been eight o'clock when this talk of theirs began, but it was two in the morning when Sidney, without the good-night kiss which had been hers for all her unmothered years, left her father and went up to her room. After that acknowledgment that she loved Alan, Major Lee paused, as though to gather all his forces of love and sympathy and wisdom to meet this crisis. That breathless " I — cannot ! " meant nothing to him. She loved, and love is at least as immortal as the lover. He saw now, clearly enough, what had blinded Sidney's reason. The theory of a God was only the first step; he was confident that she would follow it by the assertion of that belief in immortality with which Love, venturing into the same world with Death, excuses its own existence. So he must first demonstrate the folly of this extraordinary fancy of hers, which denied personality, but declared a person.

It seemed simple enough to Major Lee ; he would go over again the old conclusive arguments. He knew perfectly well that the girl's knowledge, which was only his knowledge, could not possibly stand against him. How could she fence with weapons he had given her, which were pointed against herself? She did not attempt to. Again and again he stopped, courteously, for " her reasons," and she responded, " I do not reason, father; I know." " You *feel*," he corrected her, and the anxiety in his voice seemed to her contempt. Once she attempted to say that one fact which, to her mind, proved the morality, as humanity thought of morality, — the morality of the Eternal Purpose, — was the awful pain of remorse for sin. It was in violation of the *Purpose ;* — not the palpable inexpediency ; something deeper, — the thwarted God! That Major Lee brushed this assertion away with a word produced not the slightest effect.

"The Eternal is in us," she said gently, but with a voice as determined as his own.

"You play with words, Sidney," he affirmed. "You have not moved one whit; you stand exactly where you have always stood; you know — *nothing!* Only you wish to find an excuse for choosing sorrow, and you declare yourself satisfied with — what ? A Great Nothing in Particular; a universe which is a differentiated God; nay, — the attraction of gravitation! Is it not better, instead, to have a noble acceptance of necessity, and silence ? And you say you love ? Let me tell you what love has made my life." He paused, and looked at her. "I am astounded that this should be necessary; that I, who have lived the folly of love before your eyes, should yet have to assert its misery in words!"

His surprise was so genuine that for a moment, in the half darkness of the room, they stared at each other like two strangers.

The wind twisted the flame of the lamp into a blue whirl; a moment later the storm broke, and the rain went trampling through the garden. The silence in the room could be felt. Then Mortimer Lee began to say that love was the curse of life, and life itself was only free from misery in proportion as it was free from happiness. As Sidney listened, she lived over with him his days and months of hideous anxiety and inescapable dread. She saw that the joy of his marriage walked by the side of fear. She watched his fierce struggle with death, the hand-to-hand conflict with fate, while he held a dying woman in his arms, — a woman who besought him not "to let her go." And then she listened to his life afterwards, — empty, black, hopeless; lived only to teach her how to live that she might escape such suffering.

"And now," he ended, holding out trembling and entreating hands, "you tell me you love Alan Crossan! Oh, child, if I could only see you dead instead!"

"I love him," she said, her breath coming as though she sobbed, though her eyes were without tears, "but I cannot bear it, father. Yet we are wrong, you and I."

"No!" he cried, and it seemed to Sidney that his voice was suddenly that of an old, old man, "we are right; and you shall not love him, — you shall not suffer!"

"You cannot save me from myself," she said.

"I will," he answered. He put his trembling hands on either side of her face, and looked at her as she had never seen him look before. Then he said very gently, "Go, Sidney."

She dared not intrude upon that look by a word, or by the familiar good-night. She turned, and softly went away.

XXVIII.

When his daughter left him, Mortimer Lee began to walk up and down his library. Long after Sidney was faintly smiling in her sleep as her dreams opened the doors of resolution and bade joy enter, — even after the lamp burned white in the gray of dawn, — he still kept pacing back and forth, thinking. He did not tell Sidney the conclusion of his deliberations, when, in the morning, as usual, hanging upon his arm, she walked with him to the iron gate to say good-by; there was a conscious tenderness in her manner, the major thought, which made his dim eyes burn at the very pity of it, for her and for him. When he left her, he went at once to Alan Crossan's house.

There were one or two people waiting for the doctor, and the major took his place among them. His white head was bowed a little, and the fingers upon his stick were tremulous, but that was all; there was no anger in his face, only the patient habit of sorrow. When Alan, opening the office door, caught sight of the old man, he started with surprise, and went to him at once with extended hand. "What is it?" he said hastily.

The major looked at the hand, and then at Alan's face. "I wish to see you," he answered.

Alan was confused and puzzled. "If you will

come into my library," he said, aside, " these people can wait ? "

" I will wait."

Alan went into his office, his face tingling. "It is about Sidney, — but why ? " The wild thought even occurred to him that she had sent her father to say " Yes." His two poor people were somewhat ruffled, as is the habit of non-paying patients, that the doctor did not give them the attention and interest which they felt assured their cases demanded. Instead, he hurried them away, and then begged Major Lee to come into his library.

" Very well," the major answered, and followed him through the hall and up the stairs to the pleasant room, with its sunshine, and chemicals, and stacks of music. There, when they had seated themselves, the two men looked at each other in a silence which Alan was the first to break. " I was afraid some one was ill, but I hope I can be of service in some other way than by pills and powders." He attempted to speak lightly, but it was evident that he was excited.

" You are very good," returned the other, by force of habit. " I have come to ask a favor, namely, will you kindly refrain from coming to my house ? " As he spoke his voice began to tremble with anger. Alan, instantly, was calm and joyous.

" I am sure," he said, " that you would not say such a thing unless I had offended you, and I beg that you will tell me in what way I have been so unfortunate ? "

" I have made no complaint, merely a request. If

it needs an explanation, you will, I think, find it in your own conscience."

Alan felt his face growing hard and impatient. "You are displeased because I love Sidney?"

"Pray be exact," answered the major. "I regret that you love my daughter, but I have no right to be displeased; although, indeed, had I the time and inclination for personal feeling, I might be displeased that you had told her of your love. You observe the difference? It is, however, unnecessary to discuss it further." He rose as he spoke; he was an old man, and the restraint and grief told upon him. His whole body was trembling.

"But you cannot leave me in this way," said Alan hotly. "I do not admit for a moment that it was wrong to love Sidney, or to tell her so. I will not be thrust out of your house, Major Lee, without an explanation, as though I were a rogue! She has refused me: is not that enough?" Alan's hurried breath showed that this agitation was not good for him.

"Can you not perceive that it might be"— Major Lee paused; he was not used to deception — "it might be displeasing to my daughter to see you, under such circumstances? But you admit nothing wrong? Very possibly, — very possibly. Yet when your father and I were young men, Alan, we would not have considered it honorable to have endeavored to win the regard of a woman without the consent of her father. What, then, would have been our opinion of a man who won it — who tried to win it — against the known wishes of her father?" His sad eyes had in them something beside personal injury; it was the son of his friend who had done this thing.

Alan's face flushed, but he was angry at himself that he should feel ashamed. "I cannot agree with you, Major Lee. And you have no right to suggest dishonor. We must not argue now about the wisdom of love; of course I know your ideas. But will you not grant that if it were my honest conviction that you were wrong and all the world was right, that love was good and worth the cost, then I had a right to speak of it to your daughter? Granting my conviction, you cannot speak of dishonor."

Mortimer Lee hesitated. "It was not my purpose to accuse you; I merely wished to request "—

"You have accused me, however," interposed the young man quietly.

"If you insist," returned the major, "upon pursuing this subject, yes, I do consider such conduct dishonorable. You have no right to decide upon my views, unless you investigate them, which, if I mistake not, you are entirely incapable of doing."

"Then I am to understand," said Alan slowly, "that you make this request because you do not consider me an honorable man?"

Major Lee looked straight into the stern, beautiful eyes. His own were suddenly filled with entreaty. "If you loved her, your first thought would be to spare her!"

Alan's indignation vanished with the confession of those words,— he forgot everything except that Sidney loved him, and her father knew it; and then came the tender desire to shield the major from himself, — he must not guess that his pretense at anger had betrayed his fear. (How that look in his face brushed the years aside, and showed Sidney's entreating and disdaining eyes!) As that thought came to Alan, he smiled, and the major, watching him, said to himself, "No wonder, — no wonder; but it shall not be."

"It is strange," he began to say, "that you do not see the reasonableness of my position, Alan" (he did not know that his voice had softened), "even without the investigation of which I spoke; for I should suppose that even the most superficial observer of life must at some time be struck by the sorrow of love? Every school-boy will remember his Plato, and the wisdom of moderation; and you, a man, you surely know that love is not moderation; it is the highest height and the deepest depth. And you wonder that I would protect her!"

"To gain the heights once, a man would walk in the depths afterwards!" cried the other.

"But you" — Mortimer Lee had nothing but entreaty now — "you have not the hope of a very long life before you, I have been told! Is it possible that you do not see" —

"I think I see what you mean," Alan answered gently. "I suppose I shall not live very long, but" —

The major looked at him, with a strange simplicity in his worn face. "Is — is the time short? May it not be — quite far off?" The hint of hope in his face was so unmistakable that it touched Alan into a smile; but there was a mist of pity in his happy eyes.

"Well, you know," he said, "dying is not one of those things which can be arranged by date." He bit his lip to hide his smile. It was an unusual experience, the frank intimation that his early exit from the world would give pleasure. "Sidney has refused me," he added encouragingly. "So you must not be anxious. Yes, I know what you mean. I do love Sidney, and because I love her she shall not love me. I had made up my mind to that. But if you think that she may — that — I mean, if you think it would be best, I will go away from Mercer. But" — He stopped; a quick determination came into his face. "Look here," he said; "I want to say something right here." He rose, and stood looking down at his companion. "You are an old man, Major Lee, and I am only a young fellow — but I — I am going to tell you something, sir, and I beg your pardon in advance. I think you ought to hear it; I think some healthy-minded person ought to show you how preposterous, how absurd, this idea of yours is. Why, I assure you, I can't take it seriously," protested Alan, frowning and gesticulating. "It is perfectly fantastic!"

Mortimer Lee was too much astonished for words. This boy, this light-headed boy, who knew no more of life than a frolicsome puppy, to whom love and death were only words, was going to "show" him that logic was not to be applied to life.

"If Sidney," proceeded the young man, "could just get away from this one-sided habit of thought, this dealing with death as an isolated fact; if she could fall in love," — the dignity of reserve came into his face, but his voice was gentle and his words simple, — "if she could fall in love in a natural, wholesome, human way, it would be far better for her than the egotism of the avoidance of pain which you inculcate. I trust, sir, that I have not offended you, but it has seemed to me that this should be said."

"Sir," returned the major, "you have a right to express your opinion; the more so that you have done me the favor of assuring me that you will leave Mercer."

Alan flushed. "Major Lee, you know that I did not mean to take advantage of — of that. I shall go away, but I thought it proper that you should know my going was no concession to your views. It is only because I have not a man's ordinary chances of life. If I had! — But I will go away." A man, however, cannot doff his character as he would his coat, and Alan added, "for a time."

The major was very much moved, — too moved to resent the folly of the youth who had attempted to instruct him, or to discuss his own position; he did not try to conceal his relief at Alan's acknowledgment of ill health, nor his joy that he was going away. "Young man," he said tremulously, "there is, in this distracted world, one certain thing, — compensation. You spare Sidney, and you are yourself spared the pain of leaving her." He put out his hand, and Alan took it in his brave young grasp; neither of them spoke. It was not a time for thanks or for protestations.

A moment later he had gone, and Alan was alone.

No one can contemplate the two realities of life and remain unchanged; he must be either narrower or nobler. Alan Crossan, looking into the eyes of Love and Death, in these last few weeks, had gained a point where he was not aware of himself. This talk with Major Lee was not, as it would have been six months ago, a "situation," a "scene," to be observed with interest; instead, it was felt.

"I will go away," he determined. And this solemn joy of renunciation made him decide that he would not even say good-by to Sidney. That very day he began his arrangements for departure.

The first thing to be thought of was Robert. Robert needed him. "Yet," Alan had grumbled to himself, only the day before, "the fellow does n't want me. How the deuce am I to get at him?" But after that promise to Major Lee, he had the inspiration which is so common in friendship that the wonder is it is not commonplace and futile,— Robert must feel that he was needed. (The curious part of this plan is that both sides regard it as subtile.)

As soon as this suggested itself to Alan, he went in search of his friend. "Bob, I wish you'd do me a favor," he began, as he entered Robert's room; and then he unfolded his plan that they should travel together for a time. "I am not up to going by myself," he admitted; and Robert was eager and grateful for the chance to be of use.

"See here, old man," Alan said, as he rose to go, "I'll have to prescribe for you; you've let up on morphine too suddenly?"

"No," answered the other, "it had to be done at a blow. I made up my mind to that when I made up my mind about the Church."

"The Church?"

Robert smiled faintly. "Yes. I can't manage my own life; I've made a failure of it; but I can put it where it won't do any more harm, and perhaps — I dare to hope, some good. I have entered the Catholic Church, — my mother's church, you know."

"Good Lord!" said Alan.

"*She* forgave me," proceeded the other, "but I cannot forgive myself; I do not mean for telling her, — that was right, — but for misleading her, in the first place. I cannot trust myself. The church which directs, and governs, and obliterates the individual is the place for a man like me. When you are well and strong again, I shall enter some brotherhood — and — and I shall at least be harmless."

"You will be crazy," Alan assured him. "Man alive! how can you be a Catholic? What are you going to do with your reason?"

"Have I used it so well that I can rely upon it, do you think?" returned the other. Alan looked at him despairingly. "Well," he said, "by Jove, Bob, when conscience takes the bit of common sense in its teeth, it will run as viciously as the most unbridled passions!" But Robert refused to discuss it in such a spirit; and later, when the two men talked seriously of this matter, Alan reluctantly admitted that his friend was wise.

They hastened their arrangements for departure,

and, without discussion or apparent agreement, it came about that they left Mercer the day before John and Katherine were married. The doctor was sorry for this, but he felt Robert's pain at the remembrance of what that day was to have been to him and to Miss Sally, and made no protest. He called to say good-by to Mrs. Paul the night before they went away, but she was too happily excited to regret very deeply his absence from the wedding, or to think of mentioning it to Sidney. So the girl went to the little church, that pleasant August afternoon, full of strange fear and hope; Alan would be there, she thought. She was willing to see him, she had said to herself a dozen times; with too little understanding of love to know that she was selfish.

Since the night when she had talked with her father, Sidney had changed from one opinion to another as to the expediency of love, — even when one's soul rested in the assurance of God. She was like a flower swaying into the sunshine and into the shadow, but rooted all the while in the earth from which it sprang. Sometimes it seemed to her that she would tear love out of her heart; then, that she would love Alan a little, but he should never know it; then, that he might know it, and they would both forget it; and, again, that love should end. But, no matter what temporary opinion she might hold, she never doubted that love meant sorrow, nor swerved from the determination not to marry him. There was, however, no reason, she said to herself, that she should not meet him, sometimes, and she was confused and a little troubled that he no longer came to see her.

Of course she should see him at the wedding, she thought. She was to have gone to church with Mrs. Paul, but Mrs. Paul had forgotten her; so Sidney found her way to Miss Sally's seat, which was in the shadow of a pillar and beside a blue window, that was tipped half-way open, so that she could see the glimmering line of the river across the meadows, and beyond, the hills, misty with August sunshine; nearer were the dusty roofs of the brick-kilns, and long rows of sun-baked bricks; and nearer yet was the frame of ivy leaves about the little window. With the singing murmur of the organ John and Katherine entered. Sidney had never seen a wedding before. She sat in the dark corner, leaning forward, nervously grasping the back of the pew in front of her; she listened with an intensity which made her breath come hurriedly, and her eyes blur so that she could scarcely see the bunch of white August lilies which some one had placed in the book-rack, behind Miss Sally's small shabby Prayer-Book. Scarcely a month ago, what a different scene the little gray church had witnessed! It had been Death, then, which had moved up the aisle to the chancel; and now, Love followed, joyously, in Death's very steps,—forgetting!

Perhaps the words which remained in Sidney's heart, out of all the stately and beautiful marriage service, were those least thought of in the daily careless life of husband and wife,—"till death us do part."

"Part!" she thought. "If they believe what they say they believe, that death does not end all, why is it not 'till death us do join'?"

"O Eternal God," she heard Mr. Brown say, "Creator and Preserver of all mankind, Giver of all spiritual grace"—and Sidney knelt with the rest, but with a certain terror. To presume to address the Unknown!—oh, would not silence be better?

Death had not been so solemn to Sidney as was this crown of life,—solemn and terrible; an entering into the Eternal, a yielding up of God to God. It was neither joy nor sorrow, but an acceptance of life as part of the Purpose of the universe.

She dared not look into the faces of the man and woman thus glorified, as they turned to leave the church. Still kneeling, she hid her eyes in the bunch of white lilies, and waited. Yet she might have looked. It is conceivable that Moses could have come down from the mount, good and glad, but with no glory in his countenance that need be hidden from awestricken eyes. No one saw Sidney in the dark corner; and after the gay little company had gone, she still sat there by the blue window. Some birds twittered in the ivy, rustling the leaves as they moved; the organist in the dusky loft pushed in the stops and shut the organ, and a muffled echo crept along the arches of the ceiling. A rosy finger of light from the west window pointed up the aisle and into the chancel; the shadows of the leaves moved across it like living things.

"Why do they have *words*," Sidney was thinking, "and why were we here? We had no right to see them. A wedding is love and God; it was profane to see it."

The sexton, old and wrinkled, went limping up

into the chancel to take away the flowers; he sang to himself in a soft falsetto, which cracked into unexpected bass.

> "The Lord my Shepherd is;
> He makes me down to lie
> In pastures green; He leadeth me
> The quiet waters by.'"

He did not seem to be aware that he was treading upon holy ground. Back and forth he went, carrying the flowers in his lean old arms; then, still singing, he came with a long pole to shut the windows, set deep in the gray walls. Sidney startled him, as she rose and went away.

Oh, how terrible life was; how unbearable without the Eternal Refuge of the enfolding understanding of it all! Yet, how foolish to invite sorrow as these two had done! She would not do that.

But her heart was full of Alan, as she walked home; not with any weakening of resolution, but with the human joy of love, which is not to be destroyed by reason, or time, or death itself; so that when she came into the library, and saw, leaning against the crystal ball on the oak table, a letter addressed to her in Alan's hand, her face flushed with happiness. She opened it with smiling haste; and then stood, in the yellow dusk of sunset, reading its brief and friendly words: —

DEAR SIDNEY, — I am sorry to go away — and for an indefinitely long time — so hastily that I may not say good-by to you; but I must leave Mercer to-night. [Sidney, her face settling into white calm, mechanically looked back ; it was dated the day before.] I hope to sail for Europe very soon, but just now I 'm off for the mountains for a few weeks, to 'loaf and invite my soul!' Robert Steele, who goes with me, begs to be remembered to you.

   Sincerely yours,   ALAN CROSSAN.

The yellow light faded and faded; the sparkle of the crystal ball trembled into gray; the shadows stretched themselves about the room. There was the click of the iron gate in the courtyard, and Major Lee's step upon the porch.

 " It is better so," she said, lifting her head. " I am glad that he has gone; this decides it. It is better for him."

XXIX.

ALAN went; but he took his disposition with him. He was full of the exaltation of sacrifice; yet he watched critically for the first indication of weakening resolution. After a while, with the reality of absence came a depression which was new, and in which, for once, he failed to find his own mood interesting. It became necessary that he should assure himself repeatedly that he had done well to spare Sidney his love, because he spared her also the end which was hurriedly approaching. Perhaps Alan's weakness of soul, as well as body, in those yellow September days, was good for Robert Steele. Usefulness was to be his salvation, he said to himself, and, gradually, his purpose of going into the Catholic Church became not only a flight from despair, but a hope for the future. He and Alan spoke of it often, as they wandered and rested among the hills; Alan admitting, reluctantly, that it was best, yet filled with the friendliest curiosity and wonder. He recognized in Robert the absence of that spiritual passion which, having little to do with sweet reasonableness, often hurries an impressionable man into some expression of religion. In the past, Robert had had scarcely more of a creed than Alan, yet he had felt the need of one, and to feel that is almost a creed in itself; and now he was terrified at his own nature, and sought to escape from it in the strong, wise arms of that church which nourishes the soul, and leaves the intellect to itself; here, with bitter knowledge of his cowardice, he saw his safety assured. Necessity had thrust a creed upon him!

Alan understood and sympathized with all his sweet and generous heart, but refrained from theological discussion. This for two reasons: he did not know anything about theology, and he cared less. He entered into Robert's plans, however, with the greatest interest, and furthered them by suggesting that, as soon as he himself was a little stronger, they should go together to Rome. Then he fell to thinking how rich his life had grown since he saw Italy last, and the light in his face was as though for a moment the flame of life lifted and glowed behind his smiling eyes. These moments of satisfaction with himself became rarer, however, as his strength declined, and so the date of departure for Europe was postponed, and still postponed.

October came, and yet they lingered among the hills. Alan had begun to say to himself that perhaps he was a fool; and when a man reaches that point, it is only a step to the determination to renounce his folly. Yet to break one's word to one's self is distinctly unpleasant, although, if the responsibility of it can be shared with another person it is a little less so. Alan instinctively sought approval; and who would be so ready to approve of anything he might do as Robert?

One still day, early in November, the two young men went very slowly, and resting often, up and across a ferny pasture on a steep mountain side, and stopped at last near a low, shaggy cedar. It was late in the afternoon, but the Indian-summer mildness lingered, even while the gradual amethyst of evening fell around the feet of the mountains opposite, and crept, like a tide of dreams, up the great ranges of the hills. From behind the shoulder of a peak misty with this haze of night, which yet is not darkness, the yellow sunset blurred the distance in flooding gold, and fell upon the bosom of this rocky field. Down in the valley, a little tumbling branch of the Youghiogheny grew dark in the shadows, only gleaming with sudden white where the water leaped and broke across the great stones in its path.

Alan had changed in these two months. His eyes yet smiled, but his face was white. He lay flat on his back under the cedar, where the sunshine was warm still upon the frosted ferns; his hands were under his head, his knees crossed, and there was a cigar between his lips. Robert sat beside him, looking down into the darkening valley, thinking. As he watched the twist of blue smoke from Alan's cigar, or, absently, the swing of a stalk of goldenrod under the weight of a brown butterfly, he was pressing his own weakness in upon his memory, as a fanatic will again and again open a healing wound. He would not even accept the consolation of a look into the future, with its hope of a better life, — except, as he said to himself, that he would never take any positive stand again so long as he lived; he would do only as he might be directed, and then, perhaps, he could get through life without injuring any one.

"Bob," said the doctor, "do you know, I believe I've been a fool to come up here?"

"Why?" Robert asked, turning with quick anxiety to look into his face. "You are no worse?"

"Oh, I wasn't thinking of that. I mean in leaving Mercer."

"Yes?"

"Well," Alan began slowly, "I'll tell you what I mean;" and then he told him.

It was not a long story, and the main fact his hearer had long ago guessed; but, in the middle, at the point at which he had told Major Lee that he would not see Sidney, Alan stopped, — perhaps to relight his cigar, perhaps to seek some words which might make his change of mind seem to himself reasonable, or at least inevitable. Robert looked at him with a tenderness which might have shone in the eyes of a woman.

"It was a mistake to take such a stand," the doctor proceeded; "and to stick to a blunder, when you recognize it as such, is obstinacy, not consistency. I mean the going away was a blunder; there is no reason why I should not have stayed in Mercer. I need not have — I mean, just to see her sometimes would have done no harm. There is no reason why I should not see her. As for the major, his plan of life is wicked."

"It is against nature," Robert admitted.

"How does it strike you," Alan asked, after a pause, — "the going back to Mercer?"

Robert hesitated. "I am confused," he said at last, "between the right she has to receive, even to claim, sorrow, and the right you have to withhold it from her. But that is not your question. Your promise to Major Lee is the first thing. Of course he must release you from that before you can return."

"There was no promise — exactly," Alan explained impatiently.

Robert's face flushed, and he looked away from the doctor. "It would not, however, be — honorable." He dropped his voice, miserably, at that last word.

Alan struck him on the knee with friendly roughness. "I don't pretend to be as good as you; no doubt you are right. But I'm going back. Perhaps I'll die there, but — not directly! And just to see her, Bob!"

He had only said that he loved Sidney, and she had refused him; the sacred confession of that second refusal he kept in his own heart. But the gladness in his face betrayed the truth.

Not many days later, they returned to Mercer: Robert, with faint protestations that the major should be asked to release Alan, or at least warned of the doctor's intentions; Alan, with the reckless gayety of the man who refuses to recognize his own misgivings about his duty. They went back to their old rooms in Mercer, for the agent had found no other tenants; and the sunshine dancing on the walls of the library met them with the welcome Alan's heart supplied.

"Ah," he said, "it is good to be in the same town with her. To-morrow I shall see her, — and I'll see Major Lee, of course; you needn't look at me in that way!"

But that was not to be. To-morrow came, and with it the rising tide of death. Alan was very ill for nearly a week. Robert wondered, as he watched the young man's brave fight for life, whether his friend was glad the fates had spared Sidney. But Alan, smiling with white lips, settled that question.

"Bob, if this is going to be the end," he said, with a pause between his words, "you must bring Sidney, you know." His face lighted as he spoke.

It was not the end. Little by little he came back to life, but it was some time before he spoke of Sidney again. "You have n't seen her, have you?" he asked. He was watching at dusk the dance of the flames on the hearth.

"I?" Robert answered. "No, of course not."

Alan raised his eyebrows. "I cannot imagine why not."

"Because I did n't suppose you wished her to know that you were here before you had seen her father."

Alan looked at him in despair. "As though I remembered that nonsense, with one foot in the grave. And she must have heard it from somebody." He frowned as he spoke; it had been a beautiful solace, in those sharp hours, to fancy that Sidney's thoughts were with him.

"No," Robert returned. "Mrs. Paul is away, as you know, and unless the major has chanced to hear that we are in Mercer, and mentioned it to Miss Lee (which does not seem probable), how could she know it?"

Alan shook his head impatiently. "I want her to know it!" Robert made no reply. "You must go and tell her." Alan declared.

"You will write to Major Lee?" his friend entreated gently.

"Write to nobody!" said Alan sharply. "Unless it is to Sidney, if you refuse to take my message. Do you refuse?"

"Alan," the other evaded, "do reconsider this?" Robert Steele had never been so heroic as when he raised his standard of honor out of the wreck and ruin of his own life. The sick man wearily turned his head away. "Steele," he said, "conscience, unrestrained by common sense, is worse than a nuisance, it's a snare!" He could not argue; how foolish it seemed, this straining at a gnat! Yet a little later he was able to say, with friendly cheerfulness, "All right; only you are wrong, old man." At that Robert threw his scruples to the winds. Of course he did not know that Alan had quietly made up his mind to "manage his own affairs," but that would not have made any difference. Without a word of his plans he said he was going out to walk.

Robert had not entered Major Lee's house since that day when he went to tell Miss Sally the truth, and, as he crossed the courtyard, memory assailed him like a physical pain. The little paving-stones were wet with November mist, and the fallen leaves lay in wind-blown heaps, too heavy with dampness to rustle as he walked through them. Just a year ago Miss Sally welcomed him here; the major trusted him; Alan respected him; and Sidney? The thought of seeing her now was intolerable.

He followed little Susan to the library, but with a shuddering consciousness of the yellow drawing-room, and even that strange sidewise look with which one sees a spot where perhaps a coffin has stood. Behind that closed door Miss Sally had listened to his confession. As he stood waiting, saying to himself, "She is dead, — she is dead," he forgot the terror of meeting Sidney; after all these weeks his humiliation was too absorbing for the consciousness of shame.

Sidney, when she heard who was in the library, turned white, and then a wave of color covered her face. Mr. Steele in Mercer? Then Alan must be, also! Oh, why had he come back? She went downstairs slowly, her hand resting on the banister, her mind in a tumult. Then the thought struck her of the pain it must be to Mr. Steele to enter this house where death had been, and her own confusion was forgotten. That Sidney could so forget was indicative of that change in her which Robert saw in her face. For an instant it seemed as though this woman, in her black gown, with earnest, pitying eyes, could not be the old Sidney Lee; her wide, indifferent gaze was gone, and with it self-satisfaction and a certain sweet disdain which had charmed and wounded at once. Instead, there was a quiet acceptance of life, lightened, indeed, by that great moment when she had recognized her larger self, but only by its memory, not its repetition. Such memories feed the soul; a man who has once lifted his eyes to the midnight heavens may walk forever afterwards with his face towards the dust, but he cannot forget that he has seen the stars! So Sidney, failing again and yet again, bowed by the shame of self-knowledge, struggling with her own weakness and incompleteness, was sustained by the memory of that Strength which was sufficient for her.

She had suffered, and her soul was born.

Robert and she looked at each other a moment, as she gave him her hand, and then he turned sharply away from her. Sidney did not speak; those meaningless commonplaces, which wash realities out of life, were not easy to either of these two. The tears trembled in her eyes; sympathy, which was a new sense, showed her what to say.

"Mr. Steele, the lilies in the church the day that Katherine was married were so beautiful; I knew you put them there."

"I had no right to do even that!" he answered, in a low voice. His own misery made him forget his purpose in coming, and Sidney was too pitiful to think of herself, and so remind him.

"You are unhappy," she said gently, and with that calm, direct look which made any subject fitting. "You are unhappy because you brought your engagement with my aunt to an end. That is not right, it seems to me. Truly, I think you honored truth in doing it; but you degrade truth in being sorry that you did it."

"It — it is not that!" he cried; and then, almost with a groan, "I am unworthy to speak her name!"

Sidney waited. "I wonder where Alan is," she was saying to herself; but she waited.

"No," he went on, after a pause, "I did right to tell her; but the sin — the sin was in the beginning, — that I did not see that it was not love'"

"Yes," she assented.

"And now," Robert ended, "she is dead."

They neither of them spoke for a few moments.

"Miss Lee," Robert began, his voice firm again, "will you tell me a little about her illness? I know nothing of it. I felt I had no right to ask Alan."

Sidney started. "It was not very long, you know. Alan was with us almost all the time. He was so good."

"Yes?"

"Oh, where is he?" she cried, turning, and looking straight into his face. "Where is Alan?"

"He is here in Mercer. I came to tell you."

"Here?" she faltered. "We have not seen him."

"We only came ten days ago," he explained. "I want to tell you about him, Miss Lee."

"Yes, tell me!" It would not have occurred to Sidney to disguise her wish to hear of Alan.

"I hope that he may be able to come to see you" —

"Be able?" Sidney interrupted quickly. "Has he been ill?"

"Yes; Alan has been very ill, Miss Lee."

"But not now?" she entreated breathlessly, — "he is better now?"

"For to-day, yes," he answered, "but he will never be well." She did not speak; Robert could not tell whether she understood him. "He has been so much worse, so much weaker, and — we shall not have him with us very long. I thought — I thought you ought to know it?"

"Yes." Her face was so white that Robert was terrified at what he had done. He tried to say something more of what he still dared to hope, but every word of hope was strung upon a thread of fear, and he dared not offer the comfort of a lie. Sidney was not listening; when he ended, she said quietly, "There is my father coming; tell him."

Robert met the major on the doorstep. He had forgotten that this was the first time that he had seen him since Miss Sally's funeral; for once he was so unconscious of his own sins that he did not see the questioning displeasure on Mortimer Lee's face. "Alan Crossan is in Mercer," he said, "but he is very ill. I have just told your daughter." Then, without pausing for an answer, he left him.

Sidney stood in the firelit dusk, waiting. "Father," she said, as he entered,—"father, I have something to tell you."

The major closed the door, and took her in his arms.

XXX.

With the perfect blossoming of a rose the calyx falls away, and is folded back under its shadowy fragrance. So do the small things of life, necessary in their hour, find their relative value in a great crisis. "For this cause came I into the world," the soul declares calmly: and knows no hesitation, and, equally, no determination. Its purpose and itself are one. When the environment is forgotten, the supremest individuality is reached.

Now, staring into the eyes of Death, while Grief beckoned her with extended hand, Sidney Lee's consciousness of fear, and expediency, and obedience to her father, was pushed back by this blossoming of her soul. She read her own heart, and saw her love for Alan, not as a thing bursting into existence at the touch of death, but as a tranquil and eternal fact: so much a part of her that not only did it seem that it must always be, but that it always had been, even as the perfect rose has been shut within the seed! It was not to be accepted nor rejected. It was. Her past was but the calyx of the consummate flowering of life.

She was so calm as she told her father her purpose, so ultimate, that the old man presented no argument and ventured no entreaty. There was nothing to be done or said.

Sidney kissed him gently when she ended what she had to say, and then left him. He could not touch her; he could not speak to her. "It is as though I were dead," he said to himself. This heart, which had answered his as the water answers the wind, could not be reached by his despair. "This is the pain of the dead," he thought, sitting alone in his library; "they cannot touch us!" The dead! What was he thinking of? No, they had neither this nor any other pain. A trembling comfort crept back into his heart; no one could deprive him of death. In that, at least, was no disappointment. But why had he lived so long? A strange feeling came over him, a realization of his infinite removal from all which had made his life. Surely he had died when Gertrude's lovely eyes closed upon the world? Here, in the shadows, beside his smouldering fire, that delicate and marvelous mechanism of a human mind quivered under the jar and shock of pain; in a dull confusion he seemed to forget Sidney, and the thought came to him that Gertrude was still his. To rest his head upon her bosom — ah! the hideous desolation of longing! The slow tears of age burned under his weary eyelids. Scarcely aware of what he was doing, he rose, taking the lamp in his unsteady hands, and with a feeble step left the library. He crossed the hall, and stood at the door of the yellow parlor. The house was quite silent; little Susan had put out the lamp on the staircase an hour ago, and gone up to bed; the faint glow from the library fire lay like a bridge across the darkness of the hall. He did not hesitate, but the confusion of his thoughts betrayed itself by the slowness with which he turned the knob and entered the parlor. The door stuck a little, and the jar of pushing it open moved with a muffled echo through the darkness; the room was very cold, and there was the scent of the unused fireplace and the linen covers of the furniture. Mortimer Lee went at once towards its farther end. He put the lamp down upon a small table before the portrait, stopping to move aside a little workbag of green silk, vaguely aware that it was Sarah's. Curiously enough, it reminded him of death, for he had been saying to himself that Gertrude and he were together, and that meant life.

Then he turned his dim eyes upon the portrait.

How long he stood there, his hands clasped behind him, or holding the lamp above his head, that its shifting light might fall upon that young face, he never knew. But the silence ringing in his ears was clamorous with a new desolation: in the arch sweetness of those eyes there was no comprehension of his pain. Who was she, this beautiful young woman? Not the wife who had lived in his heart all these years, — not Gertrude, whom he knew with the passion of sorrow? Mortimer Lee dropped his head upon his breast, without a sound. What was this new despair? Where was his grief? Suddenly, for one swift instant, his precious possession of pain seemed torn out of his heart, and he felt that he stood alone. That fact of the solitude of the soul is not often revealed to a man, and when it is, it crushes the mind into the numbness of despair.

Such a revelation is so overwhelming that, afterwards, the soul doubts its reality, and resumes easily the old habit of communion with whatever, in the past, has been most near and real.

That night Sidney slept as peacefully as a child. Her life, it seemed to her, had been taken out of her hands, and she knew the calm of the fatalist, which is, perhaps, the highest form of faith.

It was snowing when she looked out into her garden, the next morning; the firs in the evergreen hedge were like cowled and muffled figures stealing through the storm; her window ledge was piled high with feathery white, and the leaded outlines of the fan-lights were traced in twists of down. All the grimy, bustling town faded into misty purity while the snow fell; here and there from a great chimney a burst of flame, like a ruddy banner, flared out into the driving white, and then subsided into a roll of dark smoke, laced by hurrying flakes.

"If only it would n't stop!" Alan Crossan said, sitting at his library window, and looking at the soft depths piling up on the naked branches of the old locust tree; "but it will melt, and then I can't go out for a week."

"Do you think," Robert asked, "that you will be able to start in a week?"

"If I want to," the other replied, with gay significance. "Bob, don't worry about not getting to Rome at once. Let me die in peace at Mercer, and I'll be your patron saint. Besides, if you are really worried at the delay, I have a 'History of the

Popes' you can study. It is by an eminent Protestant; it will give you lots of information."

Robert laughed, but said he really thought Alan ought to make up his mind to start; a Pennsylvania winter was not the best thing in the world for an invalid.

Alan looked at him with interest. "You don't take the strictly moral view which you did yesterday?" he observed.

"Yes, I do; only I can't see that it makes any difference what view I take."

"Not the slightest," Alan agreed good-naturedly.

"I'd like to ask you something," Robert began, after a pause. "Do you mean, if you stay, to — try to make her love you?"

Alan's face grew suddenly grave. "No," he said quietly.

"But if she sees you, may not that come?"

Alan shook his head. "No; it must not come. I only want her to know that I am in town."

"She knows that."

"What!" exclaimed the doctor. "When?"

"I told her, yesterday."

"Bob," cried the other joyously, "you're a trump! What did she say?"

"Nothing." Robert answered, uncertain whether he should tell Alan the confession of Sidney's silence. ("It will only make it harder for him," he thought.)

"Nothing? Did you tell her I had been ill?"

"Yes," Robert admitted, still struggling to see whether he was not really helping Alan to break his word to the major.

"Well?"

"She did n't say anything."

Alan opened his lips, but seemed to find himself at a loss for words. "Did n't say anything?" he repeated blankly. "Did n't she say she was sorry?"

Robert shook his head. He had made up his mind; he had done wrong in telling Sidney, — at least it should end here.

Alan fell into gloomy silence. He was hurt. Not a message, not a word? He would not ask anything further. He began to torment himself with questions which revealed how, underneath his assurance to her and his sacrifice in going away, had lurked the hope that she loved him. "Perhaps she was angry that I did not say good-by? Perhaps my note was curt, and she felt that I had ceased to love her?" Perhaps — perhaps — Is a lover ever done with that word?

The snow whirled and drifted against his window, but to Alan's eyes all the cheerfulness of the storm was gone. Once he asked abruptly, "Did she look well?" And Robert said, "Yes; but older and graver." Alan would not read; he had not strength enough for his violin; he answered Robert's efforts at conversation by monosyllables. He looked gloomily at the fire, and said to himself that after all, life was a grim sort of thing; and he wondered whether the mere satiety of living might not bring the desire for death.

But while he brooded and wondered, turning studiously away from Robert's troubled face, the door opened, and some one stood in the doorway. Neither of the young men looked up, until Alan, realizing with vague annoyance that some one was standing behind him, turned and saw her. The wind had brought the wild-rose color into Sidney's cheeks, and the snow had caught on the rings of shining hair upon her forehead. She looked like a flower swept in out of the storm. Her long gray cloak dropped from her shoulders, as she unfastened its clasp and came quietly to his side.

"Alan, I have come," she said.

Robert Steele started to his feet with an astounded exclamation, but Alan, a sudden content smoothing the trouble and weariness from his face, as the west wind blows the clouds from the serene and open spaces of the sky, lifted his eyes to hers, without speaking. Sidney took his hand and held it against her bosom, stroking it softly.

"Mr. Steele," she said, without a tremor or a blush, and looking directly at him, "I have come to marry Alan." She did not wait to see Robert leave the room; it was nothing to Sidney if the whole world should see her now; she knelt down beside Alan, and laid her head upon his breast. He heard her whisper one word. Weakened and trembling, he could only rest his cheek against her hair, with a sob upon his lips.

XXXI.

It was just a fortnight later that Mrs. Paul returned from her first visit to Katherine and John, — a visit which was an extraordinary experience to her. She had gone full of plans for her beloved Kate's happiness, but they were quietly and quite courteously ignored. Katherine, although never unkind, was quite indifferent to her husband's mother. Life was so interesting to young Mrs. Paul that she no longer diverted herself by trying to charm the bitter and selfish old woman. Mrs. Paul was at first incapable of grasping the situation, but it dawned upon her when Katherine civilly acquiesced in her mother-in-law's tentative statement that perhaps she had better go back to Mercer?

"Yes," she said, "perhaps it is best. You would not want to travel in the colder weather."

Mrs. Paul did not understand her own emotions. She still said to herself, mechanically, that Kate was delightful, and she tried to adjust this speech to her ideal. It was inconceivable that Katherine did not love her; this willingness to have her go was really consideration; but she felt sore and baffled, and a forlorn dismay began to creep into her mind.

So, after all, it was a relief to come back to Mercer. With this new light upon Kate's character, it would be easier to talk about her than to talk to her. She wished that she could have had Sally for half an hour, but Sidney was better than no one. So, just before tea, she bade Scarlett step over to the other house, and say, with Mrs. Paul's love, "Will Miss Lee come in this evening for a little while?"

"She should come without being sent for," she added severely; "but Mortimer Lee is so selfish in keeping her with him. He made her neglect me shamefully in the summer, after Sally died."

She wondered, as she watched the fire shine and flicker, how Mortimer Lee would get along without Sally's stupid goodness. "Of course he will be uncomfortable," she said to herself, and smiled.

Thus sitting, thinking, Mrs. Paul saw Scarlett crossing the major's garden, and hurrying through the doorway in the garden wall. A moment later there was a sound of voices in the kitchen. This was so unusual and so little in accordance with Mrs. Paul's theories that she frowned, and bent her head as though to listen; but through the green baize door only a muffled discord reached her.

Scarlett, in the kitchen, with her black shawl falling off one shoulder, her small withered hands gesticulating and trembling, was at last talking. Her words came fast, but Davids, leaning against the dresser, his arms folded and his feet crossed, observed her with complacent silence.

"What has come to you?" demanded the woman. "I've been in the house since noon, and you never let on to me. And you, to hold your tongue five hours!"

"And how do you like my holdin' my tongue?" inquired Davids.

"That's neither here nor there. There's some meaning in your head, or you would n't be so close-mouthed. I know you!"

Scarlett's face was growing pale again, and her voice was steadier. She turned to take her bonnet off, that she might go to her mistress, but Davids quietly stepped in front of the door, and stood, with his hands behind him rattling the knob, observing her all the while with intense satisfaction.

"Yes," he said, " I did keep my mouth shut, and I 'd 'a' kep' it shut an hour longer if it had killed me, if I 'd 'a' bust, just for a lesson to you. You an' me 's lived in this kitchen pretty near twenty-five years, and from the very first you set out to keep a close mouth, an' you 've done it. You 've never give a bit of news that you could help. Well, it come my turn. An' I made out I could be as mean as you. I know all, — *all*; but I ain't got a word to say!"

Scarlett looked at him steadily and in silence; then a slow smile came about her lips. She turned away without a protest, to wait, with folded hands, until he chose to open the door. Her composure made Davids furious. Stammering with anger, he moved unconsciously out into the room. As he did so, the small, gray woman slipped past him, and escaped into the hall. In spite of her self-control, however, she was visibly excited when she opened the drawing-room door.

"Mrs. Paul"— she began, in a fluttering breath.

"What was that disgraceful noise in the kitchen?" interrupted her mistress sharply.

"Ma'am," cried Scarlett, "she's married!"

Mrs. Paul put on her glasses, and looked at the woman as though she thought her suddenly insane.

"She's married!" Scarlett declared again. "It's two weeks to-morrow. And — and — that Billy Davids!"

"What are you talking about?" said Mrs. Paul.

Scarlett breathed hard in the effort to compose herself. "Miss Sidney has gone and got married, and us away!" Mrs. Paul stared at her, with parted lips. "Seems he was going to die (he ain't dead yet, though; them doctors never die), and she said she'd have him; and she went to his house with a minister, — 't was n't Mr. Brown, Susan said. Yes, Miss Sidney took the preacher to him. The major was n't there, and nobody except Mr. Steele. La, madam, you're faint?" But Mrs. Paul motioned her to proceed. "She told Susan," said Scarlett, rubbing her hands to express her agitation, — "she told Susan she was going to get married, as — as natural as if it was n't anything more than to go and buy a pair of gloves, she was so easy saying it. Did n't seem to be anything to her. Susan says she ain't been home since, and she *says* the major has n't seen her. He's white mad, Susan says. And — and — that Davids!" she ended, her voice breaking as she thought of him.

"It is Alan Crossan," said Mrs. Paul, in a low voice, as though she spoke to herself.

"Yes, ma'am, it is," Scarlett assented; "and he's dying."

There was silence for a moment, broken only by Scarlett's hurried breathing.

"Bring my writing-table," commanded Mrs. Paul quietly. The woman brought it, and stood waiting, with excited curiosity on every feature. "You may go," said her mistress, looking up over her glasses; and then, with the pen between her fingers, she leaned back in her chair and thought.

"At last!" she said, under her breath, — "at last! A righteous retribution."

"My dear Major Lee," she wrote rapidly, "I hear with pleasure" — No, that was too crude to really wound him. Sympathy would be a more subtile thrust. She tore her letter across, and threw it in the fire. "How he must suffer!" she thought, and her eyes exulted. "And to think that I was not at home to see it all."

She had forgotten Katherine and her own mortification. Such grievances were superficial when placed beside this old reality, which was as enduring as a cruel rock that had been hidden, but not destroyed, by a shining tide. It was as though Katherine had never existed. Again she tried to write, but it was impossible. "I must know first how it happened," she said to herself, striking her hand sharply on the table. "Of course he is not angry with Sidney; Susan is a fool; but how much did he know about it? How does he feel towards Alan? How" — Endless questions came into her mind, but all bore upon Major Lee's discomfiture; in her exultation she had forgotten Sidney, save as the means by which her father's wickedness was baffled, and it was with almost a start of surprise that she remembered that the girl herself could best give the information she desired.

"How stupid!" she said, frowning. "I should have sent for her at once!" But, to lose no further time, she wrote a note, veiling her triumph with only the faintest pretense of sympathy and congratulation together, and bidding Sidney come at once to see her. "Scarlett will see you home," she added in a postscript, "if, as I suppose, your husband is unable to come with you." It was characteristic that, upon the receipt of Sidney's brief message that she did not wish to leave Alan and would not come, Mrs. Paul had nothing but anger and injured feelings. "I never saw so selfish a girl," she said bitterly.

That evening was intolerably long and empty. A curious feeling of being left out began to intrude upon her anger. She said to herself, "Why has no one told me this? Why did no one write to me? The world is mad!" Her chagrin had in it a sort of terror, which she refused to face, preferring, instead, to dwell upon Mortimer Lee's pain. She scarcely slept that night, and as the gray Sunday morning widened into the reluctant day she was impatient to execute some of the plans which had occurred to her. First, she sent for Robert Steele; but his response to her peremptory summons was a curt note, begging to be excused. Scarlett stood watching her as she read it, and saw her lift her head with the air of one who refuses to be rebuffed; but her voice trembled when she spoke. "Order the carriage at twelve," she said. She had made up her mind; she would go directly to Mortimer Lee. Of course he would be at home, and alone. He did not go to see Sidney, he had not a friend in the world, — save herself. — and, wicked atheist that he was, there was no hope that he might be in church.

"It is very raw and cold," Scarlett observed.

"I said twelve," Mrs. Paul answered.

"Very well," said Scarlett. She had done her duty by the protest; it was nothing to her if her mistress chose to get sick.

But when twelve o'clock came Mrs. Paul's angry mortification insisted upon words, and, while Scarlett was dressing her, she found fault with a thousand things for the mere relief of speaking.

"Why can't you fasten my cloak without fumbling about so?" she demanded. "You never try to do anything well, Scarlett; you are like all the rest of the world, and have no gratitude in you!" The woman, who had dropped on her knees to fasten Mrs. Paul's fur-lined slippers, made no reply. "There is no such thing as gratitude," continued the other; "there is not a soul I can depend upon."

Scarlett rose, her small, lean hands clasped in front of her, and her passionless eyes fixed upon Mrs. Paul's face. "I am not surprised that you should think so, madam."

"What do you mean?" returned Mrs. Paul contemptuously.

This simple question was Scarlett's opportunity; it was the small and sputtering match which may yet fire a powder magazine. She stepped back a little, swallowed once or twice, and looked steadily at a spot upon the wall, above Mrs. Paul's head. She had always meant to tell her mistress her opinion of her; as well now as any time. So, calmly, rocking slightly back and forth upon her heels, she said monotonously, " Because, madam, you are unkind, even when you do a kindness. You are unjust and you are bad-tempered. Mr. John could n't stand it, and he knew it would n't be for edification to bring his wife here to live. We get our deservings in this life, and you've got what you've earned, when you find that nobody cares for you. That is my opinion, madam."

Mrs. Paul lifted her glasses and observed the woman in silence for a moment, during which Scarlett changed color, but did not cease swaying back and forth upon her heels, and regarding the wall with a tranquil stare.

" Is the carriage ready? " said Mrs. Paul.

" Yes, madam ; " and without another word they went downstairs.

In nearly sixty years of brilliant selfishness, Mrs. Paul had had no friend who would do for her this simple office of telling her the truth, and it had to come at last from the lips of a servant. When the carriage door closed and she was alone, Mrs. Paul's face was white.

Little Susan caught a glimpse of the heavy carriage just before it left the lane and came rumbling into the courtyard, and, realizing that her master was to have a caller, she was so grateful that she

was moved to tears when she opened the door for
Mrs. Paul. "Anything," thought Susan, "to get
him like folks."

The sight of the old man sitting in his library,
his white head sunk upon his breast, his sad eyes
watching the vacant moments drag themselves away,
was very distressing to Susan. She wiped her eyes
frequently as she looked at him, or as she stood behind
his chair in the dining-room; for the major
was as careful as ever of the details of life, and
went through the form of dining as ceremoniously
as though he had his old household about him. He
even tried to eat, because he feared that the young
woman might be distressed if he did not. With the
instinct of a gentle heart he felt little Susan's unhappiness
concerning him. Indeed, the girl had
told her mother that she was that sorry for him that
she did n't know but what she must go to a more
cheerful place. Susan went each day to inquire for
"Miss Sidney's husband," and, unasked, announced
his condition to the major at tea. She could not
tell, she confided to Scarlett, whether he listened or
not, but she was n't one to be turned from her duty
by that. It was natural that she should say he was
angry. His silence, even during Mr. Steele's daily
call (Susan knew that he was silent then, she was so
interested herself, she said); the fact that he made
no inquiries concerning his daughter, that he never
went to her house, that he did not even write to her,
that he had not seen her since that morning when
she had left him to marry Alan, — what could it
mean but anger? To be sure, the expression upon

his face was not exactly anger, Susan thought; it puzzled her because she could not classify it; it was so pitiful that sometimes she could not bear to look at him.

Mortimer Lee had grown suddenly and awfully old, in these weeks since Sidney's marriage; the shock of her grief had shaken the very foundations of his life. That strange confusion which befogged his senses the night he went to look at Gertrude's picture lingered still in his thoughts. His daughter's grief seemed to be his own, not hers. He lived over again the old despair of more than twenty years ago, and then, with a start, realized that Sidney was waiting for pain which had not reached her yet. Robert told him once, hesitatingly, how calm and even glad Sidney was. The old man made no reply. Sorrow had not come yet; a false excitement upheld her, the exhilaration of present joy blinded her; the terror would but be the greater when it came. It was for that he waited; then he would go to her. As for seeing her before that moment when she should need him, it never occurred to him. This rending of the bone and marrow, this parting of two souls, was not for his eyes. Sitting here in his library, alone, night after night, without even the friendly companionship of his books, it seemed as though, with exceeding pity, his very soul wept.

And so the days passed. Alan, his hand held in his wife's, was going out into the Unknown. Sidney went step by step beside him, straining her eyes into the darkness of the future, shuddering lest at any moment her feet should touch the first wave of that dark stream upon which she must let him venture forth alone, and yet walking with a lofty serenity and peace which astounded the dying man. His own mystery of death was not half so great to Alan as was Sidney's mystery of life. He watched her with a sort of awe. Every instant was appreciation, every moment a jewel, which the divine caress of consciousness held in this light and in that, that no gleam of its beauty might be lost. Her lovely joy was set in grief, but there was no terror in it. They talked much of her assurance, but it seemed to Alan only words.

"God is enough for pain," she had told him. "Love is possible and beautiful, even though its flower is grief, because it grows from the heart of the Purpose of the universe, because it is folded about by God."

"Don't you understand me, Alan?" she said once, wistfully. He put his thin white hand under her chin, and looked down into her tranquil eyes.

"It does not seem probable that I do," he answered, smiling. "I do not very often understand myself — but I am glad."

Perhaps he was too weak to take her wider view; perhaps the exceeding simplicity of dying brought back the older thoughts, his mother's teachings of so long ago, and he rested in them with great content; but he was glad for Sidney. Once he asked her, with a pause here and there between his words, of her hope for the future.

"I cannot grasp your — willingness not to know. You do not expect to see me again?"

"If it is best," she answered, her voice quivering into calmness; "but it will be best, either way. There is no death, — never any death! It is all life; we came from it, and we go back into it again. Oh, Alan, we both belong to life; it is in it that we are really and truly *one*."

Afterwards, when he had been lying silently for a long time, he looked up at her, with a smile flickering in his eyes. "But I — shall not be I?" he said, with pitiful gentleness.

"God is," she answered. "Oh, I cannot let go of that one moment."

Their two lives shut out the rest of the world. They saw Robert Steele come and go with the same indifference to a necessity with which they saw light and darkness. Appreciation of moments may turn a day into a year, and these months together held the experiences of a lifetime. Sidney's consciousness of the pervading God took no definite shape, although she felt that she could not have lived without such consciousness. As a star opens its bosom to the sun that it may fill itself with light for the coming darkness, Sidney absorbed the present. It was at this time that she prayed, dumbly, not for Alan's life, not for strength to bear her coming sorrow, but for more, and more, and more God! There were no words in this outcry of her soul to Him who gave words, and needeth not that any should tell Him. Deep was calling unto deep, — existence was itself a prayer.

She told Alan all this, as he could listen to it; and once he said to her, "Yes, yes, I know, and I am glad. Only remember — will you, Sidney? — that I am *sure* of the rest, of the future? I am sure of it. I have come back to the old familiar things, Christ and heaven (that means having you again!); they are easier to think about than this abstraction, and I believe they are just what you have found, by another name. No, I don't reason; I trust. It is your attitude, only I go a step further than you." And then, later, "Sometimes it seems to me, do you know, that for me to go on ahead is just to teach you to take that step. And you won't forget that — *I am sure?*"

Sidney's thought of her father in these beautiful days was only that "he understood." Major Lee knew that she felt this; it would have been profane had either of them insisted upon it by words. Thus they waited: Sidney for a deeper glory, her father for the inevitable night.

That Sunday when Mrs. Paul's carriage came across the creaking snow in the courtyard, the major had been brooding over this strange pause in his life, realizing with pathetic patience that even when it ended, when Alan died and his daughter came back to him again, life could not be as it had been. His dim eyes burned as this cruel thought struck upon his heart; the insolence of time is like a blow in the face from an unseen enemy.

"There is no help for it," he was saying to himself. He was so absorbed that he did not understand Susan's summons to the parlor, or hear the name she gave, so the girl had to speak again, pleadingly: "She's in the parlor, sir, waitin'. I put a match to the fire, but it's cold in there."

"She?" said the old man vaguely. "Where?" and then brushed past her in tremulous haste. Sidney had come. But why had she waited; was Alan —

The shock of seeing Mrs. Paul, shivering in her furs, upon the yellow satin sofa was almost a physical pain. He had no words. But Mrs. Paul supplied them; her voice was full of fine anxiety.

"My dear Major Lee, pray what is this about Sidney? I was so shocked, so concerned. Such a tragedy for the poor girl! Pray tell me how you could have permitted such a thing?"

He did not answer, but seemed to look beyond her, as though he were unconscious of her presence. The change in his face since she had seen him last awed but could not silence her.

"She has grieved you, I know," she began to say, "but her disobedience will bring its own punishment; you can only pity and forgive her. And the selfishness of the young man — but tell me?"

"Not here, — not here," interposed Mortimer Lee, still gazing above her, at the further end of the room.

She turned, following his eyes, to meet those of the portrait, beautiful, disdainful, and, as she thought with sudden fury, triumphant. Standing at the feet of this dead woman, she saw the source of all her bitterness, her selfishness, her cruelty, — saw it with futile rage at her own helplessness in the hand of Fate. She had been robbed by this young creature, and she had tried to hide the desolation of her heart by worldliness and selfishness. Her loss had turned to evil everything which was good; and then, as though that were not cruel enough, Annette had been taken away. Her own son did not love her; Katherine cared nothing for her; Sidney had forgotten her; her very servant despised her. She looked again at Mortimer Lee, still staring at the picture. "Yes, not here," she repeated, "not here!" (It was strange to see how simple the primal passion of humanity made these two souls.) She motioned him to give her his arm. "I came," she said, — "I came, but I will go away; yes, I will go away!" Her voice broke.

Without a word, the major led her to her carriage. He bowed, and stood, the cold wind blowing his white hair about, watching the carriage circle around the snow-covered lawn, and disappear down the lane. Then he went back, and stood before the portrait.

"It was the only thing I ever kept from you, Gertrude," he said feebly; "but she has come and shown it to you herself. You would not have had me tell you such a thing? But she has told you" —

After the shock of that interview the confusion of Mortimer Lee's thoughts passed away. His profound dismay settled into a certain tranquillity of waiting. He was gathering up his strength to meet Sidney's need of it, when the day should come.

And so the winter failed, and fainted into the hesitating spring. Robert Steele came every evening to tell him of Alan; they never spoke of Sidney. But one day in March he did not come, and a strange excitement grew in Mortimer Lee's face. "It is near," he said to himself. It was; very near. He did not go to the bank the next morning; he must be at home to know when Sidney needed him.

All that morning he sat in his library in tense expectancy. In the early afternoon came a note from Robert Steele. "Not yet, not yet," the old man said; longing for the blow to fall, that his own work of tenderness might begin. The windy March sky lifted and lightened towards sunset, and all along behind the hills the clear and lucent air, yellow as a topaz, faded up into pale violet under the torn fringes of the clouds. Mortimer Lee stood, with his hands behind him, looking out at the peace of the coming night; but he turned at the sound of the opening door, and Sidney came swiftly to his arms.

The room had darkened in the fading light, but he could see the change in her face; not age, but living, had marked it. That ecstasy shone in her eyes which is the realization of the Infinite, and may be called either joy or grief, as both are one in it.

"I have come to tell you," he heard her say, "it is over, my life. But I am glad to have lived: Oh, I am glad!"

"*Alan?*—"

"Yes; yet I am a happy woman. Father, I wanted you to know that I was happy! It is joy, father!"

He held her fast in his trembling arms, and his tears fell upon her head. But Sidney's eyes were clear. She raised her face, and it was she who was the comforter. "It is worth while," she said tenderly. His grief moved her as her own had not; a flood of tears, as natural and unrestrained as a child's, shook her from head to foot. "He is dead, but he has lived. He is mine, always. Oh, it is worth while, — it is worth while; the past is ours, and all is — God!"

Then they went back again together to Alan's side.

. . . .

Sidney's life afterwards was as though into a dead body had come a living soul.

The old circumstances remained, the old possibilities, but the spirit which animated them was a new spirit. She and her father drew closer and closer together, the old love greater for the new love. She was strangely calm and content; entering deeper into that Refuge which had revealed itself to her, and losing her life daily in the lives of others; yet never limiting her peace by defining it, nor daring to imprison it within a creed.

Mrs. Paul called her an infidel.

Robert Steele, feeling vaguely that Sidney, religious, without a religion, drew her strength from the same source as did he, absorbed in the wonderful ritual of the most detailed religion in the world, yet prayed for her salvation with the anguished fear of the consistent Christian who hears his Lord denied.

The major only waited.

"It cannot last," he said to himself sadly; "it is unreal. And when it breaks down — even I cannot help her! Oh, the cruelty of love!"

And still he waited.

www.ingramcontent.com/pod-product-compliance
Lightning Source LLC
Chambersburg PA
CBHW051740300426
44115CB00007B/640